GOURMET *Vegetarian* M·I·C·R·O·W·A·V·E C·O·O·K·E·R·Y

GOURMET
Vegetarian
M·I·C·R·O·W·A·V·E
C·O·O·K·E·R·Y

Clare Ferguson

GRUB STREET · LONDON

I dedicate this book to my mother and father with all their
ideals of love, laughter, gardens and learning.
It is also for my husband, Ian, without whose sustained
support it could never have been completed, and for Maurice
who taught us to see with his eyes.

I also wish to thank my assistants and helpers Kerry,
Alexandra, Sally and Kate.

Published by
Grub Street
Golden House
28–31 Great Pulteney St
London W1

Copyright © 1986 Grub Street, London
Text Copyright © Clare Ferguson
Design Copyright © Grub Street, London

Photographs by Bryce Attwell
Food prepared and styled for photography
by Clare Ferguson
Illustrations by Clare Ferguson
Photograph styling by Penny Markham

British Library Cataloguing in Publication
Data

Ferguson, Clare
    Gourmet vegetarian microwave cookery.
    1. Vegetarian cookery   2. Microwave
cookery
    I. Title
    641.5'636   TV837
    ISBN 0-948817-02-X
    ISBN 0-948817-05-4 Pbk

Computerset by Tradespools
Printed and bound in Italy by New
Interlitho

FOREWORD

'Cooking is like love – it should be entered into with abandon or not at all.'

Harriet van Horne (Vogue Magazine 1956.)

Boredom is often the enemy of appetite and good cooking. Beset as we are by unnecessary additives and the synthetic, it is a relief to turn, for inspiration, to the vegetable kingdom, with its truthful colours, flavours and textures, its aromatics, its variety. Fruit and vegetable foods, carefully selected in prime condition, are largely responsible for the maintenance of our day to day vitality. They contain many nutrients and constituents which cannot be stored or made by the body itself. Health-loving good cooks, chefs, gourmets, and gourmands, many of whom had previously seen the microwave oven merely as a culinary convenience, a time-saver, a short-cut defrost mechanism, or a means of reheating ready-cooked dishes now accept it as an energy saver, and a nutritional bonus in a busy life.

Although for some years I have been aware of the potential that microwave cooking possesses even I have been newly exhilarated by the aesthetic, technical and nutritional advantages of this ingenious kitchen appliance in regard to vegetarian cookery. Many are the dishes improved, simplified and even revolutionized by its imaginative use.

Herbs, fruits, vegetables, grains, nuts, seeds, dairy produce and cheeses not only keep lively good flavours, but have a concentration of taste altogether new. This is what I call their 'true taste'. In the past we frequently lost much of this in the cooking water (along with water-soluble vitamins) or allowed other tastes (added fats, sugars, salts and caramelization) to somewhat obscure the original savour. Colours, too, will often remain magically pristine: flower petals and seed heads stay pretty as a picture; while jewel-like fruit preserves and ices tend to convert many sceptics to new ways of thinking. By the same token, certain foods look and taste unfamiliar when cooked by microwave. I have taken great care in creating this highly personal selection of new recipes to capitalize on this new style of cooking.

I readily admit to being an uninhibited omnivore, so appreciate good wines, spirits and dairy products and use them often throughout this book. We have a wealth of food from many countries and many sources, besides good local produce, so it is a pleasure, hopefully, to extend the lacto-vegetarian repertoire. Many cooks like myself are curious to find new ways to sustain well-being through food. Too often vegetable foods are the metaphorical 'ladies in waiting' but never the queen. Once meat, fish and poultry no longer hold absolute sway of the kitchen and of the menu, a reappraisal takes place. Exploring a different pattern can be fascinating, informative, rewarding.

May I amicably point out that this is a recipe book of original ideas. It follows no strict regime: nor does it constitute a complete lacto-vegetarian diet. Vegans, fruitarians and others will find some sections more relevant than others. I have tried to break some new ground for those who have not cooked or eaten 'vegetarian-style' before, for those not consciously vegetarian, for those who simply wish to extend their culinary horizons, and for 'part-time' vegetarians.

Since I cherish civilized and healthy eating and drinking (preferably in amiable and witty company) as one of life's greatest joys, I hope that this book may enlarge the pleasures of your table and promote your very good health.

Clare Ferguson

CONTENTS

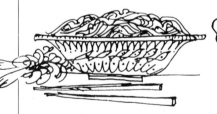

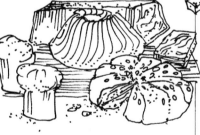

INTRODUCTION

New discoveries often require new approaches, and so successful microwave cooking involves various new techniques to be mastered and understood. In this book, the greatest care has been taken with instructions on the preparation of ingredients and techniques of working: methods of cutting; the shapes and sizes of mugs, measuring jugs, bowls, ring dishes, casseroles, flan dishes, terrines or loaf dishes; the forms and weights of the foods; the preparation and even arrangement of the food on or in its container; the need for the food to be halved, pierced, cross-cut, slashed, left whole, cooked covered or uncovered. All these factors greatly influence the success or failure of each recipe, for employing the correct microwave technique is of paramount importance in this sort of cooking. Mistakes can occur so very quickly and, alas, are often irreversible.

Timings given in the recipes are accurate for a 700-watt microwave cooker and should be carefully followed. If your cooker is of a different wattage, the *Cooking Times Adjustment Guide* on page 10 will help you to make the necessary corrections.

HOW A MICROWAVE OVEN WORKS

Microwave ovens transmit electrical energy by means of microwaves, which are electro-magnetic waves of very short length and high frequency. This way of disseminating energy is called radiation. Radiation can be of two types: ionising (which can be hazardous) and non-ionising (which does not damage human cells). Microwaves are of this second type and are particularly attracted to water molecules. By means of agitating (to thousands of millions of times a second) these water molecules in food, the temperature within the food itself is raised. In traditional cooking, the oven temperature is raised by transference of heat. But in microwave cooking, heat is produced essentially within the food itself, particularly by water, fat and sugar molecules.

Domestic models of microwave cooker run off a 13 or 15 amp power supply and socket.

Inside the oven, electrical energy from the mains is changed from high direction voltage to indirectional voltage. This is then converted by a fuse called the magnetron into electro-magnetic energy. In some cases a 'waveguide', 'stirrer fan' or 'revolving antennae', set in the side, base or roof of the oven, concentrates the waves and (to help equalize distribution) bounces them in all directions off specially constructed walls and the specially sealed door and door frame. Other models have a turntable to assist in the distribution of the microwaves. This action can only take place if the safety door is shut, completing the safety seal. It can never happen if the door is even slightly ajar. If the door is accidentally opened the process automatically shuts off. Stringent official regulations check the safety of all machines permitted entry to this country, but safety checks may also be made by qualified specialists. If you are concerned about the rate of cooking or the efficiency of the door seal mechanism, then ask your local dealer or the relevant department of the local authority to monitor the safety levels for you, for a nominal fee. (Consult your manufacturer's instruction manual for maintenance details.)

MICROWAVE ACTION

In a microwave cooker, microwaves are deflected by metal (also china with gold, silver and platinum decoration and lead crystal) but pass through glass, china, plastics, paper, oven bags and wood to act upon the molecules of the food itself.

Microwaves penetrate to a depth of 4.5 cm (about 2 inches) into the top, bottom and sides of the food so that pieces less than 9–10 cm (4 inches) thick start to cook immediately from internal heat, and not because they are surrounded by hot air or are touching a hot surface. This is why heatproof glass, completely baked (ie, *not* earthenware) ceramics, plastics (not melamine or urethane types), paper and oven bags can be used as cooking vessels. Microwaves pass through them without the containers themselves becoming hot, unless heat from the hot food transfers itself to them. No metal cooking vessels should ever be used. Microwaves do not penetrate metal; they

——— TABLE 1 ———
POWER SETTINGS, CALIBRATIONS
AND COOKING TIMES

Descriptions used in this book	VERY LOW		LOW		MEDIUM		MEDIUM HIGH		HIGH	
Descriptions given on author's microwave cooker	Warm 1	Low 2	Defrost 3	Braise 4	Simmer 5	Bake 6	Roast 7	Reheat 8	Sauté 9	High 700 Watt
Calibrations commonly used on other microwave cookers	1	2	3	4	5	6				7
% power *input*	10%	20%	30%	40%	50%	60%	75%		90%	100%
Approximate power *output* in watts	70W	140W	210W	280W	350W	420W	490–560W		630W	700W
Approx/ estimated cooking time in minutes		4 8 12 16 20 24 28 32 36 40	$3\frac{1}{4}$ $6\frac{3}{4}$ 10 $13\frac{1}{4}$ $16\frac{3}{4}$ 20 $23\frac{1}{4}$ $26\frac{3}{4}$ 30 $33\frac{1}{4}$	$2\frac{1}{2}$ 5 $7\frac{1}{2}$ 10 $12\frac{1}{2}$ 15 $17\frac{1}{2}$ 20 $22\frac{1}{2}$ 25	2 4 6 8 10 12 14 16 18 20	$1\frac{3}{4}$ $3\frac{1}{4}$ 5 $6\frac{3}{4}$ $8\frac{1}{4}$ 10 12 $13\frac{1}{4}$ 15 $16\frac{1}{2}$	$1\frac{1}{4}$ $2\frac{3}{4}$ 4 $5\frac{1}{4}$ $6\frac{3}{4}$ 8 $9\frac{1}{4}$ $10\frac{3}{4}$ 12 $13\frac{1}{4}$			1 2 3 4 5 6 7 8 9 10

TO USE TABLE 1

For example: ✒ If one of my recipes states 5 minutes at 60% and your 700-watt output microwave cooker has a calibration of 50% (not 60%) then you must look at the figure in the relevant column (50%) which is *6* minutes (and not 5 minutes).

But ✒ If your cooker is 600-watt output, with a calibration of 50%, not 60%, then as well as the calculated 6 minutes (see above adjustment) you will need to refer to Table 2, *Cooking Times Adjustment Guide* (page 10) and add on the relevant 10 seconds per minute, which gives $10 \times 6 = 60$ seconds extra. So total cooking time will be 6 + 1 minute = 7 minutes.

When manufacturers refer to a 700-watt oven they are referring to the oven's power *output*; its *input*, which is indicated on the back of the cooker, would be double that figure. The higher the wattage of a microwave cooker, the faster the rate of cooking. Thus food cooked at 700 watts on full power will cook in twice the time as food cooked at 350 watts. That said, the actual cooking performance of one 700-watt oven may vary from another with the same wattage because factors like oven cavity size affect cooking performance.

Unlike conventional ovens, the various microwave ovens have yet to be standardized. A HIGH or full power setting on one oven may be 500 watts while, on another model, HIGH or full power is 700 watts. The vast majority of ovens sold today are either 600, 650 or 700-watt ovens, but there are many ovens in use which have between 400 and 500 watts, and others of 720 watts.

IN THIS BOOK

700W is full power or HIGH
MEDIUM refers to 50%–60% of 700W
LOW refers to 30%–40% of 700W

If your cooker power output is lower than 700 watts then allow a longer cooking time for all the recipes in this book. Refer to Table 2 *Cooking Times Adjustment Guide.*

bounce off it and may therefore damage the magnetron. In most models, however, tiny amounts of metal foil may be used to protect small areas from overcooking (this is called shielding) since they deflect the microwaves from that one place. The foil must not touch the sides, base or top of the oven cavity or else 'arcing' (seen as a blue flash of light) may occur and this may pit the surfaces, reduce cooking efficiency or even render the cooker unusable. Certain 'new generation' microwaves which have dual function (browning and microwave function) or triple function (browning and conventional as well as microwave function) may safely employ metal utensils and metal cooking foil because of their different construction. In all circumstances, follow the manufacturer's instructions for best results.

◣ ———— TABLE 2 ———— ◢ COOKING TIMES ADJUSTMENT GUIDE
FOR EACH MINUTE OF COOKING TIME AT 700 WATTS (HIGH) IN THE RECIPES
Add 5 SECONDS at 650 WATTS per minute of cooking time
Add 10 SECONDS at 600 WATTS per minute of cooking time
Add 25 SECONDS at 500 WATTS per minute of cooking time
Add 45 SECONDS at 400 WATTS per minute of cooking time

For example: 4 minutes on HIGH at 700 watts would be adjusted to + 45 seconds × 4 for a 400-watt oven (ie, 180 seconds = 3 minutes). So cooking time would be adjusted to 4 + 3 = 7 minutes for a 400-watt cooker.

The microwave oven used to create these recipes
The recipes in this book were created, cooked and tested using a free-standing 700-watt cooker with a stirrer fan (no turntable).
    Its cubic capacity is large: .03 cubic metres (1.3 cubic feet).
    Its dimensions are: 23.5 cm (9½ in) high
                                      32.5 cm (13 in) wide
                                      42.5 cm (17 in) deep.
Ovens of smaller size may require an adjustment to the amount of food (both size of individual items and the volume) that can be cooked at any one time. Take this into account when considering individual recipes.

BROWNING

In order to 'brown' food in microwave cookers with no browning mechanism, heat must be attracted to the surface of the food, which must therefore contain some fats and/or sugars (although browning occurs naturally with some long-cooked foods). Certain glazes, marinades, seasonings (and treatments with herbs and spices) will contain these substances and may be used to help in the browning process. Better still, however, one should 'build in' naturally colourful ingredients to the recipe, so that the food itself is attractive without additional 'modification'.

BROWNING DISH WITH LID/FOR BROWNING FOODS
ON→
EMPTY DISH
PREHEATING: the empty browning dish.

    Certain conventional cooking processes produce crisp, crusty surfaces of bread, toast and fried potatoes through surface caramelization by transferred heat. A 'first generation' microwave oven (of purely microwave function) cannot easily perform this feat unaided. 'Browners', 'browning skillets' or 'crisper-griddles' are all examples of browning dishes or pans which are useful for the purpose and these I strongly recommend. After preheating, such dishes can act like a griddle or frying pan. The retained heat in their base is transferred to the surface of the food, thereby browning it when the two come into contact. In this book, and in my kind of cooking, I frequently specify use of these indispensable tools, which come in different materials, colours, sizes and proportions. They not only impart golden surfaces but also create delicious stocks and sauces (as a result of the sautéeing process) making microwave cooking far more versatile.
    Many 'second generation' combination microwave cookers have (as previously mentioned) dual or even triple functions: cooking by microwaves, by browning elements and by fan-assisted and/or conventional oven techniques, sometimes singly, sometimes in combination. Microwave cookers as part of a double oven are another arrangement.
    Some of my recipes which employ initial pan-browning may be satisfactorily adapted (refer to your particular manufacturer's instructions); others are better left unchanged, so use your own discretion in this matter.

TECHNIQUES

Microwave cooking requires knowledge of certain procedures to ensure evenness of cooking and heating and to produce thorough, consistent results.

SHAPES, SIZES AND ARRANGEMENT OF DISHES

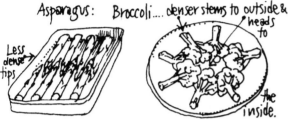

A straight-sided, shallow vessel with the minimum of corners gives the best results (corners produce overcooking). Microwave energy can enter such a dish from both sides as well as the top and base (if a trivet or rack is used). Round or oval dishes (or rectangular or square dishes with very well-rounded corners, such as the shape of certain browning dishes) promote most even cooking. Food in larger, shallower dishes cooks more quickly than food in smaller and deeper dishes. If the dish is rectangular or oval, then arrange each portion of food alternately, with the denser areas towards the outside as shown.

If the height of each portion is more than 6 cm (2½ in) then assume that the portions should be turned over halfway through cooking time.

If the dish is circular or square, then point the thinner or less dense parts of the portion towards the centre as shown. If using a bun or ring dish, tray or equivalent, rotate the whole dish a quarter turn four times, or a half turn twice during cooking to counteract hot (or cold) spots and promote even results, since microwave efficiency may vary. If using several dishes (as for individual desserts), place them on a heatproof plate or dish and rotate using the same technique. Many, if not most, microwave ovens have 'hot spots' which tend to overcook food in one particular area. Test for this by putting nine identical glasses or cups, with identical volumes of water, in an even pattern in the microwave oven. Microwave on HIGH, uncovered. The first water to boil is positioned on the 'hot spot'.

STIRRING, COVERING, PIERCING, WRAPPING, SHIELDING

⊕ Food that cannot easily be rotated or turned over should be stirred from the outside of the dish towards the centre, to help spread heat evenly. Certain sturdy foods, such as cubed vegetables, covered with cling film, or with lids, may be shaken (as well as rotated a little) instead of stirred, to produce similar results.

⊕ Covering during cooking prevents splattering and retains natural and added moisture. Plastic cling film and heavier grade microwave film often make ideal coverings because:

(1) they enclose any and all shapes of food and dishes (otherwise lidless)

(2) they can retain steam even when lightly pierced (which is essential) and so can retain pressure, ensuring that food cooks more efficiently

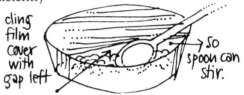

(3) a small opening may be left at one side, to insert a spoon for stirring (although less of a 'steamed under pressure' effect occurs)

(4) food may also be very loosely covered for a 'minimal steam' effect.

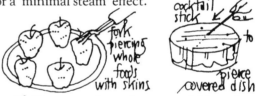

⊕ The natural membranes and skins of foods must always be pierced (use fine wooden satay sticks or wooden cocktail sticks, for example), as must applied membranes such as cling film. This prevents a build-up of pressure which may cause splitting and/or exploding of food. Assume that most dishes are to be microwave-cooked covered, unless otherwise stated. The exceptions are pan-fried or stir-fried dishes, or foods such as jacket potatoes. Sauces and stocks to be boiled down or reduced, and certain foods being dried, are left uncovered.

⊕ If covering a dish with a lid, always remove it carefully. The build-up of heat and steam and heat conduction will make the lid hot.

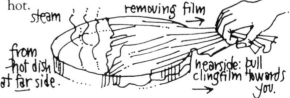

⊕ When food has been cooked on HIGH for a long time, always peel off cling film from the side furthest away so that steam does not accumulate near the face.

COVERING FOOD

🌶 Use greaseproof paper or baking parchment when partially covering food to prevent it from becoming soggy, and to help spread the heat. Cocktail sticks are useful for securing the paper in place if the food needs no turning.

🌶 When reheating, warming or cooking food which should have no surface moisture (such as bread rolls) or when splattering of fat could cause problems, cover the dish loosely with one or two sheets of absorbent kitchen paper. *Waxed* paper, plates or cups are unsuitable for use in microwave cookery.

🌶 Some experts advise that the surface of the food should *not* touch the plastic wrapping itself.

🌶 Table napkins of natural fibres (such as cotton and linen) may be used to wrap bread rolls and suchlike, but avoid all synthetic fibres.

🌶 Foods can be completely cooked in edible leaves, en papillote, in greaseproof or baking parchment or even in dampened rice paper, twisted loosely or folded beneath, in paper bags, in heavy duty plastic bags (perhaps with a plate inside), in heatproof oven bags, baskets, and so on. No metal fastenings, however, must be used. String, rubber bands, or non-metal ties will suffice to secure the bag loosely. Pierce it in several places.

🌶 Microwave cooking efficiency is reduced by an accumulation of juices (spilled foods or stains should be removed from interior cavity surfaces for they also absorb microwave energy), so the bag should be untied part way through cooking time and the liquid contents removed using a bulb baster. These may be retained for later use.

SHIELDING, HEAT RETENTION, STANDING, TENTING

When cooking any unevenly proportioned food for a medium to long time, it may be advisable to shield the smaller, thinner extremities with metal foil to prevent them from becoming overcooked (the foil should never be allowed to touch the walls of the oven).

The internal temperature of many dishes continues to rise so that they 'cook' even after they are removed from the microwave oven. Allow 'standing time' for the residual heat in food to be evenly distributed. This can also 'plump up' the tissues as in traditional cookery. Absolute timings are not always indicated for this stage so use your own judgement.

Foods with a high water content will retain heat longer than smaller, less dense foods, which cool more quickly. Some foods (including rice, beets or sauces) actually improve their texture, taste or consistency during standing time.

Because food continues to cook after it has left the oven, it may be necessary to arrest the process sometimes. Do this by 'cooling over ice' and stand the container over a bowl of ice or iced water. Smaller items such as pasta, for example, cool down very quickly and should be served soon after cooking.

Cover large foods, while making sauces or dressings, for example, in a loosely folded 'tent' of metal foil so that they do not lose heat but become succulent and complete their cooking process.

Note that jacket potatoes and similar foods can be very hot even after standing time and tenting, so beware!

The use of probes (sensors), memory, hold-warm function and the microwave oven rack can all assist in keeping foods at the desired serving temperature. Study your manufacturer's information.

EQUIPMENT FOR MICROWAVE COOKING

Metal containers must NEVER be used in a microwave oven or cooker; however it is important to follow the manufacturer's guidelines for use of each specific machine, since the range is now so great. To ascertain the suitability of other types of dish, mug, plate or casserole, stand it in the microwave oven and place a glass half filled with cold water inside or

beside it. If the dish remains cool and the water is hot, then the dish is 'heatproof' and suitable as 'microware'. If the dish becomes warm and the water is hot then the dish is less suitable, but usable. If the dish becomes hot and the water stays cool, then the dish is absorbing too much microwave energy and may break. Some containers used in conventional cookery will make excellent microware dishes, once tested as safe.

Certain items of equipment are invaluable. Among them are speciality heat-proof microwave cookware such as browning dishes or 'browners'. The type used in creating recipes for this book are of white ceramic with clear heatproof glass lids, in sizes of 25 cm (10 in) and 20 cm (8 in) diameter. They are essential for the execution of many dishes in this book. Other types of specialized dishes include 'crisper-griddles' or 'skillets'; ring dishes (plain and fluted); deep casserole dishes (with multi-purpose lids, useful for quiches); loaf dishes; bun dishes (with 6 or 8 holes, adaptable for ramekins, mousse or jelly moulds, timbales or brioche moulds); also roasting racks, trivets and individual cocotte-type dishes. Other equipment, such as plate stackers, domed 'all purpose cookers', pizza dishes, and so on, may add versatility if selected wisely. These, together with your 'own-tested' equipment (particularly a range of sturdy, calibrated, curved-base measuring cups and jugs, useful for everything from butter-melting to sauce and cocktail making, and dissolving gelatine mixtures) can make your microwave cooker more adaptable and convenient, so that creating meals becomes more fun and less effort.

USEFUL FOOD-RELATED TIPS AND TECHNIQUES

glaze or marinade

Colour Glazing, marinating, adding freshly squeezed juices, frosting or toppings, decorative seasonings (herbs, spices, nuts, seeds, etc) can all add taste and food value, as well as colour to certain recipes. If food is cooked in an oven bag it is more likely to deepen in colour (use no metal ties for such bags). Soy sauce, sesame oil, honey or caramel based glazes will add surface colour to certain foods, if required, without recourse to the browning dish.

Cross cutting   slashes

Cutting In certain instances, whole, dense foods may have a series of slashes, cross-cuts, or spiral cuts applied. These treatments increase efficient heat penetration.

stirrers of Wood, plastic.

Stirring Use a wooden spoon or spatula to stir fry or stir vegetable, fruit and sauce mixtures. This avoids scratching surfaces of vessels, and is more efficient. Stir from edges towards the centre for even results.

Seasonings Although salty foods and strongly flavoured foods are often not recommended for microwave cookery, I have found their limited use to be perfectly satisfactory. Use of salt should, however, be minimal and it should be dissolved in liquid quickly. Since many foods in microwave cookery retain their own 'distinctiveness', the amount of added salt becomes a matter of very personal taste. For both culinary and health reasons, try to develop a 'critical level' of seasoning, which suits your specific needs, but allows the true taste of each dish to triumph. Freshly ground pepper (and salt) and freshly crushed or ground spices (toasted or plain) almost always give savour. Use my recommendations as a guide.

no boiled eggs.   pierced eggs cooked out of shell   Use satay sticks.

Eggs No eggs in the shell (even if pierced) can ever be cooked in the microwave cooker – they will explode. Select fresh, preferably free-range eggs from a reliable source. Unless otherwise stated, all eggs used in microwave cookery should be at room temperature and are normally size 3. Raw, shelled eggs can satisfactorily be cooked whole only if the yolk membrane is first pierced, otherwise it will rupture and explode. Rather than use the tip of a sharp knife I prefer to keep small, sharp, wooden cocktail sticks, skewers or bamboo satay sticks to hand. With these I make several tiny holes round the edge of each yolk, without noticeable leakage (which is not only unsightly but interferes with the cooking process).

Fresh fruits, vegetables and herbs All those chosen for cooking in the microwave oven should be ripe, fresh, unblemished and as even in size as possible. Minimally sprayed, processed and stored products fresh from their growers are always most desirable. Many kinds of soft fruits should be scented when purchased, and feel heavy with juice.

Food is best purchased in season, but in recent times international air transport has made unseasonal, but hours-from-picked foods available in excellent condition, and hard-to-locate fungi, for example, eminently available within their short season. Best of all, try to grow your own! Herbs can thrive in pots and window boxes with sympathetic treatment. In many cases, the water that clings to leafy vegetables after washing is almost all that is needed to cook them. Salt added dry may cause discoloration and surface 'burn'. Follow the instructions given with individual recipes for best results. Jacket potatoes or similar vegetables, or fruit cooked 'au naturel' or whole must be pierced several times using a skewer or fork to prevent them exploding, or splitting.

Store produce carefully and prepare as near as possible to cooking time (not before) to retain goodness. Then use sharp, stainless steel knives to avoid damage to tissues and nutrients.

Contrary to popular belief, fruit and vegetables should always be brought to poaching or boiling temperatures as quickly as possible: cooking potatoes in cold water is positively wasteful of nutrients and foolish, no matter what you have been told!

If foods need to be 'held' or quickly reheated, it is good to know that the efficiency of microwave technology greatly reduces nutrient losses, compared to the old techniques.

NOTES ON RECIPES AND INGREDIENTS

My selection of recipes is to some degree a matter of personal taste. It also reflects personal experience in experimenting with the microwave cooker. In general I have tried to exploit its strengths and versatility. Wherever possible, I have shown through Cook's and Serving Tips and recipe introductions how to make the food just a little more special; I have also tried to emphasize how versatile some foods can be. For example, certain vegetable 'au naturel' dishes may be served as salads, luncheons or starters. Some preserves would be excellent as digestifs, desserts or cocktail bases, and so on. By the same token, a large section on stocks and soups is included, primarily because these give the cook so many different possibilities and options for bringing out the best in whatever chosen dishes they will enhance.

As a gourmet always prefers to seek out food in season and in the freshest condition possible, I have not advocated the use of frozen foods in these recipes. A few call for bottled, canned or cured ingredients or condiments. This is because they offer some specific advantage of taste, quality or texture. Certain dried foods are also used, for the same reasons and for their convenience.

For the best results, use the ingredients stipulated in the recipes. If these are difficult to obtain, acceptable substitutes may be used. The original 'gourmet' ingredients will, however, add that all-important 'extra' quality to the dish.

CREAM, CHEESE, YOGURT AND TOFU

My recipes include single, whipping and double creams, clotted cream, thick and soured creams. They provide, in sauces, mousses and purées, a richness and texture of particular subtlety. Imported French crème fraîche is a superb product, silky in the mouth, sharper than whipped cream yet lighter and more clean-tasting. Cream products, used discreetly within the context of a balanced diet high in whole grains, raw fruits and vegetables and relatively low in other saturated fats, yet fibre-high, give palatability and pleasure (as well as useful nutrients) to the diet.

Fromage frais and fromage blanc, once used as generic names for all 'fresh' cheeses (no matter what their fat content) now generally refer to popular, refreshing, low-fat products, with such names as Jockey, Bon Blanc or Petit-Suisse. Their taste is somewhere between crème fraîche, yogurt and cheese, and they possess a delicate graininess and great allure. These products should be refrigerated and kept away from the light.

Many of the cheeses mentioned in this book are imports from France, Italy, Switzerland, Greece, Spain, Scandinavia, Holland, or even the Middle East. Many good versions of these cheeses are now made in this country, although goats' cheeses, for example, tend to be sold here fresher and younger than, say, their French counterparts, so do not always produce the same effects.

Among cheeses I use and enjoy in cookery are: ricotta, curd, cream and quark cheeses, caboc, and occasionally a full fat cheese flavoured with garlic and herbs, or peppercorns, for example.

Plain or 'natural' yogurt now comes in a bewildering number of varieties. I tend to use the thickest strained Greek variety, which is far

creamier in texture than most yogurts. For drinks, soups or to achieve a lighter effect, use a low fat variety if you must, but nothing can replace the perfection of good Greek yogurt. (I always prefer to buy plain yogurt and flavour it myself than buy prepared products, though these are becoming better and less sweet in response to public demand.)

Tofu, or soya bean curd (fresh, or 'silken') or the more firmly pressed type is available from many Asian, oriental, wholefood, and health food stores. Dried soy bean cakes, or ready-dried tofu, which have very different qualities, can also be found. Soya milk may be substituted for milk if wished, but results will not be quite the same. For strict vegetarians or vegans, or those who wish to eat no animal-derived products, these are the high-protein alternatives to cheese, milk and yogurt.

SETTING AGENTS

Powdered gelatine and natural pectin (which forms its own gel in homemade fruit jellies) are the two setting agents I prefer and use. Sheet gelatine, of high quality, is also sometimes available. In all cases, follow recipe method when using gelatine in microwave recipes. (For sheet gelatine follow instructions given with the pack.) Agar-agar (for those who wish to avoid animal-derived products) is a seaweed product, bought in stick, flake or powder form. It must be added to cold liquid and then boiled, in order to set, but will do so without refrigeration. I have found, however, that the 'gel' tends to fracture when a jelly is turned out, and the texture in homemade foods is less acceptable than gelatine. Substitution may be made, however, if wished: 10 ml (2 level tsp) of powdered agar-agar should be allowed to set 600 ml (1 pint) of liquid, for a cold soufflé, ice cream or mousse. Work out the total of liquids in the recipe and measure out the requirement. Add this to some (or all) of the recipe liquid. Heat to boiling then add to remaining ingredients without delay: it will set very quickly. Agar-agar is available from Asian, oriental, wholefood, vegetarian and specialist stores. One sachet contains almost 60 ml (4 level tbsp) of powder.

WINES AND STOCK

I make no excuse for using wines and spirits in my cooking. I regard them, quite simply, as the best flavoured 'basic stock' imaginable for savoury dishes, sweet dishes and beverages alike. The amounts needed are often small, yet the benefits bestowed immense. Many of the specified spirits, vermouths, apéritifs, liqueurs and digestifs are available as miniatures.

Fruit eaux-de-vie (or fruit brandies) are clear, potent spirits which contain the absolute essence of the original fruit. They are, to my mind, gastronomic tours de force, not to be missed: one bottle can transform many meals. Buy them whilst travelling abroad. Fraise, Framboise, Poire, Quetsch, Mirabelle (and Boukha from Tunisia) are my favourites.

Whenever possible use homemade stocks (see Chapter 1) made from fresh raw materials, herbs, spices and aromatics. Not only do these give the best flavour, but, when reduced, add the particular pungency so often necessary for good soups, sauces and composite dishes. Select a stock suited to the dish or dishes you intend to cook or use vegetable or fruit stocks or juices saved from conventional cooking (microwave cooking yields little or no waste liquids, on the whole, for it is so efficient). Keep these liquids refrigerated or frozen for later use. Vegetable stock cubes are also an alternative, though many contain additives. Aerated and spring mineral waters are useful to have on hand.

SEASONINGS AND YEAST

Ready-made sauces, specific seasonings (such as horseradish), seasoned salts and peppers, seeds, herbs, dried 'petales' or 'boutons' (of citrus flowers), salted bean preparations, flavoured mustards, vegetable extracts, purées, chilli and bean pastes, mango and lime extracts, pickles, pastes or sauces, syrups, sugars, honeys, fruit jellies and conserves, are used with specific purpose throughout these recipes. Substitutes or omissions cannot be expected to produce the desired results.

The yeast chosen for bread recipes is a super-quick variety called micronized ('Easy-Blend' or 'Easy-Bake') dried yeast, in powder (not granule) form. It is added to the dry ingredients (without liquid) as one adds baking powder and is available in sachets from good supermarkets, many of whom stock their own brand; it makes bread-making simple. Ordinary dried yeast or fresh yeast must be 'sponged' before it is combined with the remaining liquid, then dry ingredients. If converting recipes, one sachet of Easy-Blend Yeast (used with 750 g or 1½ lb bread flour) is equivalent to 25 g (1 oz) fresh yeast or 15 g (½ oz) of ordinary dried yeast.

Vinegars these days are available in an enormous variety, but the best are costly, made by the old Orleans process. Champagne vinegar and Aceto Balsamico (from Modena, Italy) are two superb specimens suited for salad-making. Fruit vinegars (strawberry, raspberry, blackcurrant and even blueberry vinegar) can contribute greatly to many recipes, while rice and chilli vinegars are delicious. Tarragon vinegar has its uses, but many other flavoured vinegars, to my mind, use stale herb flavours to overcome indifferent vinegars. Spirit or distilled vinegars are strong, colourless and may be used in pickling.

AROMATICS, OILS AND BUTTERS

Aromatics often featured in my recipes include orange, lemon, mandarin and lime peel; green or scented teas; green, white and black peppercorns; fresh (in brine) or dried wasabi; fresh Laos root (lesser galangal); root ginger; knobbly but tender-fleshed lime leaves (fresh and dried); tamarind pulp; fresh haldi (turmeric) root; white and red garlic; and red shallots and onions.

All kinds of chillies are available these days: fresh and dried, from the tiny bird's eye kind (scorching hot) to the plumper, triangular green jalapeno type (sweet, mildly hot) and the long curved Guajillo chillies. Habanearo (tiny, irregular, green and potent) are also used. Approach all chillies with caution; do not rub eyes, nose or other delicate tissues or else wear rubber gloves.

Many aromatics such as lemon grass, cinnamon sticks, vanilla pods, freshly extracted seeds, berries, nuts, leaves, flower-heads and stems may be twisted, crushed, shredded, puréed, bruised, crumbled or slit in my recipes. These treatments help to extract the maximum aroma during the shorter cooking times, though in many cases microwave ovens tend to accentuate such flavours. Many nuts, seeds, and even coffee beans can be microwave 'toasted' to enhance and develop flavour. Sea vegetables (seaweeds), particularly the dried kinds, available from Japanese and oriental food stores, can contribute greatly as aromatics. Triple-

distilled citrus and rose flower waters and others are non-alcoholic and superb.

Finest Olive Oil

Olive oil comes in many grades, the finest being extra virgin olive oil and then virgin olive oil. Both of these have been cold pressed (no heat applied during manufacture); they have low oleic acidity, wonderful aroma, colour and taste, and a mellow 'fruitiness'. Containing monounsaturates (considered desirable for health), olive oil seems a time-honoured classic winner. It is best kept out of the light: cans or coloured glass bottles will protect it from the ravages of sunlight. 'Pure' olive oil, a lower grade, has been hot pressed and is perfectly good for many recipes, in blends or in dressings.

good oil ... good health ... select & use carefully ... for great taste

Seed oils such as safflower, sunflower and corn oil (polyunsaturates), rape seed and peanut oil are good for most uses in cooking where no particular added taste is required. Sesame seed oils (especially cold-pressed varieties) are delicious and beneficial, though the darker sesame oil has great appeal for many. Almond oil, almost tasteless, is useful.

nut oils

Nut oils, such as hazelnut and walnut, though expensive, and not recommended for normal cooking at high temperatures, seem to give good results in microwave cooking when used with another oil or butter, or when used to dress freshly-cooked food for use hot or cold.

Butters, too, vary in taste, colour, quality and degree of saltiness. (I find no place for any kind of butter-substitute in a gourmet regime.) Use the type you most prefer, although unsalted butter does give a delectable, clean taste. On the other hand, I like the vigour that many salted butters provide and use them often. Clarified butter is specified for one or two recipes and should not be confused with *ghee*, which has a very distinctive flavour. For use in the microwave oven, butter should be at room temperature, unless otherwise stated.

Nut butters, such as tahini (toasted sesame seed purée), peanut butter (some without additives) and even cashew butter, are available and delicious.

STOCKS, SOUPS AND APPETIZERS

POLISH BEETROOT STOCK

This rich red, sharp-flavoured stock lends itself to any borscht-type variation and is delicious with any addition (such as cabbage, dill pickles and dill and sour cream) or with cooked apples, béchamel and extra grated fresh beets, as a hot thick soup. Fresh radish, dill, chives and firm-cooked egg can be added to the chilled soup, together with smetana or yogurt. Jellied, this soup is exquisite served with soured cream and caraway seeds.

Makes about 600 ml (1 pint)

15 ml (1 level tbsp) olive oil
175 g (6 oz) red onions, cut into eighths
3 garlic cloves, skinned and crushed
125 g (4 oz) carrots, chopped
125 g (4 oz) radishes, trimmed and quartered
10 g (¼ oz) dried porcini or cèpes fungi, crumbled finely
125 g (4 oz) raw beetroot, shredded or cubed
30 ml (2 level tbsp) red wine vinegar
150 ml (¼ pint) dry red wine
900 ml (1½ pints) boiling water
2.5 ml (½ level tsp) salt
15 ml (1 level tbsp) sugar

1. Preheat a 25 cm (10 inch) browning dish for 5 minutes.
2. Add the first 7 ingredients and toss in the heated dish. Microwave, uncovered, on HIGH for 2 minutes.
3. Add the vinegar, wine and boiling water, cover with a lid, and microwave on HIGH for a further 10 minutes. Adjust seasonings to taste. Use as a chunky soup or strain for stock.

ROSY VEGETABLE STOCK

An almost instant, one step, highly-flavoured stock for a variety of uses. With most vegetable, cereal, grain or pasta dishes this stock gives added body and emphasis. With appropriate additions it forms the basis of a good soup.

Makes about 600 ml (1 pint)

125 g (4 oz) onion, skinned and quartered
125 g (4 oz) carrots, chopped
2 celery stalks, sliced
2 garlic cloves
4 allspice berries
15 ml (1 level tbsp) black peppercorns
2 cloves
4 juniper berries
125 g (4 oz) tomatoes, quartered
15 g (½ oz) parsley stalks, chopped
600 ml (1 pint) boiling water
2 ml (½ tsp) salt

1. Put all the ingredients, except for the liquid, in a food processor or mincer and process to a coarse purée.
2. Turn into a large, deep soup dish, bowl or ring mould and add the boiling water.
3. Cover with cling film and microwave on HIGH for 20 minutes, giving the dish three quarter turns during cooking period. Add salt to taste. Allow to cool a little, strain through a plastic sieve and use as stock, soup or freeze for future use.

TAMARIND, GALANGAL AND CHILLI STOCK

Once strained, this stock looks rather like tea and it is actually interesting enough to drink in little glassfuls, like a tisane. Its real use, however, is for soup bases, composite dishes and with noodle, rice and cereal dishes. Some of the ingredients may be difficult to locate but once purchased can be kept for a long time (tamarind in a dark glass jar; galangal in a plastic bag in the vegetable drawer of the refrigerator). There is an almost medicinal 'cleanness' to the taste.

Makes 600 ml (1 pint)

1 large fresh red or green chilli, halved
125 g (4 oz) spring onions, trimmed and halved
125 g (4 oz) carrots, chopped
15 g (½ oz) pressed tamarind (cake form), crumbled
10 ml (2 level tsp) fresh galangal (Laos root), thinly sliced
600 ml (1 pint) boiling water
salt and/or soy sauce to season

Garnish

fresh herbs of choice, noodles, bean curd, tiny dumplings or wontons as wished

1. Put the first 6 ingredients, in order, into a large heatproof measuring jug. Cover and microwave on HIGH for 8 minutes, stirring occasionally. Leave to stand for a further 8 minutes, stirring from time to time.
2. Strain through a plastic sieve or jelly bag,

taste, adjust seasoning as wished and add herbs and other garnishes of your choice.

SERVING TIP

This makes excellent soup for Mongolian hot pot (also called fire pot or sha jang jou), which is kept hot at the table in a charcoal-filled utensil. To the soup are added sliced vegetables, noodles, bean curd and rehydrated mushrooms.

CLASSIC VEGETABLE STOCK

A mellow but persuasive, fresh taste makes this stock eminently useful for all cooking purposes. Fortified with some dry white wine or vermouth and additional freshly-chopped seasonal green herbs, it becomes an elegant soup. Add some sweet corn kernels and stirred egg and it gains a different appeal.

Makes 700 ml (1¼ pints)

30 ml (2 level tbsp) fruity olive oil
125 g (4 oz) onion, skinned and cut into eighths
1 celery stalk, roughly chopped
125 g (4 oz) carrots, roughly chopped
2 cloves garlic, skinned
15 g (½ oz) parsley stalks, chopped
1.1 litres (2 pints) boiling water
15 ml (1 level tbsp) white peppercorns
1–2 cloves
1 fresh bay leaf, crushed
5 ml (1 level tsp) coarse sea salt

Garnish

fresh green herb

1. Preheat a large 25 cm (10 inch) browning dish for 5 minutes.
2. Add the olive oil, onion, celery, carrots, garlic and parsley stalks. Microwave on HIGH for 2 minutes, uncovered, stirring once.
3. Pour over the boiling water and add the spices. Cover with a lid and microwave on HIGH for 15 minutes.

4. Stir in the salt, cover, and microwave on HIGH for a further 5 minutes.
5. Allow the stock to cool a little, then strain through a stainless steel or plastic sieve or jelly bag. Use as a stock, soup or freeze for future use.

SPICED HALDI STOCK

Fresh turmeric root (haldi) is sometimes to be found in good Asian and oriental supermarkets. Its brilliant orange flesh and subtle aroma are delectable. Somewhere near the same effect can be obtained by using powdered/ground turmeric. This delicate, mild golden stock or soup base has an interesting 'bite' of chillies, a surprise to the palate. If wished, add coconut cream or water to the cooked stock and sprinkle with crisp 'Bombay Mix'.

Makes 700 ml (1¼ pints)

30 ml (2 level tbsp) grapeseed oil
15 g (4 oz) onions, skinned and quartered
125 g (4 oz) carrots, chopped coarsely
1 celery stalk, chopped
2 garlic cloves, skinned and crushed
5 ml (1 level tsp) coriander seeds, crushed
2.5 ml (½ level tsp) ground cumin
1 small fresh or dried red chilli, split or crushed
1 cinnamon stick, crushed
4 cm (1½ inch) turmeric root, sliced finely, or 2.5 ml (½ level tsp) ground turmeric
1.1 litres (2 pints) boiling water
5 ml (1 level tsp) salt

1. Preheat a large 25 cm (10 inch) browning dish for 5 minutes.
2. Add the oil, vegetables, spices and aromatics. Microwave, uncovered, on HIGH for 2 minutes.
3. Add the boiling water and stir well. Cover with a lid and microwave on HIGH for a further 15 minutes. Taste and adjust seasoning.
4. Microwave, covered, on HIGH for a further 5 minutes.
5. Allow the stock to cool a little, strain through a stainless steel or plastic sieve or jelly bag. Garnish if used as a soup with sliced spring onions or leek tops, and cooked rice or potato cubes.

HI JIKI SEAWEED STOCK

This smoky-hued stock has an elemental Japanese appeal (though traditional dashi, or stock, would use bonito shavings from tuna to provide extra body). If more astringency is required then some green tea could be infused in the boiling water, but to most tastes the hair-like seaweed provides the authentic 'sea flavour'. Add tamari or soy according to your own personal preference. This is a good stock for use with noodles and rice, with delicate leafy vegetables and in sauces to accompany vegetables such as salsify, scorzonera and artichokes. Hi Jiki is available in sachets from oriental stores.

Makes 700 ml (1¼ pints)

175 g (6 oz) leeks, green and white parts, chopped coarsely
100 g (4 oz) carrots, chopped coarsely
1 medium fennel bulb, quartered
60 ml (4 tbsp) dried Hi Jiki shreds (seaweed)
1.1 litres (2 pints) boiling water
60 ml (4 tbsp) mirin (sweetened sake) or sweet sherry
30 ml (2 tbsp) rice or white wine vinegar
2.5 ml (½ level tsp) Wasabi (green horseradish powder or paste)
tamari or soy sauce (optional)

1. Put the first 4 ingredients into a large, deep soup dish, bowl or ring mould and pour in the boiling water.
2. Microwave on HIGH, covered, for 10 minutes. Add mirin, vinegar and the Wasabi to give a 'bite' that is not overpowering. Use less if preferred.
3. Stir well, cover and microwave for a further 3 minutes on HIGH.
4. Leave to stand, covered, for 5–10 minutes. Strain the cooled stock through a stainless steel or plastic sieve or jelly bag. Taste and add a little tamari or soy sauce if wished.

SOUP STOCK VERDE

In an age when colour and flavour 'enhancers' are constantly being added to foods, it is important to know how to make an absolutely pure, unadulterated stock which has its own good colour and also retains the scent of fresh-growing produce. By chopping the food finely just before cooking, goodness and flavour are quickly extracted. Make this stock to use fresh as soup, or for any recipe calling for flavoursome cooking stock. The proportions of the six green vegetables may vary somewhat as long as the total weight is no less than 700 g (1½ lb).

Makes 900 ml (1½ pints)

175 g (6 oz) onions
175 g (6 oz) spinach or spinach beet leaves
125 g (4 oz) fennel bulbs
125 g (4 oz) fresh green beans
125 g (4 oz) celery sticks
4 fresh bay leaves, crushed
5 ml (1 level tsp) coarse sea salt
1.1 litres (2 pints) boiling water

1. Skin and quarter the onions, tear the spinach leaves into pieces, slice the fennel and break up beans and celery into similar length pieces.
2. Put half the volume of vegetables into a food processor and process until roughly chopped, then put them into a deep 3.4 litre (3 quart) heatproof casserole. Repeat this process with the second volume of vegetables. Add to the casserole together with the crushed bay leaves. Add salt and boiling water, cover with a lid and microwave on HIGH for 12–15 minutes or until aromatic.
3. Strain contents of the casserole through a non-metal sieve or jelly bag, pressing down to extract all the liquid. Discard the solids. Use the stock as a soup (adding herb and/or cooked and drained pasta) or for cooking rice, grains and other composite dishes.

SERVING TIP
Try stirring homemade Pesto San Lorenzo (see page 29) into the soup at serving time: fragrant gusts of basil rise from the bowl! This soup is also a superb vehicle for Bugialli's Pasta (see page 92) previously cooked, drained and added to the soup, with the pesto as additional bonus.

See photograph page 66–67

CHAYOTE AND SPROUT SOUP WITH TORTILLA CRISPS

Chayote (also called Xu-Xu, Choko or Cristophene) are pear-shaped members of the squash family, with soft seeds which should be discarded. They grow easily (indeed the soup's name has additional point since my chayote actually sprouted during its sojourn in the refrigerator!). For this recipe the brussels sprouts are halved and cooked quickly in a ring dish. The method is energy-efficient, convenient, and allows no time for bitterness to develop. Use some medium dry wine such as Vouvray or dryish cider to give balance to the taste. Heat the tortilla crisps just before serving and pass them with this curious but satisfying thick green soup, or use as a garnish on top.

Makes 900 ml (1½ pints)

50 g (2 oz) onion, shallots or spring onions, skinned and chopped
15 ml (1 tbsp) olive oil
450 g (1 lb) small brussels sprouts, trimmed and halved lengthwise
300 ml (½ pint) vegetable stock
225 g (8 oz) medium chayote, halved, seeded and sliced
150 ml (¼ pint) medium white wine or cider
50 g (2 oz) cream cheese, cubed
5 ml (1 tsp) freshly squeezed lemon juice
salt and freshly ground pepper

Garnish

1 packet tortilla crisps (tostadilla)
chopped parsley (optional)

1. Put the onion, olive oil and the washed sprouts (with the moisture still clinging to them) into a large heatproof ring dish. Cover with

cling film and microwave on HIGH for 6 minutes, giving the dish a shake and rotating it every 2 minutes. Test sprouts to see if they are ready; they should be tender and sweet.

2. Put the contents of the dish into a food processor or blender and process, in short bursts, to a rough purée with half of the stock.

3. Put the chayote, with a little more of the stock and a splash of the wine, in the ring dish. Cover with cling film and microwave on HIGH for 4 minutes, shaking and rotating the dish halfway through cooking time.

4. Reduce the chayote and all the remaining stock and wine, together with the cream cheese and lemon, to a smooth purée. Add the sprouts and process again. Taste, adjust the seasonings and either serve warm or reheat, if wished, for 2–3 minutes (or until hot) in a large heatproof serving dish.

5. Place 8–12 tortilla crisps on kitchen paper and microwave on HIGH for 1 minute. Serve with the soup and chilled white wine or cider.

CAPSICUM SOUP ORTIZ

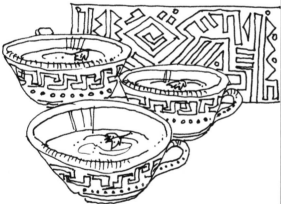

This delicious, rosy-coloured, Caribbean-style soup is best served in small soup cups or china pots, as it has quite a powerful flavour. At serving time, each bowl should have a spoonful of cool, fresh fromage blanc or fromage frais added, with perhaps one or two coriander leaves. The concept of a red pepper soup is one I learned from Elizabeth Lambert Ortiz while working with her during a recent television series. My recipe uses a preheated browning dish to 'pan grill' the peppers, so making the skins easily removable after leaving them to stand in a plastic bag (another Ortiz tip). The soup may be served hot, warm or chilled.

Serves 4

two 225 g (8 oz) large red capsicums
15 ml (1 level tbsp) harissa paste (hot pepper-spiced purée)
60 ml (4 tbsp) fromage blanc 'battu' or fromage frais
1.25 ml (¼ tsp) sea salt
300 ml (½ pint) well flavoured vegetable stock

Garnish

60 ml (4 tbsp) fromage blanc or fromage frais
coriander leaves (optional)

1. Preheat a large 25 cm (10 inch) browning dish for 8 minutes. Remove stem and seed ends of capsicums, cut off bases and slit flesh down one side to allow the peppers to be rolled out flat. (Try to waste as little as possible.)

2. Quickly place the capsicums, skin side down, in the pan, flattening them with a heatproof plate until they have softened and will stay in position. Remove the plate.

3. Microwave on HIGH, uncovered, for 4 minutes, giving the pan a quarter turn halfway through cooking time.

4. Remove the capsicums, put into a plastic bag and seal. Leave for 3 minutes or until the skin feels loose. Remove the capsicums from the bag and slide the skin away, using kitchen paper. Dice the flesh and put into a food processor or blender with the harissa, the first 60 ml (4 tbsp) measure of cheese and the salt. Process, in short bursts, to a purée. Add the stock and purée again.

5. Serve warm, garnished with a little extra fromage blanc and a coriander leaf. If the soup is preferred hot, reheat, covered, for 2 minutes or so. Alternatively, chill and serve icy cold, garnished as above.

—— COOK'S TIP ——

Fromage blanc 'battu' is whipped (it has a light, yogurt-cheese texture) and is often known by its brand name of 'Jockey'. Fromage frais will do equally well if forked until creamy and, if neither is obtainable, Greek sheep's milk yogurt is excellent but may have a higher fat content. Harissa is available in small cans from many delicatessens and from Asian and North African stores.

GREEN REVIVAL SOUP

A brilliant, aromatic and utterly delicious soup such as this makes one feel full of life and vitality – hence the name. Many diners who neither like nor eat watercress or coriander as garnishing herbs will gladly consume them when served this way. The soup takes very few minutes to make, yet has an accomplished suavity. Provide each diner with a half lime to squeeze into the soup when serving, so that the fragrance is absolute.

Makes about 600 ml (1 pint)

3 bunches fresh watercress, cleaned and chopped
1 bunch fresh coriander, cleaned and chopped
½ bunch flat leaf parsley, cleaned and chopped
25 g (1 oz) butter
30 ml (2 level tbsp) flour
2.5 ml (½ level tsp) sea salt
pinch cayenne
300 ml (½ pint) buttermilk, or natural yogurt

To serve

extra buttermilk or natural yogurt (optional)
sesame or poppy seeds, toasted (optional)
2 fresh limes

1. Check through the herbs, discarding any dirty or damaged parts, then chop (including the stalks) into 2.5 cm (1 inch) chunks. Put the herbs into a colander, rinse in cold water and leave to stand.
2. Put the butter, flour, salt and cayenne into a large 1.1 litre (2 pint) heatproof measuring jug and microwave on HIGH, uncovered, for 50 seconds to 1 minute, stirring once until the mixture is bubbly and golden. Add the buttermilk or yogurt, whisking constantly.
3. Microwave on HIGH, uncovered, for 3 minutes, whisking or stirring 3 times during cooking. Whisk again to obtain a smooth sauce.
4. Put the herbs, with the water still clinging to their leaves, into a food processor or blender and process to obtain fine shreds. If necessary do this in several batches.
5. Add the hot sauce, a little at a time, and process in short bursts until an evenly green mixture is obtained. (Do not over-process.) Taste and adjust the seasoning as necessary.
6. Serve hot (or chill and serve cold) with spooned buttermilk or yogurt on top and some seeds if wished.
7. Cut the limes crosswise with a diagonally cut 'spout' (see photograph page 28) and encourage diners to squeeze a little juice over each spoonful. A malty granary loaf or some light lacy French bread would be the ideal companion for this soup.

See photograph page 28

CARROT, ORANGE AND CHARENTAIS SOUP

Radiantly colourful, delicious and effortless, this soup is served hot, warm or cold over ice-cold segments of charentais. The tastes are so true that no seasoning whatsoever is required and the contrasts of textures, temperatures and smoothness make a bold impression.

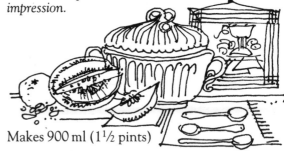

Makes 900 ml (1½ pints)

700 g (1½ lb) charentais melon, chilled
350 g (12 oz) carrots, peeled and coarsely shredded or grated
150 ml (¼ pint) vegetable stock
1 large orange
150 ml (¼ pint) dry white wine or cider

1. Remove and discard the skin and seeds from the melon. Slice into segments over a serving dish so that no juice is lost.
2. Put the carrots and stock in a medium-sized heatproof bowl, cover with a lid or cling film and microwave on HIGH for 5 minutes.
3. Meanwhile remove the zest of the orange in fine shreds and remove and discard the pith. Slice the orange flesh into cubes and put into a food processor or blender with the zest. Add the cooked carrot and stock and half of the melon (reserve half for serving) and wine or cider. Process to a smooth soup consistency in short bursts.
4. If serving the soup warm, pour over the

reserved melon and serve straight away. If the soup is preferred hot, return the serving bowl to the oven, cover with a lid or cling film and microwave on HIGH for 4 minutes or until very hot. (This will depend on how long the soup has been standing.) Do not overheat. If the soup is to be served cold, chill for ½–¾ hour before pouring over the chilled melon segments.

PALESTINE VICHYSSOISE

Velvety Jerusalem artichoke and leek soup has the twin attributes of a beautiful green hue and superlative flavour. Although it is considered healthier to retain the skin of vegetables whenever possible, I make an exception here, preferring the absolute smoothness of colour and texture of the peeled vegetables. The leek, however, should include both white and green parts and must be well washed to remove any grit. The soup can be served thick and nourishing, accompanied by some crusty granary rolls, or diluted to a thin cream and served with Melba toast or crisp cracker biscuits.

Makes 700–900 ml (1¼–1½ pints)

15 ml (1 tbsp) olive oil
700 g (1½ lb) Jerusalem artichokes, skinned and cubed
350 g (12 oz) leeks, trimmed, sliced thinly and washed
175 g (6 oz) potatoes, peeled and cubed
150 ml (¼ pint) milk
150 ml (¼ pint) vegetable stock
coarse sea salt and freshly ground black pepper

Garnish

15 ml (1 level tbsp) finely shredded leek rings, spring onions or chives

1. Put the oil, artichokes, leeks and potatoes into a 3.4 litre (3 quart) casserole and stir until lightly coated with oil. Cover with cling film and microwave on HIGH for 10 minutes.
2. Put half the cooked vegetables into a food processor or blender with the milk and process, in short bursts, to a smooth purée.
3. Repeat the process with the second half of the vegetables, using stock in place of milk.
4. Pour the puréed vegetables back into the casserole. Add salt and pepper to taste. Microwave, uncovered, on HIGH for 4 minutes to bring back to boiling. Serve sprinkled with the herbs of your choice.

—— COOK'S TIP ——

If preferred, the soup may be diluted by the addition of extra milk, stock, white wine or a mixture of all three. Increase the final heating time correspondingly.

HERB AND SPICE CROÛTONS

Croûtons cooked in a microwave oven are deliciously crisp and easy to make. Serve them with any food which needs 'texture enhancing' or simply to provide interest to bland-flavoured dishes.

Serves 2–4

40 g (1½ oz) clarified butter (see below)
2.5 ml (½ level tsp) paprika
1.25 ml (¼ tsp) turmeric
2.5 ml (½ level tsp) celery salt
15 ml (1 level tbsp) freshly chopped parsley
5 ml (1 level tsp) dill, dried or fresh
freshly ground pepper
75 g (3 oz) or 2 thick slices wholewheat bread, cubed

1. To clarify butter, put it in a heatproof jug and microwave on HIGH for 35–38 seconds, or until it begins to spatter. Leave to stand a few seconds. Pour off and (or) strain the clear golden liquid, leaving the sediment behind. Allow enough butter to leave 40 g (1½ oz) for use in the recipe.
2. Heat the clarified butter in a large, 20 cm (8 inch) browning dish on HIGH for 1 minute.
3. Add the spices and herbs and microwave on HIGH for a further 30 seconds.
4. Add the croûtons (seasoned) and stir well to combine all the ingredients. Microwave on HIGH for 3½ to 4½ minutes (depending on crispness required), stirring each minute. Serve with soups or with vegetable accompaniments.

MAURICE'S PICK-ME-UP

This little treasure is one of many imparted by a dear friend, Maurice Duault, who first made it while staying as a guest in our house. It was the morning after some very late and lively carousing. He decided that a certain frivolity made from the very same cognac that he had whisked through customs, and the Roquefort left on the cheeseboard after our party, was a veritable reviver of the spirits. How right he was! This potted cheese recipe is not for the faint-hearted: it is pungent with salty flavour and redolent of cognac. We enjoyed it as a late breakfast (with a little of the same excellent liquor and copious cups of strong black coffee) followed by a handful of fresh cherries. Since this recipe keeps well, the remainder may be left in a cool larder or refrigerator and used with crisp biscuits or crackers, croûtes or French bread as an appetizer or after-dinner savoury.

Makes 350 g (12 oz)

---

25 g (1 oz) unsalted or lightly salted butter

---

2 shallots, skinned and finely chopped

---

275 g (10 oz) Roquefort, broken into 15–18 pieces

---

15 ml (1 tbsp) Rémy Martin cognac

---

freshly ground black pepper

---

crusty ficelle bread, toasted

---

1. Put the butter and chopped shallot into a medium sized heatproof pot or china terrine. Microwave on HIGH, uncovered, for 1½ minutes or until the shallot has 'melted' to transparency and the butter is hot.
2. Stir in the crumbled cheese, mashing it roughly with a fork.
3. Measure out then trickle in the cognac with one hand, constantly mashing and blending with the fork in the other hand. The mixture should become creamy but slightly rough. (Too much refinement is not desirable.)
4. Bring to the table while still warm. Serve with good bread or toast, smearing only a little at a time on to tiny corners of crust. Remember also to provide the imperative accompaniment of excellent coffee.

BACHELOR'S CROISSANTS ST ANDRÉ

An elegant and less-than-2-minute dish which utilises excellent 'deli' ingredients, namely the delicious 'triple crème' St André cheese (which melts to a perfect topping layer) upon best quality croissants. These snacks would make a main course dish if accompanied by a leafy salad and preceded by a soup. The timing of the croissants is important – too little cooking and they are cool; too much and the crustiness disappears. Try Pont l'évêque or Savarin cheese if St André is unavailable.

Makes 4

---

1 garlic clove, skinned and crushed

---

4 French croissants, halved crosswise

---

5 ml (1 tsp) fruity olive oil

---

5 ml (1 level tsp) fresh marjoram or oregano, chopped

---

125 g (4 oz) St André cheese

---

15 ml (1 level tbsp) parmesan cheese, freshly grated

---

1. Rub the garlic over the cut surfaces of the croissant bases. Trickle oil all over and sprinkle with oregano. Slice the cheese thinly and use to cover. Put a small sprinkling of parmesan in the centre of each croissant.
2. Position evenly on a heatproof plate lined with kitchen paper. Keep the lids aside.
3. Microwave, uncovered, on HIGH for 45 seconds then give the dish a half turn and place the four lids on top.
4. Microwave, uncovered, on HIGH for a further 25 seconds. Serve hot or warm (the lids continue to heat from inside) as a snack or main course.

See photograph page 25

Bachelor's croissants St André (above) with Jack-in-the-box aubergine kebabs (page 70) and Red onion lotus flowers with pistachio butter (page 79).

OVERLEAF
Salsify mustard preserve (page 44), Dulcissima preserve (page 43) with a wedge of stilton and Carrot preserve Constantinides (page 43). All served with warm scones.

FLAUBERTIAN CAMEMBERT EN CROÛTE

This recipe is reminiscent of a quote from the book Flaubert's Parrot *by Julian Barnes – 'I feel I am liquefying like an old camembert' – for when cooked and cut into, the molten interior of this camembert pours out. It is a phenomenon devoutly to be savoured. Quick freezing is the key to success in this recipe: the crumb coating is thus quickly firmed and united with its host cheese.*

Serves 4–6

one 225 g (8 oz) whole small camembert, chilled

1 egg (size 2), beaten

2.5 ml (½ level tsp) salt

25 g (1 oz) dried breadcrumbs, uncoloured

25 g (1 oz) freshly grated parmesan cheese

15 ml (1 level tbsp) red sweet paprika

1.25 ml (¼ tsp) cayenne pepper

30 ml (2 tbsp) olive oil

cranberry and melon preserve (page 41)

1. Completely coat the camembert in beaten egg. Toss the salt, crumbs, parmesan, paprika and cayenne together well and use these seasoned crumbs to coat the cheese evenly. Freeze for 8 minutes.
2. Repeat this process, freezing for a further 8 minutes or until the crumb layer seems firmly adhered.
3. Meanwhile heat a 20 cm (8 inch) dish for 5 minutes. Add the oil and put the crumbed, chilled camembert in one corner of the dish. Allow it to sizzle for a few seconds, shake the dish to loosen it, then flip it over (using a fish slice) to the opposite side of the browning dish and microwave, uncovered, for 2 minutes.
4. Serve this appetizer or savoury course with ice-cold slices of melon and some fruit preserve of your choice. Accompany with some crusty bread and a good Beaujolais.

Green revival soup (page 22), Japanese sushi with nori (page 30), and Carrots in toffee upon wild rice (page 84).

PESTO SAN LORENZO

The San Lorenzo covered market in Florence is one of the most astonishing and fascinating places I have ever visited. A veritable tapestry of produce dazzles the eye with its intricacy, brilliance and freshness. Buckets of fresh basil release their fragrance as one pushes past. Great bouquets of the herb, in unceremonious newspaper-wrapped dampness, are snapped up within hours, for basil is an integral part of Florentine cuisine. My pesto paste recipe is a pungent one which should be used sparingly. It is meant to be stored in its concentrated state, covered, in a china pot in the refrigerator. It should be diluted somewhat with extra olive oil as it is used and so can last over a course of weeks, even months.

Makes 225 g (8 oz)

50 g (2 oz) shelled pine nuts

125 g (4 oz) parmesan (grana) in 3 or 4 pieces

50 g (2 oz) fresh basil leaves, torn

2 large garlic cloves, skinned and chopped

45–60 ml (3–4 level tbsp) extra virgin olive oil

salt and freshly ground black pepper (to taste)

1. Put the pine nuts on a heatproof plate and microwave on HIGH, uncovered, for 8 minutes, stirring from sides to centre every two minutes. The nuts should become a mellow golden brown. Leave to cool somewhat.
2. Using the grater attachment of a food processor, grate or shred the cheese coarsely. Replace the chopping blade, add the nuts, basil leaves (roughly torn if large) and the garlic. Process in several short bursts until the mixture resembles fine breadcrumbs.
3. Trickle in the olive oil gradually, stopping when the mixture has achieved the consistency you wish. Taste and, according to the saltiness and strength of the parmesan, add salt and pepper as desired.
4. Put into a china pot with a non-metal lid and use immediately (diluted by the addition of more oil) or store in the refrigerator.

VARIATIONS

Pesto Aeginis Use toasted halved pistachios (the best come from Aegina, in Greece) in place of pine nuts.
Pesto Filbertius Use toasted halved hazelnuts with half olive oil and half hazelnut oil for a mellow variation.

See photograph page 66–67

JAPANESE SUSHI WITH NORI

This Westernized sushi is made with flavoured, slightly sweetened rice and, in this recipe, is rolled up inside a layer of nori (a sea vegetable). Nori is available in thin dried sheets from Japanese specialist food stores, good delicatessens and health food shops. It can be filled with a central stuffing of your choice. Don't underestimate the green horseradish paste, Wasabi, if you have never tried this dish before – it is a revolution of flavour. If unavailable, mash a little avocado with horseradish and/or cayenne for an alternative serving. The rice used is in fact a type of risotto rice (semi-fino or fino), small grain and slightly sticky when cooked. The type I used is termed 'Japan rice'.

Serves 4

225 g (8 oz) Japan risotto rice (semi-fino or fino)

600 ml (1 pint) boiling vegetable stock

2.5 ml (½ level tsp) sea salt

25 g (1 oz) butter

15 ml (1 tbsp) mirin (sweetened rice wine) or dry sherry

15 ml (1 level tbsp) dried verveine (verbena) leaves, crumbled

10 ml (2 tsp) shoyu (or soy) sauce (optional)

15 ml (1 tbsp) mirin or dry sherry

15 ml (1 level tbsp) sugar

three 20 cm (8 inch) squares of nori (seaweed)

Stuffings

2 kiwi fruit, skinned and cut into 1 cm (½ inch) cubes

and/or 1 egg omelette, cut into 1 cm (½ inch) strips

and/or 1 avocado, skinned and cut into 1 cm (½ inch) cubes

1. Put the rice, hot stock, salt, butter, mirin and verveine into a heatproof ring dish and stir. Cover with a lid or cling film and microwave on HIGH, without stirring, for 10 minutes. Leave to stand for 3–4 minutes with the cover removed. Stir in the shoyu, mirin and sugar. Leave until sufficiently cool to handle.
2. Divide the mixture into 3 portions. Half cover one sheet of nori with rice in an even layer. At the centre of the rice put a lengthwise line of one of the stuffings. Roll up the nori, starting from the rice-covered edge, to enclose the filling completely. Wrap firmly and leave to stand for 5 minutes.
3. Repeat the process twice more using your choice of fillings. Slice each cylinder, using a sharp knife, into 8 little drum shapes and stand them upright so that the filling shows. Arrange on a serving dish (or dishes) with a dot of green Wasabi paste, about 1 cm (½ inch) per person, on one side. Add edible garnishes such as spring onions or cucumber strips.

See photograph page 28

COCKTAIL OLIVES CHANSONETTE

Stylish titbits like these are tailor-made for a party or, if served uncut, to take on a picnic or use as a light lunch with salad. Some people say that money talks. I reckon that garlic sings – read on!

Makes 20 or 40

½–1 head of garlic (containing at least 20 cloves)

20 large green or black olives, stoned

275 g (10 oz) cream cheese

50 g (2 oz) citrus herb and nut seasoning (page 36), or other seasoning

1. Pierce the head of garlic all over with a needle, pin or fine skewer. Microwave whole, on HIGH, uncovered, for 2 minutes. Do not be surprised if the garlic seems to 'sing' as the juices become hot; this is quite normal. Wait for the garlic to grow cool enough to handle.
2. Slide the garlic cloves out of their skins and push one down into each olive. Dry the olives in kitchen paper.
3. Divide the cream cheese into 20 portions. Roll each olive completely in cream cheese. Put the seasoned salt on a plate and roll each olive-cheese ball in the seasoning. Chill for 15 minutes then serve cut neatly in half. Supply cocktail sticks and have on hand some good jugsful of Bloody Mary, ice-cold dry Martini or even a Gibson or two.

SAUCES, SEASONINGS AND SAMBALS

APRICOT AND CHILLI SAUCE

You can use this hot sauce as soon as it is made, serve it chilled or keep it in the refrigerator indefinitely to use with South-east Asian, Thai or Chinese food. It is simple, decorative and quite delicious, but do be warned about its hotness – and use sparingly. The consistency makes it perfect as a dip for titbits of food. Provide an egg cup-sized dish of the sauce for each serving.

Makes 150 ml (¼ pint)

5 ml (1 level tsp) fresh root ginger, skinned, shredded and chopped

10 ml (2 level tsp) garlic, skinned and crushed

15 ml (1 tbsp) peanut or soya bean oil

45–60 ml (3–4 tbsp) chilli-flavoured sherry or dry sherry

45 ml (3 level tbsp) white wine vinegar

125 g (4 oz) apricot jam

1 large dried red chilli, finely chopped

2.5 ml (½ tsp) rich soy sauce

1. Put the ginger, garlic and oil into a heatproof measuring jug, bowl or ring dish. Microwave on HIGH, uncovered, for 1 minute, then stir well.
2. Add the chilli sherry, vinegar, jam, chilli and soy sauce. Stir again and microwave on HIGH, uncovered, for a further 3 minutes until the mixture is hot and bubbling and the chilli skin and seeds look rehydrated.
3. Use hot or pour into a heatproof jar with a non-metal lid and allow to cool before placing in the refrigerator. Use as a dipping sauce, in small quantities, for won tons, dumplings, noodles and stuffed pastry parcels.

SAFFRON ORANGE SAUCE APOLLON

This sauce is guaranteed to enchant with its brilliant, radiant colour and pure taste. Rather like a new version of sauce Maltaise, it is rich (but then so are many of life's good things!) and therefore not needed in huge quantities. Indeed, moderation is the word to remember when people mutter pessimistic indictments of any food containing egg yolks and cream! Apollo being the sun god, I should like to dedicate this golden-warm recipe to him.

Makes 150 ml (¼ pint)

15 ml (1 tbsp) fruity olive oil

25 g (1 oz) onion, skinned and finely sliced

1.9 grain (small) sachet saffron

juice of 1 large orange

75–90 ml (5–6 tbsp) crème fraîche

salt (optional)

1. Put the oil, onion and saffron into a heatproof jug or sauce boat and microwave, uncovered, for 2 minutes or until hot, bubbling and deep orange in colour.
2. Add the freshly squeezed juice of the orange, about 45–60 ml (3–4 tbsp), the crème fraîche and the egg yolks, in that order. Whisk together quickly with a fork.
3. Microwave, uncovered, for 3–3½ minutes, or until creamy and thick, whisking occasionally.
4. Taste, add salt if wished, and use while pleasantly hot as a sauce or dip. It adds relish to anything from brown bread to pasta, or from salads to broccoli.

RAW TOMATO SAUCE PRIMORDIO

Many of the 'health and beauty conscious' restaurants in London, New York and Florence now serve one version or another of a fresh (as opposed to long-cooked) tomato sauce with pasta. Sometimes the sauce is wholly raw; sometimes it is part-cooked and part-raw (as in my version here). Use whatever tomatoes are the fattest, reddest and most bursting with taste. The sweetness of fruit vinegar accentuates the fruitfulness of the tomato flavour. If no fresh oregano or marjoram is available, this is one situation in which I do not flinch at half measures of the dried version, particularly if it is an aromatic, sun-dried herb from somewhere like Provence, Sicily or Zakynthos.

Makes 600 ml (1 pint)

50 g (2 oz) carrots, diced
2 garlic cloves, skinned and crushed
125 g (4 oz) red or white onion, skinned and chopped
2 celery stalks, chopped
2.5 ml (½ level tsp) rock or sea salt
1.25 ml (¼ tsp) cayenne pepper
50 g (2 oz) potato, diced very small
30 ml (2 tbsp) fruity olive oil
2 fresh bay leaves, crushed
10–12 parsley stalks, snipped small
2.5 ml (½ level tsp) fresh oregano or marjoram
450 g (1 lb) plum, marmande or other tomatoes
15 ml (1 level tbsp) tomato purée
30 ml (2 tbsp) raspberry or other fruit vinegar

1. Put the carrot, garlic, onion, celery, seasonings, potato, oil and herbs into a 25 cm (10 inch) browning dish. Stir to coat the potato well with oil. Microwave on HIGH, covered with a lid, for 6 minutes, giving the dish a quarter turn and a stir every 1½ minutes.
2. Meanwhile, cross-score the tomatoes with a knife. Pour on some boiling water and then refresh the tomatoes in iced water. Peel away and discard the skin. Halve the tomatoes and squeeze out the seeds (keep these for another recipe). Chop the flesh and put it into the food processor or blender. Process briefly until coarsely chopped.
3. Add the contents of the hot pan to the tomato, first removing and discarding the bay leaves. Process minimally, in short bursts, until a purée-sauce is obtained. Stir in the tomato purée and the vinegar, blending these quickly through the mixture.
4. Serve the sauce as it is (warm) or reheat briefly in the serving jug or dish.

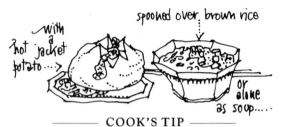

with a hot jacket potato...→   spooned over brown rice   or alike as soup.....

--- COOK'S TIP ---

This sauce may also be stirred into brown rice or spooned over baked jacket potatoes. It may be eaten as a soup, if preferred, or as a dip when chilled. For more vivid colour, double the amount of tomato purée.

RICH MUSHROOM SAUCE

This earthy, strongly coloured and flavoured sauce uses wholemeal flour, red wine and stock. If homemade stock is used (see Polish Beetroot Stock page 17) the sauce becomes very suitable for barley, buckwheat and pancake dishes.

Makes about 300 ml (½ pint)

25 g (1 oz) butter, softened
225 g (8 oz) field mushrooms, finely chopped
30 ml (2 level tbsp) wholemeal flour
175 ml (6 fl oz) fruity red wine
175 ml (6 fl oz) Polish Beetroot Stock (page 17) or vegetable stock
1 fresh bay leaf, crushed
30–45 ml (2–3 tbsp) cream or sour cream
salt and freshly ground black pepper

1. If necessary, soften the butter by microwaving on LOW (30%) for 30 seconds.
2. Stir in the chopped mushrooms and microwave on HIGH, covered, for 8 minutes.
3. Stir in the flour and microwave on HIGH, uncovered, for 30 seconds.
4. Gradually blend in the wine and stock. Add the bay leaf then microwave on HIGH, uncovered, for 7 minutes, stirring three times during cooking. Taste, add cream and season well.

HERBED WHOLEMEAL CREAM SAUCE

This version of béchamel sauce is nutty and delicious in taste, and speckled like a bird's egg. The herbs can be added with a light or heavy hand, depending on personal choice and use. The variations listed below make this adaptable sauce invaluable for a host of occasions.

Serves 4

½ onion, coarsely grated

1 clove, crushed

½ carrot, cut lengthwise

1 fresh bay leaf, crushed

6–8 parsley stalks, crushed

300 ml (½ pint) milk

25 g (1 oz) salted butter

30 ml (2 level tbsp) wholemeal flour

salt and freshly ground black pepper

fresh herbs such as parsley, chives, thyme and chervil

1. Put the onion, clove, carrot, bay leaf, parsley stalks and milk into a 900 ml (1½ pint) heatproof measuring jug. Microwave on HIGH for 2 minutes. Leave to infuse for 5 minutes then strain into a bowl, discarding the solids. Keep the milk aside.
2. Put the butter and flour into the measuring jug and microwave on HIGH, uncovered, for 45 seconds. Stir and microwave for a further 20 seconds. Season with salt and freshly ground black pepper.
3. Stir the infused milk into the roux. Microwave on HIGH, uncovered, for 3 minutes then stir and/or whisk thoroughly to obtain a perfect smooth sauce, slightly speckly in texture. Add herbs and serve.

—— VARIATIONS ——
Add some sliced and quickly sautéed fresh fungi, such as chanterelles, mousserons, blewits or cèpes, and a spoonful of natural yogurt for a delicate mushroom sauce.
Add 5–10 ml (1–2 level tsp) of curry paste (homemade or of a reputable brand) and some coconut cream, with, perhaps, some finely chopped pistachio nuts, for an exotic spiced sauce.
Add some asparagus sharpenings (see Asparagus Pencils page 78) which have been cooked 'au naturel' in a little water, then puréed with a dash of dry white wine and some chervil for an indulgent pale green asparagus sauce.
Add some sliced shallots (sautéed in butter), a touch of parmesan and a dash of cognac for a soubise par excellence.

TOMATAUBERGINE SAUCE

This mellow, fresh tasting and fruity sauce has a host of uses. Puréed, it takes on a quite different, more elegant, character and is delicious with cooked potatoes or eggs, for example.

Serves 4

30 ml (2 level tbsp) fruity olive oil

225 g (8 oz) aubergine, cut into 1 cm (½ inch) cubes

1 garlic clove, skinned and chopped

350 g (12 oz) tomatoes, cut into 1 cm (½ inch) cubes

1 small onion or 2 shallots, skinned and finely chopped

5 ml (1 level tsp) dried oregano or fresh marjoram

15 ml (1 level tbsp) chopped parsley or chopped fresh basil leaves

1. Preheat a large 25 cm (10 inch) browning dish for 6 minutes. Add the olive oil, aubergine and garlic, stir quickly to coat them, then microwave on HIGH for 2 minutes, uncovered.
2. Add the tomatoes and microwave on HIGH for a further 3 minutes, uncovered, stirring occasionally. Taste to check when tender.
3. Add the onion or shallots and herbs of choice.

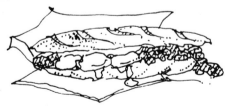

—— COOK'S TIP ——
Leave rough and chunky for an earthy sauce to use with potatoes and egg dishes, pasta and whole grain rice. For a lunchtime snack, try it in hollowed-out rolls, topped with mozzarella and reheated until the cheese melts.

GOLDEN QUAIL'S EGG MAYONNAISE

This deceptively delicate and golden mayonnaise has an undeniably assertive mellow taste and colour. The addition of the whites of the quails' eggs (which should not be chilled) gives particular lightness. Use any light-tasting oil for consistent results, but vary the herbs according to season and availability.

Serves 4

30 ml (2 level tbsp) Dijon mustard
15 ml (1 level tbsp) corn meal
60 ml (4 tbsp) white wine or dry cider
1 garlic clove, skinned and chopped
6 quail's eggs, at room temperature
300 ml (1/2 pint) rapeseed, safflower or grapeseed oil
chopped chives (optional)
salt and freshly ground pepper (optional)

1. Put the mustard, corn meal, wine and garlic into a medium heatproof bowl and microwave, uncovered, on HIGH for 2 minutes, stirring twice, until a hot, thick paste is formed.
2. Break the quail's eggs into the goblet of a blender, add the still-warm paste, and process for a few seconds or until smooth.
3. Switch on the blender and add the oil in a thin, continuous stream until about half is used. Stop the blender every 20–25 seconds and stir the mixture, scraping down the sides of the goblet with a spatula.
4. Taste, add herbs and seasonings if wished, and use on a warm salad (of wet leaves microwaved, uncovered, on HIGH, very briefly until wilted and warm) or on any cold salad leaves as a dressing. This mayonnaise also blends well with apple and cheese salads and slaws.

GREEN AVOCADO AND LIME MAYONNAISE

What would purists make of this recipe? A mayonnaise made in the normal way is reinforced with a purée of freshly-cooked avocado, to which the juice and zest of a fresh lime is added for sparkle. The avocado should feel tender under gentle thumb pressure, but not soft. The rough, black-skinned variety seem to me to have the best flavour for this recipe. Vary the amount of lime juice according to the intended use of the mayonnaise.

Serves 4

2 egg yolks (size 3), at room temperature
juice of 1 lime, freshly squeezed
1.25–2.5 ml (1/4–1/2 tsp) lime zest, finely shredded
1.25 ml (1/4 tsp) salt
freshly ground black pepper
150 ml (1/4 pint) fruity olive oil
1 large ripe Hass avocado, about 225 g (8 oz)

1. Put the yolks, 10 ml (2 tsp) of lime juice, the zest and seasonings into a 600 ml (1 pint) measuring jug or small high-sided bowl.
2. Use one hand to pour in the oil, in a thin continuous stream, while operating an electric whisk with the other. Towards the end the oil can be added more quickly. The resulting mayonnaise should be light but thick.
3. Halve the avocado, scoop the flesh from the stone-free half and then chop it quickly. Put it into a heatproof jug or small straight-sided bowl with the remaining lime juice.
4. Microwave on HIGH, uncovered, for 50–60 seconds or until the avocado is hot. Mash roughly using a fork.
5. Put approximately quarter of the mayonnaise into the avocado mixture and whisk until just smooth and no more. Fold the resulting avocado mixture quickly through the mayonnaise using a spatula, wooden spoon or serving spoon until fairly evenly blended.
6. Store, skin and cube the remaining avocado flesh neatly and stir through the sauce.

—— SERVING TIP ——
Use this fascinating sauce to dress rice or pasta salads, with vegetable crudités, or with raw sliced fruit such as mangoes, pawpaws, or even peeled mangosteens or lychees.

SALSA AVGOLEMONO

Although all the cooks I know in Greece tend to use cornflour or nothing in their traditional avgolemono, my version is curdle-proof, delicate and not too modest in flavour. The egg yolks, added with the freshly squeezed lemon to the already thickened sauce, need minimal cooking. Use herbs or not, depending on the effect you prefer and the food this sauce will accompany. The herb sellinos is often erroneously sold as flat leaf parsley – a quite different herb. Smell the crushed leaves to see which it is – sellinos has a celery smell. Otherwise use green leafy tops of mature celery. Do use fresh golden-yolked farmyard eggs if you can: their shell colour doesn't matter but the yolk colour does. Thin the sauce with stock, wine or Greek yogurt if it thickens on standing.

Makes about 225 ml (8 fl oz)   *greek picnic......*

225 g (8 oz) onions, skinned and sliced
15 ml (1 tbsp) Greek olive oil
15 ml (1 level tbsp) fécule (potato flour)
300 ml (½ pint) hot vegetable stock
50 ml (2 fl oz) retsina (white)
1 large or 2 small lemons
2 egg yolks (size 3), at room temperature
freshly ground black pepper
chopped fresh sellinos, or celery leaves

1. Put the sliced onions and olive oil in a medium, high-sided heatproof jug or bowl and microwave on HIGH, uncovered, for 1 minute, stirring once.
2. Stir in the fécule, then the stock and retsina and microwave on HIGH, uncovered, for 4 minutes or until hot and bubbling, stirring well at the end of cooking time.
3. Remove and finely shred the zest of the lemons and squeeze the juice.
4. Add the 2 egg yolks to the hot sauce and 45–60 ml (3–4 tbsp) of the lemon juice. Whisk quickly to incorporate the yolks into the sauce.
5. Microwave on LOW (40%), uncovered, for 2 minutes or until the egg yolks have increased the thickness of the sauce and it is very warm, but not near boiling.
6. Stir in the finely shredded lemon zest, the pepper and sellinos or celery leaves. Use the sauce hot or cold on a variety of dishes, including soft cooked eggs, beans, other green vegetables or pasta.

STRANGERS' SEASONING

Here is a rather free adaptation of a garam masala-type seasoning described by a horticulturist (hitherto unknown to me), Jelena de Belder, in Harpers and Queen magazine. My microwave version of this condiment includes a fascinating burgundy-red powder called somaq (or sumac) which comes from a decorative tree and possesses a fruity gentle astringency, far less harsh than tamarind. I was first made aware of its usefulness by a total stranger from Uzbekistan, who took pity on my ignorance as I fired questions at the perplexed Arab shopkeeper in a supermarket. I owe thanks to all three strangers.

Makes 125 g (4 oz)

15 ml (1 level tbsp) black peppercorns
45 ml (3 level tbsp) green peppercorns in brine, drained
15 ml (1 level tbsp) white peppercorns
30 ml (2 level tbsp) white mustard seeds
30 ml (2 level tbsp) fenugreek seeds
15 ml (1 level tbsp) coriander seeds
5 ml (1 level tsp) laurel seed buds (from bay tree)
15 ml (1 level tbsp) somaq (sumac or sammak)

1. Preheat a 25 cm (10 inch) browning dish for 6 minutes, or according to the manufacturer's instructions.
2. Add the first 6 ingredients, cover and microwave on HIGH for 3 minutes (or until a delicious aroma is noticeable), constantly stirring from edges to centre.
3. Using an electric grinder or pestle and mortar, grind to a coarse powder. Stir in the laurel seeds (pale green and delicate) and somaq. Leave to cool then pack into clean, dry jars and store in a cool, dark, dry place. Use at the table to enliven bland foods.

REMPAH

Make this rempah for use as a seasoning condiment (with added wheatgerm) or as a sauce base (without added wheatgerm) in Indian-style dishes. To use for the latter, add about 60 ml (4 tbsp) to 15 ml (1 level tbsp) of mustard oil in a heatproof dish and microwave, uncovered, for 30 seconds, or until it can be stirred together to form a paste. Stir into it 150 ml (1/4 pint) of stock, tamarind water or any coconut liquid and microwave on HIGH, uncovered, for 2–3 minutes or until a sauce forms.

Makes 50–75 g (2–3 oz)

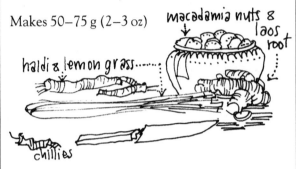

15 g (1/2 oz) haldi (fresh turmeric) root, shredded
2 bulbs lemon grass, shredded crosswise
15 g (1/2 oz) galangal (Laos root) finely shredded
25 g (1 oz) peanuts, cashew nuts or macadamia nuts, chopped
2 or 3 small dried red chillies, crumbled
1 medium fresh green chilli, shredded
60 ml (4 tbsp) creamed coconut powder (unsweetened)
25 g (1 oz) wheatgerm (optional)

1. Preheat a 25 cm (10 inch) browning dish for 6 minutes, or according to the manufacturer's instructions.
2. Put the first 6 ingredients (all finely shredded, crushed or chopped) into the pan and microwave, uncovered, for 2 minutes to toast (a noticeable aroma will arise after the correct time), stirring frequently.
3. Put half the contents of the dish into an electric grinder and grind, in short bursts, to a powder. Repeat with the second half.
4. Return the ground rempah to the browning dish and microwave on HIGH for 3 further minutes, uncovered.
5. Allow to cool completely before mixing in the creamed coconut powder, tossing it in well and breaking down any lumps.
6. Add wheatgerm (if wished) when the mixture is about to be used as a seasoning, but not before. (It is unsuitable when the mix is to be used as a sauce.)

--------- COOK'S TIP ---------

This sauce complements a wide range of vegetables and fruits, particularly tropical fruits. Store the basic rempah condiment (once it has cooked and cooled) in a cool dry dark place, or in a refrigerator, and use within 2 months.

See photograph page 65

CITRUS, HERB AND NUT SEASONING

For a number of reasons the combination of sweet, salt, aromatic, nut and herb tastes, taken all at once, provides huge gustatory pleasure. This imaginative condiment can appear on the table in place of salt and pepper and no one will miss them — yet its salt content is relatively small. Another positive feature is that it provides a useful nutritional boost from good, natural, earthy raw materials.

Makes 125 g (4 oz)

125 g (4 oz) roasted salted almonds
zest of 1 lime or lemon, finely shredded
50 g (2 oz) sesame seeds
30 ml (2 level tbsp) coarse sea salt
15 ml (1 level tbsp) alfalfa seeds
2.5 ml (1/2 level tsp) tartaric or citric acid
15 ml (1 level tbsp) dried celery seasoning (page 38)

1. Grind half of the roasted almonds to a fine powder in an electric coffee grinder. Grind the remainder in the same way.
2. Put the citrus zest on kitchen paper and microwave, uncovered, on HIGH for 1 minute or until dry.
3. To toast the sesame seeds, sprinkle evenly over a shallow heatproof dish and microwave on HIGH, uncovered, for 8 minutes, stirring from edge to centre every 2 minutes.
4. Put the ground almonds, zest and remaining ingredients into a large, shallow heatproof dish or platter and microwave, uncovered, on MEDIUM (50%) for 3 minutes, stirring occasionally.

5. Allow to cool completely. Store, in a small jar with a non-metal screw top lid, in a cool, dark place.

See photograph page 46–47

SEA-FLAVOURED SEASONING PAILLASSON

A condiment tasting of the sea, this sweet-salt seasoning can be used to enliven simply cooked foods: vegetables 'au naturel', purées, noodles, rice or egg dishes. Layered on a plate with food, it resembles an elegant black straw mat (or paillasson).

Makes 1 small jar

| 15–25 g (½–1 oz) Wakame or Hi Jiki seaweed or sea vegetable |
| 15 ml (1 tbsp) chilli-flavoured sherry |
| 30 ml (2 tbsp) shoyu (or soy) sauce |
| 45 ml (3 level tbsp) sunflower seeds |
| 45 ml (3 level tbsp) alfalfa seeds |
| 2 sheets of nori (sheet sea vegetable), shredded finely with scissors |

1. Preheat a 25 cm (10 inch) browning dish for 8 minutes. Put the seaweed into 150 ml (¼ pint) boiling water for 1 minute, stirring until the strands have softened. Pour off any liquid (reserving as stock for use in another recipe).
2. Put the softened seaweed and sherry in the browning dish and microwave, uncovered, on HIGH for 2 minutes or until the sherry has evaporated completely and the seaweed is dry. Remove the dish and stand for 2–3 minutes.
3. Microwave again on HIGH, uncovered, for 3 minutes or until dry. Put half the seaweed into an electric grinder and grind coarsely.
4. Put the shoyu (or soy) with the seeds in the browning dish and microwave, uncovered, on HIGH for 3 minutes, stirring from edges to centre several times during cooking, until the seeds have absorbed the soy and are dry. Allow to stand for 5 minutes.
5. Mix the cooked, ground and shredded sea vegetables and seeds together. Store in a cool, dark, dry place and use within 6–8 weeks.

See photograph page 45

ORANGE-ANISE SAVOURY SEASONING

This deliciously dry sambal-type seasoning has a number of well discerned yet harmoniously blended flavours. The microwave toasting of the nuts and seeds contributes largely to its success, and all the ingredients should be combined and ground while the cooked components are still hot. Use the method on page 38 to make some dried citrus peel.

Makes 150 g (5 oz)

| 75 g (3 oz) cashew nuts |
| 30 ml (2 level tbsp) poppy seeds |
| 30 ml (2 level tbsp) coarse sea salt |
| 15 ml (1 level tbsp) juniper berries |
| 15 ml (1 level tbsp) white peppercorns |
| 10 ml (2 level tsp) dill seeds |
| 15 ml (1 level tbsp) coriander seeds |
| 5 ml (1 level tsp) allspice berries |
| 10 heads star anise, broken into fragments |
| 15 ml (1 level tbsp) dried satsuma peel (page 38) |

1. Toast the cashew nuts by spreading them on a flat heatproof plate and microwaving, uncovered, on HIGH for 4 minutes, stirring 3–4 times from edges to centre to avoid scorching. Toast the poppy seeds in the same way.
2. Combine the nuts and seeds with the remaining ingredients. Put no more than ⅕th of this mixture at a time into an electric grinder (a coffee grinder is ideal) and grind to a coarse powder. Repeat this process until all the mixture is ground.
3. Allow to cool completely and store in an airtight jar in a dark, cool, dry place. Provide a small jar on the table for use as a general seasoning in place of pepper and salt. It contains little salt yet contributes great savour.

sprinkle on to · store in a pretty jar··· use on omelettes··· potatoes···· so useful····

— COOK'S TIP —
This seasoning transforms the humblest potatoes or Brussels sprouts into sophisticated offerings. Use it also for sprinkling into omelettes oeufs en cocotte and puréed vegetables, as well as on top of cottage cheese and fruit salads. Stores well.

DRIED SATSUMA PEEL

Humble dried citrus peel is an indispensable maid-of-all-work, adding subtle aroma and flavour in a host of varied ways. Use of the microwave oven makes it available almost on the instant.

Makes 1 small pot or jar

---

550 g (1¼ lb), or 6, seedless satsumas

---

1. Remove the peel carefully so as not to damage the flesh beneath. Tear the peel into 1 cm (½ inch) or 2.5 cm (1 inch) pieces.
2. Lay them, not touching, on 2 adjacent sheets of kitchen paper. Microwave, uncovered, on HIGH for 6–7 minutes or until dried and crisp. Turn them over, and give the paper a half turn, halfway through the cooking time. Towards the end of cooking time they may begin to darken in colour: remove the very dark ones as necessary so they do not over-cook.
3. Remove from the oven and leave on the paper until cooled. Store in an airtight jar (with a sachet of silica gel if possible) and use as wished.

Uses
Add 6–8 pieces to vegetable stocks when an oriental scentedness is required.
Add several pieces to a pot of tea to enliven its aroma.
Chop or crumble into caramel or chocolate sauces.
Chop or crumble into ice creams or mousses.
Add a little to the coffee jug when brewing fresh coffee and stir in some Grand Marnier at serving time for a delicious coffee-liqueur night cap.
Add to stuffings and toppings, sweet and savoury.
Nibble pieces of the dried peel as a 'breath sweetener' and/or in place of a longed-for cigarette.
Use the peeled segments of flesh for a fresh fruit salad.

DRIED CELERY OR CELERIAC SEASONING

Celeriac is often sold (in street markets and supermarkets alike) with its stems and green leaves still intact. These are far too good to waste, as are celery side-stems and leaves. To keep for future use, here is a method for drying them easily and well. Take care that the timings are carefully followed; the natural starches and sugars will caramelize if not closely watched and may spoil both flavour and colour. (Remove any pieces as they darken to avoid this.) I have found that one average head of celeriac tends to give at least a 75 g (3 oz) weight of stems and 25 g (1 oz) of leaves. To dry more, repeat the recipe rather than trying to dry too much at once.

Makes 1 small jar

---

75 g (3 oz) celeriac or celery stems, shredded

25 g (1 oz) celeriac or celery leaves, shredded

---

1. Put the shredded stems into a 25 cm (10 inch) browning dish and microwave, uncovered, on HIGH for 6–8 minutes, giving a quick stir from time to time. Spread out on kitchen paper and allow to cool.
2. Put the shredded leaves in the browning dish and microwave, uncovered, on HIGH for 4 minutes, giving a quick stir from time to time. Spread out on kitchen paper and allow to cool.
3. When both have cooled, crumble them into airtight containers and store in a cool, dark, dry place. Use as a constituent of a seasoning, a topping or in stocks and sauces.

SAMBAL ASSEMSAI

This purée (not unlike some of the sambals sold in oriental stores) brings out the taste of other foods and may be used as a relish, a chutney or to accentuate mild or spicy foods. Tamarind provides much of the sharpness. It is important that the sambal is not processed so much that it loses its texture, which should be slightly rough. If it is put into an attractive jar or pot it can come straight to the table. Warn diners that it should be used sparingly.

Makes 225 g (8 oz)

15 ml (1 tbsp) peanut or soya oil
375 g (12 oz) red capsicum, seeded and cubed
3–4 fresh red bird's-eye type chillies, sliced and seeds retained
6 garlic cloves, skinned and chopped
75 g (3 oz) onion, skinned and chopped
2.5 cm (1 inch) piece fresh root ginger, shredded
125 ml (4 fl oz) boiling water
40 g (1½ oz) tamarind in cake (pressed) form
1.25 ml (¼ tsp) sea salt
30 ml (2 tbsp) tomato purée
30 ml (2 tbsp) white liquor such as marc, grappa or vodka

1. Preheat a 25 cm (10 inch) browning dish for 8 minutes. Add the oil, capsicum and sliced hot chillies, garlic, onion and ginger to the dish and microwave on HIGH, uncovered, for 5 minutes.
2. Meanwhile, pour the boiling water over the tamarind (crumbled) to soften it, stirring occasionally. Strain off and keep the tamarind water for other uses, add the softened tamarind to the dish and microwave, uncovered, for a further 5 minutes, stirring from time to time. Add the salt, tomato paste and the chosen liquor.
3. Put the contents of the dish into a blender or food processor and reduce (using short bursts) to a rough paste. If too thick add a little tamarind juice.
4. Spoon into a small sterilized jar or pot (see page 41) with a non-metal (preferably screw top) lid. Label and store in a cool, dark, dry place. Use within several months.

See photograph page 65

SINGAPORE SEASONING SAMBAL

This mildly hot and very perfumed sambal tastes good with any dish from the Indian sub-continent and with Malaysian and Indonesian dishes. Microwave 'toasting' is a perfect way to release the scentedness from spices. If fresh haldi is not available, use 5 ml (1 level tsp) powdered turmeric

instead. Do try to locate a wholefood store which sells coconut flakes: they are considerably superior to desiccated coconut in this particular recipe. Pungent asafetida is a matter for individual choice. It is said that the late James Beard likened the flavour of this ground resin to the scent of truffles. One way or another it is a flavour quite on its own: you like it or loath it! Mine came from Singapore but good suppliers of oriental and Asian foods should stock this product.

Makes 75 g (3 oz)

50 g (2 oz) bulb fresh lemon grass
15 g (½ oz), or 4, small green chillies, sliced
15 g (½ oz) haldi (fresh turmeric root), sliced
15 ml (1 level tbsp) caraway seeds
15 ml (1 level tbsp) coriander seeds
2 cinnamon sticks, roughly crushed
2.5 ml (½ level tsp) asafetida powder (optional)
50 g (2 oz) coconut, flaked, unsweetened

1. Put the lemon grass (crosswise sliced and separated into rings), sliced chillies, haldi slices, caraway seeds and coriander seeds into a 25 cm (10 inch) browning dish. Microwave, uncovered, on HIGH for 4–5 minutes, stirring frequently. When nearly ready a strong aroma is noticeable.
2. Stir the remaining ingredients into the hot pan and toss all well together.
3. Put no more than ⅕th of the mixture at a time into an electric grinder (a coffee grinder is ideal) and grind to a coarse powder.
4. Repeat this process until only ⅕th of the mixture is left. Do not grind this but add it to the ground seasoning to provide a varied texture. Allow to cool completely. Store in an airtight jar in a cool, dark, dry place.

SERVING TIP
Serve a small bowl with spiced and curried dishes, noodles, or use over cooked fruits and vegetables and in yogurt.

SPREADS AND PRESERVES

TOMATO, ORANGE AND LEMON MARMALADE

Although in the past traditionalists would have blanched and removed the tomato skins in this recipe, I find the skin fragments perfectly acceptable and barely detectable anyway. The orange and lemon should both be plump, juicy and large. This recipe makes a delicious breakfast preserve, suitable with rolls, scones and breads.

Makes 450 g (1 lb)

| 550 g (1¼ lb) ripe firm tomatoes, quartered |
| 1 large orange, sliced thinly and seeded |
| 1 large lemon, sliced thinly and seeded |
| 450 g (1 lb) granulated sugar |
| 30 ml (2 tbsp) Curaçao or Grand Marnier |

1. Put the tomatoes into a large casserole or bowl together with the orange and lemon slices and microwave on HIGH, uncovered, for 15 minutes or until the rind feels tender.
2. Add the sugar and stir well until dissolved. Microwave, uncovered, on HIGH for 20 minutes or until the temperature reaches 113°C/235°F (jam setting point) or until a teaspoon of jam dropped onto a chilled saucer forms a skin after 1 minute, indicating a good degree of setting.
3. Allow the jam to stand for a few minutes while the jars are sterilized (page 41). Fill the jars when cool and pour a spoonful of liqueur over each. Seal, using non-metal lids, label and store in a cool, dark, dry place.

LAVENDER AND PARSLEY SPREAD WITH CALVADOS

This recipe employs the cooked unsweetened pulp previously used to make a clear jelly (see page 42). The pulp is cooked again and, once thickened, parsley (or another herb) is added before it is stored in sterile jars. The mixture has a creamy, buttery consistency and can be used in numerous ways for savoury dishes. The spoonful of Calvados helps to contribute a pungently floral flavour. This is a medium-term preserve and will keep for up to four months. Use with main course dishes, as well as a garnish, relish, dip or as a spread on savoury scones or muffins.

Makes 450 g (1 lb)

| 700 ml (1¼ pints) cooked apple, lime and lavender pulp (from recipe on page 42) |
| 275 g (10 oz) caster sugar |
| 60 ml (4 tbsp) chopped parsley (or other aromatic herb) |
| 15–30 ml (1–2 tbsp) Calvados or Applejack |

1. Remove the limes and process the apple and lavender pulp to a smooth purée. Put this into a large heatproof casserole with the sugar. Stir well then microwave, uncovered, on HIGH for 15 minutes, stirring from the edges to the centre at intervals, until a thickened buttery mixture is obtained.
2. Stir in the parsley while the butter is very hot. Leave to stand while the jars are sterilized (page 41). Pour into the sterile jars, allow to cool, pour over the Calvados, cover with non-metal screw-top lids, label and store in a cool, dark, dry place.

CLEMENTINE AND PASSION FRUIT CURD WITH VODKA

Most people enjoy lemon curd (also called lemon butter or lemon honey, depending on local tradition). This short-time preserve can achieve quite different appeal when made with the pulp of fresh passion fruit. Just scoop out the flesh as you would a boiled egg. Vodka adds a particular sparkle.

Makes 450 g (1 lb)

4 eggs (size 3)
175 g (6 oz) caster sugar
10 ml (2 level tsp) lemon zest, shredded
30 ml (2 tbsp) lemon juice, freshly squeezed
5 ml (1 level tsp) clementine zest, shredded
50 ml (2 fl oz) clementine juice, freshly squeezed
75 ml (5 level tbsp) passion fruit pulp, freshly extracted
50 ml (2 fl oz) dry white wine
125 g (4 oz) butter, cubed
15–30 ml (1–2 tbsp) vodka

1. Whisk the eggs and sugar in a large heatproof casserole or bowl, using an electric whisk, until smooth and frothy. Stir in the fruit zest and juice, the passion fruit pulp, wine and butter.
2. Microwave, uncovered, on HIGH for 3 minutes then stir well and microwave on MEDIUM (50%) for a further 6 minutes or until the mixture has thickened to a creamy consistency. Stir well from the sides to the middle during cooking time.
3. Leave to stand while the jars are sterilized (see below).
4. Pour into the hot jars, cool and pour a spoonful of vodka over each. Seal, label and store in a refrigerator. Use within two weeks.

COOK'S TIP
To sterilize jars (which must have no metal parts) in the microwave oven: pour in 60 ml (4 tbsp) water and microwave on HIGH for 1½ minutes or until boiling. Using oven gloves, pour out the water and invert the jar on to clean absorbent kitchen paper or a sterile oven rack and the hot jar is ready for use.

CRANBERRY AND MELON PRESERVE WITH COGNAC

Cranberries are too often overlooked in cookery. This recipe combines them with melon, producing a good blend of colour and flavour. If cranberries are not available, blackberries or loganberries could be substituted. Cognac provides the finishing touch.

Makes two 450 g (1 lb) jars

450 g (1 lb) melon, skinned, seeded and cubed
550 g (1¼ lb) cranberries
15 ml (1 level tbsp) shredded orange zest
15 ml (1 tbsp) freshly squeezed orange juice
15 ml (1 tbsp) freshly squeezed lemon juice
275 g (10 oz) caster sugar
30 ml (2 tbsp) cognac or brandy

1. Put the melon, berries, zest and juices in a large heatproof casserole or bowl and microwave on HIGH, uncovered, for 9–10 minutes.
2. Add the sugar, stirring well until it dissolves. Then microwave on HIGH, uncovered, for a further 20–22 minutes or until a teaspoonful of jam dropped onto a chilled saucer forms a skin after 1 minute, indicating a good degree of setting.
3. Allow the jam to stand for a few minutes while the jars are sterilized (see this page). Fill the jars and, when cool, pour 15 ml (1 tbsp) of cognac over each. Seal, label and store in a cool, dark place.

LAVENDER AND LIME SCENTED JELLY

This remarkable jelly has a pretty, delicate design of lavender heads and stems set within it. The scentedness is very special, bringing to mind Elizabethan knot gardens and a leisured past. The boon, however, is that the whole recipe, from start to finish, is made within one hour. The 'debris' of apple purée left in the jelly bag is re-used to make a herb butter (page 40). 'Waste not, want not' can still be a relevant proverb for the 1980s!

Makes two 450 g (1 lb) jars

900 g (2 lb) Granny Smith apples, roughly chopped

700 ml (1¼ pints) warm water

3 limes, halved and the juice freshly squeezed

10–12 dried lavender flowers and stems

350 g (12 oz) granulated sugar

1. Put the chopped apples, water and the squeezed dry half 'shells' of the limes (but not their juice) with the lavender stems into a large casserole or bowl. Microwave on HIGH for 20 minutes or until soft. Remove the lime 'shells'.
2. Put the contents of the casserole into a food processor and process briefly to chop roughly but not purée. Pour through a fine, non-metal sieve or jelly bag and leave to drip, undisturbed, for 15 minutes at most. (Keep the resultant pulp for the recipe on page 40.)
3. Measure the juice: there should be about 450 ml (15 fl oz). Return the juice to the pan with the lime juice and the sugar.
4. Microwave on HIGH, uncovered, for 20 minutes. Add the lavender flower heads and microwave on HIGH for a further 2 minutes, or until the temperature reaches 113°C (235°F) – jam setting point – or until a teaspoon of jelly dropped onto a chilled saucer forms a skin after 1 minute, indicating a set. Allow the jelly to stand while the jars are sterilized (page 41) then pour into the jars (first removing and setting into the hot jars the flower heads—use sterilized tongs for this). Fill the jars then seal, label and store in a cool, dark place.

SPICED MUSHROOMS MATA HARI

Somewhat like mushrooms à la grecque in style but in a more oriental, scented syrup, these mushroom preserves keep well in a refrigerator. They are helpful to have on hand to impart style to hors d'oeuvres, are a delicious way to garnish cheese, pasta and grain dishes and may be stirred into bland sauces and dressings for use with salads, much as one might use capers. Galangal and lime leaves (both of which can be stored in plastic bags in the refrigerator for weeks) are available from Asian and oriental supermarkets and particularly Thai food specialists, such as the Mata Hari chain in London.

Makes 450 g (1 lb)

45 ml (3 tbsp) fruity olive oil

2 garlic cloves, skinned and chopped

2 cm (¾ inch) length of fresh galangal, skinned and shredded

450 g (1 lb) whole button mushrooms

15 ml (1 level tbsp) coriander seeds, crushed

15 ml (1 level tbsp) green cardamom pods, seeds extracted

1 hot red chilli, slit and seeded

30 ml (2 tbsp) scented honey

50 ml (2 fl oz) sherry or rice wine

75 ml (3 fl oz) red wine vinegar

5 ml (1 level tsp) tomato purée

4–6 lime leaves, dried (fewer if fresh)

30 ml (2 tbsp) fruity olive oil

1. Preheat a 25 cm (10 inch) browning dish on HIGH for 8 minutes, or according to the manufacturer's instructions. Add the olive oil then the garlic, galangal and mushrooms. Microwave, uncovered, on HIGH for 3 minutes until the mushrooms are tender, stirring once or twice.
2. Add the coriander, cardamom and chilli and microwave on HIGH, uncovered, for 1 minute. Add the remaining ingredients (except the olive oil to seal) cover and microwave on HIGH for 4 minutes, until boiling.
3. Pour into a hot sterilized jar (page 41) but do not cover. When cold, pour the oil over the surface to act as a seal. Cover securely with a non-metal screw top lid.

CARROT PRESERVE CONSTANTINIDES

I was taught how to prepare this Greek preserve by an irascible but able cook and journalist called Tasso. He assured me that it did wonderful things for the libido! True or false, the flavour of these decorative whole carrots certainly grows better and better the longer they keep. Serve the carrots thinly sliced in a pool of their liquor with some chopped fresh parsley, chunks of feta cheese and olives.

Makes 1.1 litres (2 pints)

1.4 kg (3 lb) long, straight, even-sized carrots, peeled

1.7 litres (3 pints) boiling water

600–700 ml (1–1¼ pints) white wine vinegar

10–12 black peppercorns

10–12 whole cloves

125 g (4 oz) Greek Hymettus honey

4–5 fresh bay leaves, crushed

1 head of garlic, top sliced off to expose flesh

30 parsley stems halved crosswise and tied into 2 bundles

olive oil to seal

1. Use a fork to score the entire surface of the carrots deeply down their length.
2. Put them in a large 3.4 litre (3 quart) casserole and pour on the boiling water. Microwave on HIGH, uncovered, and bring them back to the boil, about 15 minutes.
3. Pour off the water and wedge the drained carrots upright in a large straight-sided preserving jar (previously sterilized, see page 41; jars with metal fittings should be sterilized by conventional, not microwave, means). Ideally there should be sufficient room above the carrots to take the head of garlic (perhaps broken into halves).
4. Bring the vinegar, spices, honey and bay leaves to the boil in a measuring jug covered with cling film. Wedge the halved heads of garlic flat side down on top of the carrots with the 2 parsley bundles and pour over enough of the hot vinegar to cover. Once cold, top with a film of good Greek olive oil and seal loosely with a non-metal lid. Store in a cool, dark, dry place and preferably wait for 2 weeks before using.

See photograph page 27

DULCISSIMA PRESERVE

I was first served this delicious preserve by a consummate hostess and entertainer. To put a shy young guest at her ease, Dulcie put the driest dry Martini into my hand that I have ever tasted. She proffered a gleaming dish on which were piled plump succulent prunes, a scattering of fresh herbs, and a pile of tiny ivory forks. Later, after my appreciative squawks, she divulged her method. I guarantee that this recipe will thaw any shy guests at your parties!

Makes about 30, plus syrup

450 g (1 lb) plump Californian prunes

125 g (4 oz) caster sugar

300 ml (½ pint) smoky (or else bergamot-flavoured) tea, freshly made

120 ml (8 tbsp) cognac

Garnish

fresh herbs (lovage, marjoram, chervil or angelica)

1. Put the prunes into a heatproof dish. Pour on the sugar and the hot tea. Cover with cling film and microwave on HIGH for 5 minutes. Strain the prunes through a colander, reserving the liquid. Return the liquid to the heatproof dish and microwave on HIGH for 8 minutes, or until bubbling and reduced to about 150 ml (¼ pint).
2. Sterilize a 600 ml (1 pint) jar with a non-metal screw-type top (see page 41). Pack the hot jar with the drained prunes and add the cognac, using a sterile funnel.
3. Top up the jar (using the hot syrup) to overflowing. Any excess syrup should be kept for a cocktail base. Cover and invert once, gently. Label and store in a cool, dark, dry place. Use within two months. To serve, remove as many prunes as are required from the jar. Trickle a little syrup over them and serve with a garnish of fresh herbs of your choice.

—— COOK'S TIP ——
To make the really strong tea required in this recipe, use 4 heaped teaspoons of aromatic tea. Blue cheese and crackers, if wished, make an excellent accompaniment.

See photograph page 26–27

APRICOT AND BLUEBERRY COMPOTE WITH VODKA

This compote (or short-term preserve) of fruits is delicious served with crème fraîche or fromage blanc as a dessert, or as a superb breakfast treat (with warmed brioche). As a sort of fruit 'salad' it can start a meal, icy cold, in small goblets. It has a scented, slightly alcohol-flavoured syrup, the colour of which deepens as it stands. Do try to find sun-ripened, dappled small apricots; they have real, sweet-sharp pungent flavour. The fruit cooks briefly in a prepared syrup, and goes on cooking after it leaves the oven.

Makes 900 g (2 lb)

---

225 g (8 oz) blueberries

450 g (1 lb) ripe fresh small apricots

300 ml (½ pint) dessert wine

150 ml (¼ pint) hot water

225 g (8 oz) sugar

2.5 ml (½ level tsp) tartaric acid

15 ml (1 level tbsp) cardamom seeds, crushed

4–5 fresh (or 3 dried) lime leaves, crushed

1 vanilla pod, slit lengthwise

60 ml (4 tbsp) vodka (or other white spirit)

---

1. Pierce each fruit several times all over with a needle or cocktail stick. Put the fruits (mixed) into a wide-mouthed, heatproof serving or preserving-type jar or pot.
2. Put the wine, water, sugar and tartaric acid into a large heatproof measuring jug or bowl. Stir. Add the crushed seeds, lime leaves and vanilla.
3. Pour the syrup over the fruit in the jar, allowing at least 5 cm (2 inches) headroom (stand the jar inside a bowl in case the syrup bubbles up too far).
4. Microwave on HIGH, uncovered, for 8–9 minutes or until the fruits have both cooked through and the syrup is boiling. Top up with more syrup as needed.
5. Allow the fruit and syrup to cool. Add vodka, cover and gently invert the jar or pot once. Refrigerate and use within one week.

COOK'S TIP
Even after the fruit has been eaten, the syrup can be used as a base for drinks or for macerating other fruits.

SALSIFY MUSTARD PRESERVE

Scorzonera, salsify or oyster-plant are all names for the root vegetable once de rigueur in many Victorian gardens. It is delicious to eat as an hors d'oeuvre, before rich dishes, or in a leafy salad.

Makes 450 g (1 lb) jar

---

700 g (1½ lb) (scorzonera) black salsify, peeled and cut into 5 cm (2 inch) lengths, prepared weight 550 g (1¼ lb)

150 ml (¼ pint) water

15 ml (1 level tbsp) freshly squeezed lime juice

150 ml (¼ pint) dry cider

150 ml (¼ pint) white wine vinegar

2.5 ml (½ level tsp) salt

5 ml (1 level tsp) dry English mustard powder

30 ml (2 level tbsp) coarse grain mustard

pinch cayenne pepper

125 g (4 oz) reserved cooking liquid

15 ml (1 level tbsp) honey

---

1. Put freshly peeled scorzonera in a microwave-proof ring dish with the water and lime juice. Cover with cling film and microwave on HIGH for 5–6 minutes. Drain, but keep the cooking liquid; measure and retain 125 g (4 oz).
2. Mix the remaining ingredients and pour over the scorzonera. Microwave, uncovered, on HIGH for 6 minutes. Using sterile tongs, pack the salsify into a sterilized jar (see page 41, but use conventional sterilizing methods if jar has metal fastenings), standing upright so that the close-packed batons support each other. Pour over the hot mustard syrup to overflowing. Seal while hot, label and store in a cool place.

See photograph page 26

Mange-tout stuffed with Tawny broad bean pâté (page 88) with Golden courgettes (page 78) and Thai white aubergine eggs (page 83) on Sea-flavoured seasoning paillasson (page 37). In the background is Country-style herb and pumpkin bread (page 108).

OVERLEAF
Pink pompadour potatoes, (page 58) with Spinach and pont l'évêque salade branché (page 50). Diamond potatoes (page 63)   sprinkled with citrus, herb and nut seasoning (page 36) and Broccoli with blue cheese dressing (page 80). On the side is Granary soda bread (page 110).

HOT, WARM AND COLD SALADS

LINDA'S SALADE TIÈDE

This stylish salad is adapted from the recipe of one of the most accomplished salad-makers I know. Linda's surprise additions of unexpected fruits and nuts, and a virtuoso dressing, almost always delight her assembled luncheon guests: yet her role as hostess is often simultaneously combined with managing a busy and important photographic studio. It is her husband and partner, Bryce Attwell, who photographed the dishes in this book.

Serves 4

75 g (3 oz) pine nuts

75 g (3 oz) frisée (or curly endive), torn into pieces

75 g (3 oz) radicchio, torn into half leaves

50 g (2 oz) mâche (or lamb's lettuce), separated into leaves

50 g (2 oz) feuille de chêne (red or green) or batavia lettuce, torn into half leaves

25–50 g (1–2 oz) alfalfa sprouts

2–3 fresh nectarines (or peaches, blanched and peeled)

1 ripe avocado

Dressing

2 cloves garlic, skinned and crushed

10 ml (2 level tsp) coarse grain mustard

75 ml (5 tbsp) green Tuscan olive oil

15 ml (1 level tbsp) French tarragon vinegar

salt and freshly ground pepper

handful of herbs (tarragon, chervil, salad burnet, flat leaf parsley or basil)

1. Put the pine nuts on a heatproof plate and microwave on HIGH, uncovered, for 6 minutes, stirring frequently after 4 minutes.
2. While the nuts cook, wash, dry thoroughly and tear up or separate the salad leaves. Pull apart the alfalfa into small sections. Arrange the salad stuffs at random in a large, elegant bowl.
3. Remove the pine nuts and toss them over the salad. Slice the nectarine into 1 cm (1/2 inch) segments and put on the heatproof plate. Skin, stone and cube the avocado. Bury it at the centre of the salad.
4. Microwave the nectarine, uncovered, on MEDIUM (60%) for 2 minutes (or until pleasantly warm).
5. Make the dressing by putting the ingredients into a shaker and shaking until well blended.
6. Pour the dressing over the salad and toss gently but very thoroughly, scattering the peach segments throughout. If wished, present on individual plates. Serve with lacy French bread and granary rolls.

— COOK'S TIP —

Serve after pasta or rice, followed by cheese and finally by nut ice cream, an anise-flavoured mousse or tiny pastries.

Linda's salade tiède (above) with Pomegranate granita (page 112) and Strawberry scelto cocktail (page 126).

See photograph opposite

POMEGRANATE AND CABBAGE SALAD AEGINITISSA

During New Year celebrations in Greece, pomegranates are traditionally broken against the wall of the house to ensure good fortune in the coming year. But these beautiful and distinctive fruits are also used in a number of dishes. One is cabbage salad, in which the red jewelled seeds are dotted throughout the pale strands of cabbage. Because some white winter cabbage can be tougher and less sweet than the native Greek type, it is good to blanch briefly and drain the cabbage, then embellish it with a warm pomegranate dressing as well as with the seeds. The original recipe comes from a Scottish friend, Mistress Barrabel, who wintered in the island of Aegina, but the microwave amendments are my own.

Serves 4

450 g (1 lb) white winter cabbage
150 ml (¼ pint) boiling water
5 ml (1 level tsp) sea salt
freshly ground black pepper
45–60 ml (3–4 tbsp) Greek olive oil
1 large ripe pomegranate, halved crosswise
30–45 ml (2–3 level tbsp) celery tops or flat leaf parsley

1. Shred the cabbage finely and put into a large casserole. Pour on the boiling water, toss quickly and microwave, uncovered, on HIGH for 2–3 minutes.
2. Drain well and sprinkle with salt, pepper and oil. Press one half of the pomegranate over a lemon squeezer to extract the juice. Microwave the juice on HIGH for 1 minute then quickly pour it over the salad.
3. Scoop the seeds from the other half of pomegranate and separate from any connecting membranes. Then scatter them over the salad with the herb.

COOK'S TIP

If preferred, after blanching the cabbage, refresh in iced water until cooled completely. In this case do not microwave the pomegranate juice – use it cold for a chilled (not warm) salad. This dish goes well with feta cheese, some good bread and a sustaining bean dish, if wished.

SPINACH AND PONT L'ÉVÊQUE SALADE BRANCHÉ

A cheese and spinach salad with a difference is provided by the combination of Pont l'évêque and the vegetable – half raw, half cooked – in a creamy sauce. Olives add the 'natural seasoning' and the salad should be eaten just as the cheese begins to soften. The title incorporates a sort of pun: the spinach should be little bouquets of the branched variety; the cheese comes in a wooden box, and the style is what my Parisienne friend Susie might call 'branché', in her endearing cross-cultural argot.

Serves 4

450 g (1 lb) fresh young (preferably Redroot variety) spinach leaves
1 Pont l'évêque cheese, about 225 g (8–9 oz)
1 clove garlic, skinned and crushed
150 ml (¼ pint) crème fraîche or soured cream
salt and freshly ground black pepper
30 ml (2 tbsp) dry (Normandy) cider
1 shallot, skinned and shredded finely
12 black olives, crushed, stones removed

To serve

Rye, granary or buckwheat bread if available

1. Separate the bunches of spinach into tiny and medium-sized leaves. (Keep the tiniest aside to eat raw.)
2. Put the others, with their washing water still clinging, into a ring dish, cover with cling film

and microwave on HIGH for 2–2½ minutes or so, depending on tenderness and size of leaves, until part cooked.

3. Slice the Pont l'évêque into 32 or so wedges. Crush the garlic, add it to the cooked spinach with the cream, seasonings, cider and shallot.

4. Microwave, uncovered, stirring from time to time until a creamy sauce forms and the spinach is tender, about 1–1½ minutes.

5. Add most of the uncooked spinach, stir in the cheese, serve in little mounds (with a few perfect baby leaves on top) and add a scattering of olives over all. Eat while temperatures and textures are at their best.

See photograph page 46

VASILI'S CRETAMA GREENS

Last summer, staying at our tiny cottage in Greece, I was taken exploring by a neighbour and friend whose family farms the surrounding hillside. During a walk over sun-drenched rocks we gathered cretama (a kind of sea samphire looking rather like delicate chains of tiny string beans). This we cooked in a little sea water, adding some of this family's greeny-gold olive oil, garlic, parsley and fresh lemon juice. Luckily samphire is becoming available in high street fishmongers. Ask for it and try this recipe – good alone or with fish dishes.

Serves 4

450 g (1 lb) cretama (samphire), broken up finely

45–60 ml (3–4 tbsp) salted water

30–45 ml (2–3 tbsp) Greek olive oil

2 cloves garlic, skinned and chopped

juice of 1 fresh lemon

freshly ground black pepper

handful of flat leaf parsley, chopped or snipped

Greek country bread or other good bread

1. Put the cretama and salted water in a large casserole and microwave, covered, for 3 minutes. Toss well and stir in the oil, garlic, lemon juice, pepper and parsley. Eat the salad hot, warm or cold with rough bread to soak up the juices.

MELON IN SCENTED HERB DRESSING

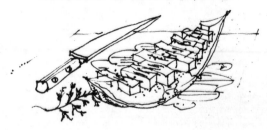

Warm or hot melon with a sweet but piquant dressing and feathery herbs gives an appealing start to a meal. It could also be the basis for a lunch or supper. Champagne vinegar is expensive but, strong and clean tasting, well worth the investment. Red fruits mustard (mine comes from Hédiard in Paris) is absolutely irreplaceable. If it cannot be located, a mild Dijon will just about suffice but cannot equal the fine taste of the former. I hope to devise my own recipe for rosy mustard soon!

Serves 4

700 g (1½ lb) Ogen melon

50 g (2 oz) spring onions

10 ml (2 level tsp) rosy (red fruits) mustard

30 ml (2 tbsp) crème de cassis de Dijon

15 ml (1 tbsp) champagne or white wine vinegar

30 ml (2 tbsp) grapeseed oil

handful of fresh chervil

1. Quarter the melon lengthwise and discard the seeds. (Dry these if wished between kitchen paper in the microwave oven, for use on another occasion.)

2. Slice the flesh, in one continuous cut, from the skin of each section, then cross cut the flesh almost to the base in 8 places, leaving it in position.

3. Put the onions, mustard, cassis and white wine vinegar in a heatproof sauceboat or serving bowl. Microwave on HIGH, uncovered, for 1 minute. Stir well. Add the oil and stir until thick and emulsified.

4. Put the 4 sections of melon on a heatproof serving plate (or plates) and microwave on HIGH, uncovered, for 1 or 2 minutes, depending on the temperature preferred.

5. Pour some sauce over each, scatter a little chervil over all and serve immediately with the remaining sauce.

MANGO FAN SALAD WITH TANDOORI DRESSING (AND POPPADUMS)

Fan-shaped servings of cooked mango on a bed of brilliant coloured and spicy sauce constitute a notable discovery! The taste is superlative and the textures memorable. What is more, deep frying or grilling of poppadums become things of the past once you own a microwave.

Serves 4

two 350 g (12 oz) ripe mangoes

10 ml (2 tsp) safflower, sunflower or grapeseed oil

2 shallots or 1 small onion, skinned and chopped

1 cm (½ inch) cube of root ginger, shredded or grated

Dressing

15 ml (1 tbsp) safflower, sunflower or grapeseed oil

30 ml (2 tbsp) white wine, champagne or fruit (such as raspberry) vinegar

2.5 ml (½ level tsp) tandoori mixture

To serve

4 spiced or garlic poppadums (papad)

1. Peel or pare the skin from the mangoes using a floating blade peeler or sharp paring knife.
2. Slice off the 2 large sides from either side of the stone of each mango (keep the stone portions). Slash each of these 4 curved halves lengthwise, almost to the base, in a series of parallel lines. Keep the shape and base section intact (to allow flesh to be opened out into a 'fan').
3. Preheat a large 25 cm (10 inch) heatproof browning dish for 5–6 minutes. Add the oil, then the prepared shallots and ginger and stir quickly until wilted and aromatic. Add the 4 halves of mango, evenly spaced and flat surfaces down.
4. Microwave on HIGH, uncovered, for 2 minutes, shaking once during cooking.
5. Meanwhile, make the dressing. Cut and scrape the remaining mango flesh from the stones. Put the flesh into a food processor or blender with the oil, vinegar and tandoori

mixture and reduce to a smooth purée. (If too thick, add a little iced water or white wine.)
6. Remove the mangoes from the cooker and place 2 poppadums on some kitchen paper. Microwave on HIGH, covered with kitchen paper, for 2 minutes, turning the poppadums over halfway through cooking time. Repeat the process with the other 2 poppadums.
7. Serve the mango halves, with the slashes spread as a fan, on a pool of tandoori dressing with some onion and ginger. Place a poppadum by each serving. Serve warm, cool or chilled.

See photograph page 101

RAW BEET AND CELERIAC REMOULADE

Nothing seems more modest than the taste of raw baby beets, yet contrasted beside the sophisticated taste of blanched celeriac in a mustardy mayonnaise, it excels. Nut bread provides the third element of this interesting assemblage.

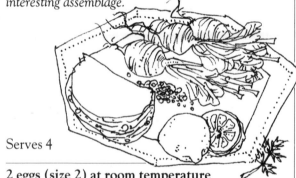

Serves 4

2 eggs (size 2) at room temperature

30 ml (2 level tbsp) coarse grain mustard

salt and freshly ground pepper

5 ml (1 tsp) freshly squeezed lemon juice

300 ml (½ pint) light olive oil

350 g (12 oz) raw celeriac

150 ml (¼ pint) boiling water

225 g (8 oz) scrubbed raw beets

crisp, lacy French bread (such as ficelle)

crushed hazelnuts

Garnish

flat leaf parsley

1. Put the eggs, mustard, salt, pepper, and lemon juice into a blender. Put the olive oil into a measuring jug.

2. Switch on the blender and, starting gradually, trickle in the oil, increasing the speed as the emulsion thickens. Stir thoroughly, taste and adjust seasonings. Set aside.

3. Put the celeriac (cut into suitably sized pieces) into a food processor (use coarse grater attachment) and shred quickly. Put the shredded celeriac into a medium heatproof bowl and pour on the boiling water. Microwave on HIGH for 1 minute , then drain very thoroughly, squeezing out any moisture.

4. Put the beetroot (cut into suitably sized pieces) into the food processor (still using coarse grater attachment) and shred quickly.

5. Using an ice-cream scoop or spoon, put scoops of beetroot on to each of four serving plates.

6. Mix half of the mayonnaise into the warm celeriac. Put scoops of this alongside the beetroot. (Serve the remaining mayonnaise separately.)

7. Slice the French bread into 10 cm (4 inch) lengths. Slice these cylinders lengthwise and parallel 3 times to give 4 slim slices.

8. Lightly butter and sprinkle with crushed nuts. Serve the dish while it is barely warm, with some long, elegant flat leaf parsley as accompaniment.

CHAVIGNOL WITH ARTICHOKE HEARTS EN SALADE

This makes a delicious salad for lunch or supper or as a first course for an elegant dinner. The artichoke must be freshly prepared and cooked (not canned) but if the salads given are not readily available, make some imaginative substitution. Do try to use the goat cheeses specified: they are particularly good. Fromagède is an alternative: it can be sliced into 4

drum shapes. If neither of these can be found, use another reputable French fromage de chèvre. Use a 175 g (6 oz) slice, cut into 4.

Serves 4

2 Chavignol cheeses or a baton of Fromagède

4 cooked globe artichoke hearts (page 56)

6–8 nasturtium leaves, torn

50 g (2 oz) rocket

50 g (2 oz) dandelion

1 miniature cos or 'little gem' lettuce

½ handful fresh mint leaves

1 handful fresh nasturtium (or caper) leaves

Dressing

45 ml (3 tbsp) first pressing olive oil

15 ml (1 tbsp) Sancerre (white) wine

1 clove garlic, crushed

salt and freshly ground black pepper

To serve

60 ml (4 tbsp) chopped parsley

crusty French or Italian bread

1. If using Chavignols, remove wrapping and labels and halve crosswise. Otherwise, slice the baton of Fromagède crosswise into 4 equal portions. Remove all the leaves from the artichokes, retaining only the base. (Scrape the soft leaf-bases before discarding and add the purée to the fonds.) Put a cheese portion, cut surface upwards, on each artichoke heart.

2. Mix the 6 types of salad leaves together, separating leaves from central stems and cores, and tearing large leaves into halves. Prepare the dressing: put the oil, wine, garlic and seasonings into a non-metal screw-top jar.

3. Evenly space the prepared cheese-topped fonds around a heatproof plate and microwave on HIGH, uncovered, for 1 minute or until the cheese is soft (about to dribble) and fonds are warmed.

4. Quickly shake the dressing to mix, then pour over the salad leaves and stir. Divide the salad between 4 serving plates.

5. Serve each with an artichoke and cheese centrepiece with a scattering of parsley and eat whilst the temperatures and textures are at their best. Drink the remaining Sancerre.

YUCCA, YAM, PAWPAW AND MOOLI SALAD

Exotic root vegetables such as yucca, with its rough, hairy outer skin, and rosy-skinned yams, are beloved basic fare for many people. To those more accustomed to potatoes and carrots such vegetables may appear somewhat daunting. This fruited version of a potato salad should help improve the acquaintance. Yucca should be peeled under water and prepared and cooked quickly, along with the yams, for all to be at their best. Cubes of 1 cm (½ inch) are suitable size. The texture of pawpaw, cool and smooth, and crispness of mooli, provide interesting contrasts. Slice these while the other vegetables cook. Eat the salad while it is half warm and half cool. The coriander provides a final touch but if it cannot be located, fresh mint would be moderately acceptable.

Serves 4

---

225 g (8 oz) yucca (cassava or manioc) root, peeled and cubed

450 g (1 lb) small yams (sweet potato), scrubbed and cubed

75 g (3 oz) spring onions

60 ml (4 tbsp) stock verde (page 20)

30 ml (2 tbsp) mustard oil (or safflower or sunflower oil)

shredded zest and squeezed juice of 1 lime

1 ripe pawpaw, skinned, seeded and sliced

125 g (4 oz) mooli (daikon) radish, scrubbed and cut into julienne strips

To serve

coriander leaves, chopped

natural yogurt (optional)

1. Put the peeled and cubed cassava root (you will need a floating blade peeler and a cleaver or very sharp knife for this), the yams (also cubed) and the white parts of the spring onions (reserve tops) into a ring dish with the stock.
2. Cover with cling film and microwave on HIGH for 10–12 minutes (or until cubes are very tender), giving the ring dish a half turn halfway through cooking time.
3. Shred the remaining green tops of the spring onions and add these to the vegetables with the oil, zest and juice. Toss well to mix.
4. Pile on to a large flat dish, making an indentation at the centre. Add the pawpaw and

mooli in a decorative pattern. Scatter coriander over all and supply fresh natural yogurt as additional dressing for those who enjoy it.

STIR-FRIED CELERIAC RIBBONS

Certain delicious foods, such as salsify, celeriac and artichokes, too often seem shrouded in myth, mystery and superstition as far as their preparation is concerned. Rather than lemon juice, flour and water pastes and other dated techniques, I propose that they should be prepared quickly, cooked minimally and served at once! It can be a revelation. Celeriac cooked this way has a deliciousness which is hard to define – substantial, rich, flavoursome.

Serves 4

---

700 g (1½ lb) celeriac root, washed

30–45 ml (2–3 tbsp) safflower, sunflower or grapeseed oil

2.5 cm (1 inch) portion of root ginger, peeled and slivered

2 garlic cloves, peeled and crushed

seeds of 4 green cardamom pods

seasoned salt (of choice) to taste

Garnish (optional)

radicchio leaves

a few drops of hazelnut oil

1. Preheat a large 25 cm (10 inch) browning dish for 5 minutes.
2. Meanwhile peel and quickly cut the celeriac into 1 cm (½ inch) by 5 cm (2 inch) rectangles so that they can be fed easily into the food processor. Using the slicer attachment, slice the celeriac into fine ribbons.
3. Pour the first measure of oil into the hot pan, add the ginger and garlic, stirring quickly to stir-fry it. Add the celeriac and toss well in the oil of the still-hot pan, then microwave on HIGH, uncovered, for 10 minutes. Stir well halfway through cooking time, adding the cardamom seeds.
4. Serve sprinkled with homemade seasoned salt or herb seasoning (page 36) and piled round a circle of cupped radicchio leaves. Eat at once. If wished, add a few drops of nut oil.

INSALATA TRATTORIA

It is the dressing that distinguishes the dish. I once ate a somewhat similar salad in a cheerful hilltop trattoria not far from Fiesole's Roman baths and the Museo Bandini, which I discovered quite by chance. Thus I made several pleasant discoveries in one day! Have the pine nuts toasted prior to starting the salad or else the timing will be ruined: they take about 6–7 minutes on HIGH, uncovered, stirring frequently.

Serves 4

450 g (1 lb) French or string beans, trimmed to 5 cm (2 inch) lengths

30 ml (2 tbsp) green (or other vegetable) stock

Dressing

1 egg yolk (size 3), at room temperature

15 ml (1 level tbsp) whole grain mustard

5 ml (1 tsp) tabasco sauce

15 ml (1 tbsp) plum or other fruit sauce

2.5 ml (½ level tsp) paprika

pinch nutmeg

3.75 ml (¾ tsp) salt

6 fresh mint leaves

6 fresh basil leaves

12 fresh tarragon leaves

1 sprig fresh lemon thyme

90 ml (6 tbsp) pure virgin olive oil

To serve

fresh parsley sprigs

75 g (3 oz) pignolia (pine nuts), freshly toasted

1. Put the beans and stock into a ring dish. Cover with cling film and microwave on HIGH for 4–5 minutes, shaking the dish and giving it a half turn halfway through cooking time. Leave to stand.
2. Meanwhile, make the dressing. Put the ingredients, in order, into a blender (having torn the herbs just as they are added to retain full flavour) and process in short bursts until a smooth, speckled sauce is obtained.
3. Pour the sauce over the beans and juices, scatter with parsley and nuts and serve warm.

See photograph page 68

INSALATA MACCHIAIOLI

'Macchiaioli' means 'blotch-painters' – a name given to the Tuscan painters' movement which was important during the 1860s. The salad is so called because it should be served on a flat dish, square or rectangular (like a canvas), with the two vegetables spread at random across it. The dressing is poured in 'impressionistic blotches' over it. Serve, perhaps with asparagus pencils (page 78) and some fettunta (crusty, lightly-toasted bread rubbed with a cut garlic clove and touched with olive oil) to complete the effect.

Serves 4

675 g (1½ lb) small new potatoes, scrubbed and pierced

450 g (1 lb) young branched (Redroot) spinach, separated into leaves

Dressing

2 medium tomatoes, cubed

90 ml (6 tbsp) thick cream

2.5 ml (½ tsp) salt

15 ml (1 level tbsp) soft dark brown sugar

5 ml (1 level tsp) paprika

6–8 fresh basil leaves

1 clove garlic, peeled and chopped

1. Put the potatoes, with their washing water still clinging, into a ring dish. Microwave, cling-film covered, on HIGH for 8–10 minutes, stirring potatoes from base to top halfway through cooking time. Remove and keep aside.
2. Put the spinach, with its washing water still clinging, into the ring dish. Microwave, cling-film covered, on HIGH for 4–4½ minutes. Do not chop.
3. Put the dressing ingredients in a blender and reduce to a thick purée. Taste and adjust seasoning as necessary.
4. Slice the warm potatoes thickly and crosswise into 'coins'. Scatter over the serving dish.
5. Arrange the spinach attractively among the potatoes. Pour over the dressing so that some parts are left uncovered. Serve while still warm, and the dressing cold.

See photograph page 68

INSALATA DI ZUCCHINI

You will find diners asking for the recipe of this five-minute salad immediately, believing that ingredients and method must be complex and difficult. On the contrary! In my experience this salad, so simple, yet so interesting in taste, texture and temperature, is quite enough (if preceded by say, pasta, and followed by fruit and cheese) to make an excellent main course, though it is also a good starter or accompaniment. Good bread is, of course, essential.

Serves 4–6

900 g (2 lb) medium sized courgettes (zucchini)
1/2 young leek, trimmed and washed
15 ml (1 level tbsp) safflower oil
10 ml (2 level tsp) sesame oil
15 ml (1 level tbsp) raspberry or strawberry vinegar
45 ml (3 level tbsp) blue poppy seeds

1. Using a food processor's slicing attachment, slice half the courgettes finely and keep aside. Replace the slicer with the shredder or coarse grater attachment and coarsely shred the remaining courgettes. Keep the two piles separate.
2. Shred the leek and put into a ring dish or heatproof serving dish with the two oils. Microwave, uncovered, on HIGH for 1 minute or until very hot. Add the sliced (not shredded) courgettes and toss in the hot mixture. Microwave, uncovered, for another 2 minutes.
3. Add the vinegar and stir quickly. Push the sliced courgettes to the outside of a serving dish to make a border.
4. Toss the remaining raw shredded courgettes with the poppy seeds and pile into the centre of the dish. Serve immediately, to enjoy the difference in the temperatures.

GLOBE ARTICHOKES, SAUCE MOUSSELINE

There is a delightful anecdote in my Penguin Alice B. Toklas Cookbook, which tells of two brothers at lunch in the French countryside, in the company of their parents, the author Gertrude Stein and Janet Scudder, a sculptress friend. One boy fell silent, and was asked why he did not converse with his brother. He explained that he never spoke when artichokes with sauce mousseline were served. I hope that the following recipe can provoke a similar respect and pleasure among the diners around your table.

Serves 4

4 medium-sized globe artichokes, each 175 g (6 oz) before trimming
juice of 1 lemon
15 ml (1 tbsp) olive oil
150 ml (1/4 pint) mayonnaise (homemade)
150 ml (1/4 pint) crème fraîche
salt and freshly ground pepper

To serve

fresh herbs

1. Lying each artichoke on its side, slice off and discard the top 2.5 cm (1 inch) of leaf tips in one movement, using a serrated stainless steel knife. Trim back the stem ends so that the artichokes can sit upwards comfortably. Cross-cut the stem base. Using a pair of tongs or tweezers, pull up and out the middle leaves. Then remove the fluffy tender leaves and inner 'choke' portion, scraping with a teaspoon and taking care not to cut away any of the precious fond or base. Squeeze a few drops of lemon juice into the centres of each artichoke.
2. Place the four artichokes in a ring dish. Pour 15 ml (1 level tbsp) boiling water inside each artichoke. Pour another 60 ml (4 tbsp) of boiling water into the dish. Carefully and quickly cover the dish with cling film and microwave on HIGH for 8 minutes. Then uncover. (An inner and outer leaf should pull away easily and there should be a distinct aroma of artichoke.) Drain, upside down, then stand them up. Pour a few drops of oil into each. Leave for a few minutes.
3. To the mayonnaise (classic mayonnaise made with lemon, or quails' egg mayonnaise, page 34), add and stir in the crème fraîche, seasoning the sauce as needed.
4. Spoon a measure of sauce inside each warm artichoke. Insert some herbs. Pass the remaining sauce separately, also scattered with herbs. Have some delicious, nutty brown bread thinly cut and buttered and rolled on the diagonal into water lily shapes. Serve a good full-bodied white wine such as a Chardonnay, or a crisp Riesling (though there are many who will tell you that artichokes spoil the pleasure of a good wine).

MAIN COURSE DISHES

ELEMENTAL LUNCH

*What more simple, elemental vegetable meal could
there be than gently-cooked fresh tomatoes, in whose
sweet-sharp pulp thin-sliced courgettes are tenderly
softened? A handful of fresh herbs, generous
seasoning with pepper and salt and a welcoming
bowl, with perhaps an accompanying muffin or roll,
complete the picture. This lunch is a joy: tasty,
effortless, healthful, inexpensive and ready in
minutes. But note two essential points: use a ring
dish if you can – it's easy and cooks best that way;
and slice the courgette (as thin as a coin) just before
cooking for full goodness.*

Serves 1

4 small or 3 medium tomatoes, quartered
15 ml (1 level tbsp) butter in 4–5 pieces
1 medium courgette, sliced thinly
salt and freshly ground pepper to taste
fresh herbs of choice (spring onion tops, chives, basil, parsley, tarragon)

1. Dot the tomato quarters with butter and
place in a microwave ring dish. Cover with a lid,
heatproof plate or cling film and microwave on
HIGH for 4 minutes.
2. Stir in the courgettes until coated, cover and
microwave on HIGH for a further 45 seconds.
Stir, season, add herbs and serve in a bowl. Eat
with a spoon to scoop up the last of the juices.

─────── VARIATIONS ───────

For a change, add fromage blanc, fromage frais
or yogurt.
For the frugal, stir in left-over pasta, rice,
lentils, barley or beans and reheat briefly.
For sophisticates, stir in cubed avocado.
For epicures, stir 2 quails' eggs into the hot sauce
and reheat briefly.
For toddlers, add cubed wholewheat bread or
croutons.
For those with jaded palates, add cubed
cucumber and pickled walnuts to make a hot
salad.

DILL, YOGURT AND LEEK TART

*This is a dish for spring or autumn. Dill is a splendid
herb to use with vegetables – too often it is forgotten
or relegated to fish dishes only. Its sweet delicacy
gives leeks a 'garden fresh' sort of taste in this quick
but interesting recipe. Try to use really young leeks
or late season thinnings. (Dill seed and flower heads,
as well as the green fronds, are worth microwave-
drying when in season.)*

Serves 4

350 g (12 oz) baby leeks, trimmed and cut into ¼ inch slices
90 ml (6 tbsp) natural strained Greek yogurt
2 eggs (size 2)
100 g (4 oz) strong farmhouse cheddar, grated
salt and freshly ground black pepper
45 ml (3 level tbsp) fresh dill, chopped or snipped
19 cm (7½ inch) pre-cooked poppyseed pastry pie shell (page 76)

1. Put the leeks into a microwave ring dish and
rinse thoroughly under running water, checking
for any grit between the outer layers. Do not
separate the rings, however. Drain, and with the
washing water still clinging to the leeks,
microwave on HIGH, covered with cling film,
for 3 minutes, giving the dish a shake halfway
through cooking time.
2. Add the yogurt and eggs, stirred, to the still-
warm leeks and 75 g (3 oz) of the cheddar with
the dill and seasonings. Spoon this mixture into
the poppyseed pastry shell.
3. Sprinkle on the remaining cheddar and
microwave on MEDIUM (50%) power,
uncovered, for 9–10 minutes. The leeks should
remain green and fresh and the sauce creamy
and dense.

See photograph page 101

PASHA'S PILLOWS

These rectangular green parcels with their exotic-tasting (yet simple) filling conjure, in my imagination, miniature velvety cushions of the type one might expect to find in a harem, for languid creatures to recline upon! This dish is easy to make well if the leaves used are large undamaged ones, so buy from an obliging greengrocer or a store where you may choose your own. (Better still to pick them from your own garden.) Both the powdered pure saffron and the golden sultanas add to the essential charm of this recipe so try not to use substitutes.

Serves 4

---

225 g (8 oz) button mushrooms, cleaned and halved lengthwise

---

15 ml (1 tbsp) pure virgin olive oil

---

50 g (2 oz) spring onions, sliced

---

2 garlic cloves

---

75 g (3 oz) golden sultanas

1.9 grain (small) sachet powdered pure saffron

---

salt and freshly ground black pepper

---

50 g (2 oz) strong cheddar cheese, grated

---

100 g (4 oz) cream cheese with chives

---

1 egg (size 2)

---

8 large spinach or Swiss chard (blette) leaves with washing water still clinging

---

30 ml (2 tbsp) moscatel or vermouth bianco

---

1. Put the halved mushrooms in a ring dish with the oil and toss to coat. Microwave, uncovered, on HIGH for 2 minutes. Add the spring onions, garlic, sultanas, saffron and seasonings. Stir well and microwave, uncovered, on HIGH for a further 2 minutes. Stir in the cheeses and egg.

2. Evenly arrange the wet spinach leaves overlapping on a large baking tray or roasting rack. Microwave on HIGH for 1 minute to soften and blanch them.

3. Working quickly, place one quarter of the mushroom mixture in the middle of each of 4 of the leaves (underside up). Fold the leaf edges in and over to form neat rectangles. Re-wrap each 'pillow' in a second leaf.

4. Oil a large shallow casserole or dish and evenly arrange on it the leaf 'pillows' (folded sides down). Microwave, uncovered, for 6 minutes, giving the dish a half turn halfway through the cooking time.

5. Carefully lift out using a fish slice, and place on a serving dish. Pour the vermouth or moscatel into the casserole, stir to mix with the juices and microwave on HIGH, uncovered, for 30–45 seconds or until hot. Pour over and serve while still hot.

PINK POMPADOUR POTATOES

This astounding purée is adapted from the Penguin edition of the Alice B Toklas Cookbook, where it serves as the accompanying garnish for sea bass. My microwave version is served alone but for some sautéed walnuts, spring onions and a garnish of flat leaf parsley – a curious, splendid centrepiece for any table. Do not be tempted to use purchased beetroot. It is necessary to cook your own, 'au naturel'. This amount takes 8 minutes to cook, on HIGH, in a covered ring dish. Serve this purée after a clear soup course, and accompany or follow it with a favourite cheese or cheese salad then a fruit sorbet, or fresh fruit.

Serves 4

---

900 g (2 lb) even-sized potatoes, preferably King Edward or Desirée, washed

---

450 g (1 lb) beetroot (cooked 'au naturel' and skinned)

---

15 ml (1 level tbsp) fruity olive oil

---

30 ml (2 level tbsp) freshly squeezed lemon juice

---

5 ml (1 level tsp) freshly ground sea salt

---

freshly ground white pepper

150–200 ml (5–7 fl oz) thick cream

To serve

5 ml (1 level tsp) fruity olive oil

125 g (4 oz) fresh walnuts, halved

6–8 spring onions, sliced

2.5 ml (½ tsp) freshly ground sea salt

8–12 fresh flat leaf parsley sprigs

1. Using a sharp knife, make a series of diagonal and parallel slashes almost to the base of each potato, at 1 cm (½ inch) intervals. Make another series at right angles to these, to give diamond shapes. Space the potatoes evenly around a heatproof plate and microwave, cling-film covered, for 10 minutes, giving the dish a half turn halfway through cooking time.
2. While the potatoes cook, put the beets, cubed finely, with 15 ml (1 level tbsp) oil, the lemon juice, salt and pepper and most of the cream into a food processor (or blender) and process, in short bursts, to a thick purée.
3. Once the potatoes have cooked, leave them to stand for 5 minutes, then uncover and separate them into 'diamonds'. Put them into a deep, straight-sided bowl. Use an electric whisk to reduce to a purée with the remaining cream. (Alternatively, put through a potato ricer, not a food processor.) Add the beetroot purée, and blend until moderately well mixed (but not ultra-smooth).
4. Put the oil, walnuts, spring onions and salt into a ring dish and microwave on HIGH, uncovered, for 2 minutes, shaking the dish once or twice. Keep hot. Spoon, mound or pipe the crimson purée into or onto a serving dish, plate, bowl or china stand. Surround the base with a garland of flat leaf parsley sprigs and add the hot walnut-onion mixture.
5. Serve while still hot, with garlic bread, fougasse, wholewheat toast triangles or crusty rolls.

See photograph page 46

CHANTERELLES EN BRIOCHES

In this dish, delectable and decorative fresh chanterelles tumble from a lemon-scented rich bread case. Although bread of this type does not normally become crisp when reheated with a filling, it is the nature of the crumb which is so appealing – absorbent and tender, perfect for the sauce.

Serves 4

25 g (1 oz) butter

2.5 ml (½ tsp) freshly shredded lemon zest

15 ml (1 tbsp) freshly squeezed lemon juice

215–225 g (7½–8 oz) large brioches (purchased)

15 ml (1 tbsp) fruity olive oil

2 garlic cloves, skinned and chopped

50 g (2 oz) shallots, skinned and chopped

1 red onion, skinned and sliced

275 g (10 oz) fresh chanterelles (girolles)

60 ml (4 tbsp) white bordeaux (Graves)

45 ml (3 tbsp) double or thick cream

45 ml (3 level tbsp) fresh chervil, chopped

30 ml (2 level tbsp) fresh flat leaf parsley, chopped

2.5 ml (½ level tsp) freshly ground sea salt

1.25 ml (¼ level tsp) freshly ground black pepper

1. Put butter, lemon rind and lemon juice into a heatproof measuring jug and microwave on HIGH for 1 minute, uncovered.
2. Preheat a 25 cm (10 inch) browning dish for 5 minutes.
3. Meanwhile, use a grapefruit or other short-bladed but serrated knife to remove a cone-shaped section from the top of the brioche. Retain the top crusty section as a lid. Remove and discard the crumbs from the lower part. This should leave a lid and a hollowed-out brioche case. Enlarge the lower case if necessary.
4. Brush the inside and outside of the brioche case and its lid with the butter-lemon mixture.
5. Add the oil, garlic, shallots and the red onion to the browning dish. Toss them together briefly and then microwave, uncovered, on HIGH for 45 seconds. Add the cleaned mushrooms (halved if large) and microwave on HIGH for a further 2 minutes, uncovered. Add the wine and microwave, uncovered, for a final 30 seconds or until minimally cooked but hot.
6. Quickly fold the cream and herbs through the mixture, adding seasonings to taste. Spoon the filling into the prepared brioche. Cover with the lid. Place on kitchen paper and cover loosely with another sheet of kitchen paper. Microwave on HIGH for 1½ minutes or until the case and its contents are very hot indeed. Serve while the mushrooms are steaming and aromatic.

See photograph front cover

ELGIN MOUSSAKAS

My neighbour and friend, Fionnuala, served delicious meatless moussakas one cold Sunday night recently. She wasn't sure, she said, if it would work. It worked, and her two brothers and I regaled ourselves with the bounty. She accompanied the moussakas with plain boiled potatoes, followed it with a garlicky-dressed red and green leafed salad, cheese, then muscat grapes. We drank a good red wine and I hoped fervently that she would never forsake our neighbourhood for new pastures. This microwave version is substantial and probably needs only a leafy salad to accompany it. Don't be surprised to find the chickpeas quite firm – that is to be expected – but they are delicious even so.

Serves 6–8

225 g (8 oz) chickpeas
1.1 litres (2 pints) boiling water
5 ml (1 level tsp) garlic, skinned and chopped
30 ml (2 tbsp) fruity olive oil
5 ml (1 level tsp) fresh root ginger, shredded
1 vegetable stock cube
225 g (8 oz) Spanish onion, skinned and sliced
550 g (1¼ lb), or 3 small, aubergines
275 g (10 oz) courgettes, trimmed and sliced thinly lengthwise
60 ml (4 tbsp) tomato purée
150 ml (¼ pint) boiling stock or water
2.5 ml (½ level tsp) salt (optional)
5 ml (1 level tsp) oregano or marjoram
225 g (8 oz) Greek strained yogurt
15–30 ml (1–2 tbsp) milk
1 egg (size 1)
45–60 ml (3–4 level tbsp) kephalotiri or parmesan-type cheese
¼ nutmeg, finely grated

1. Cover the chickpeas in hot water, stir well, then cover and leave to stand for ½ hour.
2. Drain. Add 1.1 litres (2 pints) boiling water, put into a large 25 cm (10 inch) browning dish, cover and microwave on HIGH for 45 minutes, by which time most of the liquid will have been absorbed. Remove the dish from the oven.
3. Strain off any liquid left from the chickpeas and reserve. Cover the chickpeas with a layer of garlic, oil, ginger and onion.

4. Pierce the aubergines in 10 or 12 places, arrange on a sheet of kitchen paper and microwave on HIGH, uncovered, for 5 minutes, turning them over once. Remove the tops and slice into .5 cm (¼ inch) thick slices, lengthwise.
5. Cover the onions with an even layer of cooked aubergines and then the sliced courgettes. Mix the tomato purée with the boiling water and salt and pour over all.
6. Microwave, covered, on HIGH for a further 30 minutes. Mix the oregano or marjoram, yogurt, milk and egg together to make a custard. Remove the lid, pour the custard evenly over the moussakas and sprinkle with the cheese. Microwave on HIGH, uncovered, for another 4 minutes. Grate nutmeg over the top and serve hot, cut into large wedges.

PLEUROTES EN PAQUETS

In a unique song called 'The piano has been drinking (not me)' the American singer Tom Waits laments that, among other things, 'the menus are all frozen', in a certain establishment. It took me some time to unravel the imagery: not only plastic, glossy cold-to-handle menus but frozen food, treated impersonally, which has lost its charms! But frozen menus need not be catastrophic: freezers are a brilliant invention if properly used. This recipe responds well to freezer treatment. Together with the other items found on the illustrated menu (and taken from elsewhere in this book), they can be stored in a freezer, thawed and reheated in the microwave oven, and provide a tasty, full-bodied meal. Here's to Tom Waits' Frozen Menu.

Serves 4

4 sheets filo pastry (purchased), cut in 4
30 ml (2 tbsp) peanut oil
15 ml (1 tbsp) sesame oil
125 g (4 oz) pleurotes (oyster) mushrooms, quartered
3–4 spring onions, chopped
pinch of 5-spice powder
30 ml (2 level tbsp) coriander leaves
10 ml (2 level tsp) soya bean paste

1. Prepare the filling. Mix the two oils and add

half to a heatproof ring pan with the quartered mushrooms and spring onions, tossing well to coat. Microwave on HIGH, uncovered, for 2 minutes. Add the 5-spice powder, the coriander and half the soya bean paste. Stir to mix.

2. Cut the 4 sheets of pastry lengthwise into 4 (giving 16 slices). Use the remaining mixed oil to brush over the surface of each filo pastry strip. Put a small 1/16th dot of the soy bean paste on the right hand corner. Spoon 1/16th of the cooked filling on to each strip.

3. Make continuous rolls and folds from right to left, tucking in any loose filo pastry to keep the little paquets neat. Work quickly, keeping the pastry strips in a pile under a damp cloth to stop them drying out.

4. Brush or rub a film of oil over the surface of a large 25 cm (10 inch) browning dish. Place 8 of the prepared paquets, arranged like the spokes of a wheel, in the browning dish and brush the tops with oil. Microwave, uncovered, on HIGH for 4 minutes or until the paquets have puffed up and look crisp.

5. Quickly but carefully turn them over. Microwave on HIGH, uncovered, for a further minute. Remove the first batch.

6. Repeat the process with a second batch of 8. Served hot with some apricot and chilli sauce (page 31) these are utterly delicious.

HOT SPINACH SANDWICHES EVESHAM

This simple but inventive brunch, lunch or supper snack for two employs classic ingredients. Use unpasteurised cheese made lovingly and carefully, for this sandwich is one in which each ingredient must triumph. The spinach should be brilliantly green, young and tender. I particularly like the type which grows into 10-cm (4-inch) high bunches still jointed at their rose-tipped bases and looking like a quaint bouquet. Much comes from Italy or France but it is also grown and marketed in England (mine came from Evesham, Surrey).

Serves 2

125 g (4 oz) young spinach leaves (preferably Redroot variety)

two 125 g (4 oz) crusty baguettes

butter to spread (optional)

125 g (4 oz) pays d'Auge camembert, unpasteurised brie, Neufchâtel, or goat's cheese (such as Chavignol)

sea salt and freshly ground pepper

1. Wash and drain the spinach (leaving the water that clings), separating the leaves. Tear them if large. Put them into a medium heatproof bowl or ring dish, cover with cling film and microwave on HIGH for 1½–2 minutes.

2. Meanwhile split the bread lengthwise and lightly butter if wished. Cover the base thinly with sliced cheese.

3. Season the spinach and quickly pack it into the sandwich, leaving some visible at the edge. Halve crosswise and eat while the spinach is hot and the cheese softened.

VARIATION
HOT SPINACH SANDWICH FLORENTINE

Add one soft cooked egg, yolk pierced, microwaved at 50% MEDIUM (en cocotte with a little butter or cream) for 1½ minutes. Uncover it, then mash with a fork and spread it over the sandwich.

CHEESE, WHOLEWHEAT AND HERB PASTRY CASE WITH FILLING AU CHOIX

Microwaved pastry must, to my mind, have definite ease of preparation, flavour appeal and healthful ingredients to make it worthwhile, for the texture is somewhat unusual. This recipe justifies the choice, for the finished article comes out hot and crisp from the oven in under 15 minutes from starting the recipe, which must be some sort of record! While the pastry stands, a filling can be quickly prepared (I suggest an egg and fromage blanc type), spooned into the warm case and quickly reheated.

Makes a 20 cm (8 inch) shell case

75 g (3 oz) wholewheat flour

75 g (3 oz) plain unbleached flour

75 g (3 oz) cold butter, cubed

25 g (1 oz) freshly grated parmesan or cheddar cheese

15 g (½ oz) parsley, finely chopped

30 ml (2 tbsp) cold milk

10 ml (2 tsp) rich soy sauce

1. Put the flours into a medium sized bowl and cut or rub in the butter until the mixture resembles coarse breadcrumbs. Add the cheese and parsley and stir to blend.
2. Add the liquids all at once and stir quickly to form a firm dough, using the heel of the hand if necessary to obtain a compact ball.
3. Wrap in cling film and chill by placing in the freezer for 2 minutes.
4. Roll out into a 25 cm (10 inch) diameter circle. Invert a 20 cm (8 inch) diameter round pie plate and lift pastry, on its cling film, on to it. Fold back the edges (moistening them with water) to form even ridges or flutes.
5. Prick at 1 cm (½ inch) intervals with a fork and microwave on HIGH, uncovered, for 6 minutes, pricking again if pastry 'bubbles' during cooking. Leave to firm up before removing shell from its plate and inverting it. Remove cling film.
6. If wished, prepare a filling from eggs, gruyère, fromage blanc, spring onions, seasonings and watercress and spoon it into the still-warm shell. Microwave on MEDIUM (60%) until gently cooked, firm and hot.

COLCANNON CON AMORE

Colcannon, which correctly should contain kale, not cabbage, was always a delicious, useful and homely dish. My version has become less Irish and more European. Fennel gives it a special charm and good English cheese containing walnuts provides the final loving touch. Drink some lusty red wine of any reputable origin and rejoice in simplicity! A separate bowl of walnuts, a nut cracker and some crusty bread complete the pleasure.

Serves 4

700 g (1½ lb) potatoes (such as King Edward or Red Desirée)

120 ml (8 tbsp) soup stock verde (see page 20) or other good vegetable stock

350 g (12 oz) spring greens, shredded

225 g (8 oz) Florence fennel (with green fronds), thinly sliced

2 garlic cloves, skinned and chopped

125 g (4 oz) spring onions, thinly sliced

60 ml (4 tbsp) thick Jersey cream

salt and freshly ground pepper

50–75 g (2–3 oz) grated Walton cheese

To serve

fennel bulbs separated into scoops

1. Cut the potatoes into 1 cm (½ inch) cubes and put them into a roasting bag with 60 ml (4 tbsp) of the stock. Secure loosely with string or plastic ties. Puncture the bag in one or two places near the mouth and put it on its side in the oven with the potatoes in one layer. Microwave on HIGH for 7 minutes.
2. Use a slotted spoon to remove the potatoes to a deep, high-sided bowl. Put the shredded greens and sliced fennel, garlic and spring onions into the bag with the remaining 60 ml (4 tbsp) of stock. Seal again then microwave for a further 5 minutes. Meanwhile, purée the potatoes with an electric hand-held whisk or potato masher (do not use a food processor). Add the cream and seasonings.
3. Drain the contents of the bag into the potatoes and mix again. Pile the colcannon into a majestic mound and cover with the cheese and the reserved fennel fronds. Surround the dish with extra sticks of raw fennel to use as scoops. This dish is very hot so beware of burning an eager mouth!

PAPER-WRAPPED MIXED VEGETABLES

A tiny packet of steamed vegetable exotica permeated with the scent of rich sesame provides a novelty for guests. Serve complete for each diner to unwrap at the table. Add a starch-based accompanying dish.

Serves 4

25 g (1 oz) dried cloud ear fungus or Chinese black fungus

25 ml (5 tsp) dark sesame oil

2.5 cm (1 inch) ginger root, shredded

2 garlic cloves, skinned and shredded

125 g (4 oz) crosnes (baby Chinese artichokes) or small Jerusalem artichokes

125 g (4 oz) tindori, or else baby patty-pan squashes 2.5 cm (1 inch) across

75 g (3 oz) hop shoots (jets de houblon) or beansprouts

125 g (4 oz) young courgettes

125 g (4 oz) young fresh broad beans, shelled or fresh flageolet Chinese beans, shelled

50 g (2 oz) bean curd, cubed

1. Pour boiling water over the dried mushrooms and leave to stand.
2. Brush four 30 cm × 20 cm (12 inch × 8 inch) sheets baking parchment or greaseproof paper with half the sesame oil. Fold the papers lengthwise into thirds and then unfold, leaving a mark.
3. Shred the ginger and garlic finely; sprinkle some over the mid-portion of the centre third of each of the four papers.
4. Diagonally slice the crosnes and tindori. Divide these between the four papers on top of the ginger and garlic. Add halved hop shoots.
5. Slice the courgettes into 5 cm (2 inch) cylinders, then slice lengthwise into thin rectangles. Add these to the pile of vegetables.
6. Divide the broad beans or flageolets between the four piles, adding bean curd cubes, and the drained (but rehydrated) cloud ear mushrooms. Trickle the remaining sesame oil over the piles.
7. Fold the side flaps over the central third of the oiled paper to cover the filling. Fold under, or crimp and seal, the narrow ends to form envelopes.
8. Position the envelopes evenly round the edge of a large heatproof dish (folded or crimped edges downwards).
9. Microwave on HIGH for 4–5 minutes, giving the dish a half turn halfway through cooking time.

See photograph page 65

DIAMOND POTATOES

Criss-cross cutting of whole potatoes gives a large surface area into which to insert seasonings and, in this case, spices. The incisions then self-seal. Cling-film wrapped, the potatoes cook in their own scented steam. The colour and appearance are enjoyable in their own right but the flavour and texture achieved by this technique are even more noteworthy. Fresh herbs could be substituted for the sugar, if wished, for another quite different effect.

Serves 4

four 225 g (8 oz) potatoes, preferably oval

5 ml (1 level tsp) 5-spice powder

2.5 ml (½ level tsp) soft dark brown sugar

2.5 ml (½ level tsp) seasoned salt, such as citrus, herb and nut seasoning (page 36)

To serve

butter, yogurt or soured cream (optional)

1. Scrub the potatoes and position them flattest surface downwards. Using a sharp knife make a series of diagonal, parallel slashes almost to the base at 1 cm (½ inch) intervals. Make another series at right angles to these, forming diamond shapes. Carefully open up (almost like a pack of cards) and sprinkle in the spice, sugar and seasoning.
2. Position the potatoes evenly round the edges of a heatproof dish. Cover tightly with cling film and microwave on HIGH for 10–12 minutes or until the potatoes feel soft to the touch. Allow to stand for a further 2–3 minutes, covered.
3. Serve with accompanying butter, cream or yogurt if wished.

See photograph page 46–47

SFOGATO-TAJINE

According to Theodora FitzGibbon, sfogato denotes a Rhodian dish and uses a selection of foods, mainly vegetable (sometimes meat), in the omelette-custard mixture. In Tunisia I have tasted many different, ingenious versions of similar dishes called tajines. The spicing can be very individual indeed, allowing considerable freedom, so substitute favourite spices if wished. Serve with harissa.

Serves 4

30 ml (2 tbsp) fruity olive oil
5 ml (1 level tsp) fenugreek seeds, crushed
5 ml (1 level tsp) cumin seeds, crushed
5 ml (1 level tsp) celery or black mustard seeds
225 g (8 oz) onions, skinned and sliced
275 g (10 oz) courgettes, sliced
275 g (10 oz) aubergines, cubed
6–8 pickled walnuts, quartered
4 eggs (size 2)
salt and freshly ground pepper
30 ml (2 tbsp) crème fraîche or soured cream
50 g (2 oz) fromage blanc or frais, battu
45 ml (3 level tbsp) coriander leaves

To serve

6–8 fresh mint sprigs
harissa paste

1. Oil a rectangular heatproof glass casserole or loaf dish about 1.4 litres (2½ pints) in volume. Preheat a 25 cm (10 inch) browning dish for 8 minutes, or according to manufacturer's instructions. Put in the olive oil, spices, onions and aubergines. Stir and microwave on HIGH for 5 minutes, stirring from time to time.
2. Add the pickled walnuts, stir and microwave for a further 1 minute or until tender. Whisk the eggs with seasonings, cream and cheese and fold in the coriander leaves.
3. Pour the egg mixture over the vegetables and stir quickly. Spoon the mixture into the prepared glass dish, stand on an inverted saucer and microwave on MEDIUM for 15 minutes until puffy and set. Leave to stand for 2–3 minutes, covered.
4. Invert the dish and turn out. Decorate with mint sprigs. Serve in slices, hot, warm or cold.

ONE-POT FRUITED COUSCOUS

Traditional couscous is made and then cooked by laborious methods. My version is a 'one-pot' variety which takes 3 minutes to prepare and cook. This simple recipe uses 'instant' couscous available in packets in many ethnic groceries (described as 'moyen' or medium grade). Use it with dates, figs or fresh pineapple. Substitute harissa for tomato purée if you prefer.

Serves 4–6

30 ml (2 level tbsp) tomato purée or harissa
5 ml (1 level tsp) salt
15 ml (1 tbsp) fruity olive oil
5 ml (1 level tsp) ground turmeric
2.5 ml (½ level tsp) ground cumin
125 g (4 oz) leek, finely shredded crosswise
700 ml (1¼ pints) boiling water
225 g (8 oz) medium 'instant' couscous
225 g (8 oz) muscat or other white grapes, halved
25–50 g (1–2 oz) seedless raisins
25 g (1 oz) sunflower seeds

1. Put the first 6 ingredients, in order, into a medium-sized casserole or heatproof serving dish.
2. Add the boiling water, stir then add the couscous and stir again. Cover and microwave on HIGH for 2 minutes.
3. Add the fruit and seeds, stir, and microwave on HIGH for a further 30 seconds. Serve immediately or use warm or cold.

Paper wrapped mixed vegetables (page 63) served with Rempah (page 36) on noodles with a bowl of Sambal assemai (page 38).

OVERLEAF
Morel funghi pastinata with salad garnish (page 91), Brianza alchemist's risotto (page 84) and Bugialli's parsley pasta squares (page 92) in Soup stock verde (page 20) with a knob of Pesto San Lorenzo (page 29) on top. On the teatowel is Saffron tagliarini (page 90), Patrician pasta (page 93) and Five-spiced fine noodles (page 92).

BRIK À L'OEUF

Among Tunisian street snacks offered for sale are delicious, semi-circular, thin pastry envelopes in which a whole egg, some capers, cheese and various other ingredients are enclosed. This 'brik' is then deep fried, and when cut into, the barely set yolk pours out like a sauce. Deep frying is not possible in a microwave oven but these small square envelopes of filo pastry (in Tunisia a pastry called 'malsouka' is used) are a modified version of their tasty snacks. Harissa, available in cans, is an essential ingredient of these pastries, as are quails' eggs, which are just the right size and weight.

Serves 2 or 4

---

4 sheets filo pastry (purchased)

---

60 ml (4 tbsp) olive oil

---

4 quail's eggs

16–20 capers

---

50 g (2 oz) feta type cheese, crumbled

---

10 ml (2 level tsp) harissa

---

1. Brush one pastry rectangle with some oil, working quickly. Break a quail's egg straight into the centre of the pastry, dot it with 4–5 capers, crumble a quarter of the feta around it and top with half a teaspoon of harissa.
2. Fold the narrower ends of pastry over each other so that one completely covers the other. Fold the 2 unsealed ends towards each other (they will overlap a little) to form a square. Flip it over so that it rests on the thicker side.
3. Complete the process with the other sheets of pastry and their share of the ingredients. Flip them over in the same way.
4. Pour or brush a generous layer of oil over a 25 cm (10 inch) browning dish. Put in 2 'briks' at a time and microwave on HIGH, uncovered, for 2 minutes. Turn them over and microwave on HIGH, uncovered, for a further minute.
5. Repeat the process with the remaining 'briks'. Serve still warm with a fresh date, orange and avocado salad and perhaps some Tunisian wine.

Insalata trattoria (page 55) and Insalata macchiaioli (page 55) with Asparagus pencils (page 78).

GNOCCHI COLVILLE

The red, yellow and green of these moist cheesy little mouthfuls makes me think of the Rastafarian colours often worn by the West Indian youngsters who live, work and make music in our quarter of London. Plump, juicy chillies are often sold in local ethnic food shops and stalls and they enliven this very straightforward but tasty dish. Sometimes I serve gnocchi such as these with a warm salad of microwave-'wilted' leaves embellished with some lemony dressing or with a fresh tomato sauce or tomato salad. Eat the gnocchi hot; they lose their appeal cold.

Serves 4

---

225 ml (8 fl oz) warm water

---

15 ml (1 tbsp) olive oil

2.5 ml (½ level tsp) sea salt

---

75 g (3 oz) coarse semolina

---

50 g (2 oz) freshly grated parmesan cheese

---

50 g (2 oz) freshly grated gruyère cheese

30–45 ml (2–3 level tbsp) chopped flat leaf parsley

1.25–2.5 ml (¼–½ tsp) fresh red chilli flesh, shredded

---

semolina (to roll out)

⅙–¼ whole nutmeg, grated

---

1. Put the water, oil, salt and semolina (in order) into a large heatproof measuring jug or bowl. Stir well. Microwave on HIGH, uncovered, for 3 minutes, stirring thoroughly with a wooden spoon halfway through cooking.
2. To the hot paste add the parmesan, half the gruyère, the parsley and the chilli. Mix with a wooden spoon until thoroughly incorporated.
3. Scatter a little semolina onto a flat surface and pat out the still-warm mixture until it makes a rectangle about 20 cm (8 inches) by 15 cm (6 inches). Scatter a little more semolina on top.
4. Use a 5 cm (2 inch) circular, fluted cutter to cut out 12–14 rounds. Rub a little oil over a shallow heatproof serving plate about 15 cm (6 inches) in diameter.
5. Using a palette knife or spatula, arrange the gnocchi, overlapping, over the surface of the dish. Scatter on the remaining cheese and grate the nutmeg over all.
6. Microwave on HIGH, uncovered, for a final 2 minutes and eat while still hot. Crusty or crisp bread and a chilled beer or dry red wine would make an appropriate companion for this dish.

JACK-IN-THE-BOX AUBERGINE KEBABS

To find that, by cutting aubergines in a certain but quite simple manner, they open up like a toy and expose their inside surfaces beautifully to take a marinade, is a fascinating discovery. Since size and form matter in microwave cookery, this was an exercise in lateral thinking and it results in a visually intriguing and convenient-to-eat result. The satay-style sauce is rosy coloured and delicious served hot with the kebabs. Chinese Taste Powder is a flavouring which can be bought ready made and perfectly suits such dishes as this. If preferred, use your own citrus herb and nut seasoning instead (page 36).

Serves 4

4 'slim jim' thin purple aubergines, about 350 g (12 oz)

Marinade

2.5 ml (½ level tsp) Chinese Taste Powder or citrus herb and nut seasoning (page 36)

15 ml (1 tbsp) palm sugar or honey

15 ml (1 tbsp) dry sherry

30 ml (2 tbsp) sesame oil

1 garlic clove, peeled and crushed

15 ml (1 level tbsp), freshly chopped parsley

Sauce

30 ml (2 level tbsp) smooth peanut butter

5 ml (1 level tsp) fresh red or green chilli, shredded

2.5 ml (½ level tsp) tomato purée

2.5 ml (½ level tsp) Chinese Taste Powder or citrus herb and nut seasoning (page 36)

45 ml (3 tbsp) dry sherry

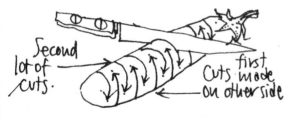

1. Cut parallel slashes at 1 cm (½ inch) intervals down one side of 4 long, 'slim jim' aubergines. Roll the aubergines over and cut alternate slashes on the opposite side of the aubergines, between the slashes already cut. In this way the aubergines can be pulled out, like a jack-in-the-box spring, to twice their length, for cooking on a wooden skewer or heatproof chopsticks, rather like a kebab.
2. Cut off and discard the stalk ends if wished. Push the aubergines lengthwise onto wooden chopsticks, satay sticks or wooden skewers. Pull out to open up the surfaces.
3. Mix the marinade ingredients together in a heatproof bowl or jug and microwave on HIGH, uncovered, for 30 seconds. Brush this marinade quickly over the cut surfaces.
4. Arrange the aubergine kebabs around the edges of a microwave roasting rack or a large heatproof plate. Microwave, uncovered, on HIGH for 5½–6 minutes.
5. While the aubergines cook, mix the sauce ingredients in a heatproof serving bowl or sauce boat, reserving a tablespoon of sherry. Remove the kebabs and cover while the sauce is cooked.
6. Microwave the sauce on HIGH, uncovered, for 1 minute or until hot, stirring once. Add the sherry to the sauce and serve poured over. If wished, serve the aubergine on a bed of finely-shredded salad or on plain or scented rice or noodles.

VARIATION

Insert slivers of mild, easily-melted cheese in folds of the aubergine for a more substantial dish.

See photograph page 25

QUAIL'S EGGS AU NID

Le Phare .....

Last March, after a visit to Sidi Bou Said, just outside Tunis, and a sojourn in a famous tea salon there, two friends and I walked to the lighthouse of Le Phare and mounted the spiral stairs to the top, from which we could survey the view and the lantern itself. On my way down I discovered a tiny gull's nest, full of eggs, in one of the arrow-slit windows. This recipe, with the quail egg neatly contained and the somewhat Mediterranean topping, reminds me of that sunny, beautiful place.

Serves 4

4 medium sized Desirée potatoes, scrubbed

30 ml (2 level tbsp) curd cheese

30 ml (2 level tbsp) snipped chives (reserve 5 ml [1 tsp])

15 ml (1 level tbsp) fromage frais or thick yogurt

15 ml (1 tbsp) olive oil

salt and freshly ground black pepper

4 quail's eggs

Topping

15 ml (1 level tbsp) capers

10 ml (2 tsp) caper juice (vinegar)

15 ml (1 tbsp) olive oil

8–12 black olives, stoned

1. Prick each potato several times with a fork. Place on absorbent kitchen paper and microwave on HIGH for 10 minutes, turning each potato over after 5 minutes.
2. Leave the potatoes to stand for 5 minutes then cut off the tops and scoop out the flesh. Mix this with the cheese, chives, fromage frais, oil and the salt and pepper.
3. Pack back into the jacket and place evenly around a plate. Microwave, uncovered, on HIGH for 1½ minutes. Using the back of a round 5 ml (1 tsp) measuring spoon, make an indentation in each. Break into each hollow one quail's egg, yolks pierced carefully. Meanwhile process the capers, juice, oil and olives and spoon some over each egg.
4. Dip the potato lids in the reserved chives and replace on the potatoes. Microwave on HIGH for 1½ minutes then leave to stand for 15–30 seconds. Serve immediately.

SALADE DES COGNOSCENTI

Fontina is a supple Italian cheese of delightful texture: pan-grilled red capsicums are 'meaty' in the extreme: while a dressing of good yogurt and balsamic vinegar (available from informed food suppliers) proves definitely memorable. Combine these elements and you have an extremely pleasing salad for a summer or autumn meal. The final flourish is red basil – an ingredient most likely to be familiar to the cognoscenti, the fortunate or the green-fingered. It was first introduced to me by a Norwegian friend, Bille. My greengrocer began to stock this red-leaved, red-budded version of the herb last summer and I dried some very successfully in the microwave oven. It makes an enchanting finish to this salad.

Serves 4

4 large red capsicums, seeded and cored

350 g (12 oz) fontina cheese, cubed

90 ml (6 tbsp) thick Greek strained yogurt

30 ml (2 tbsp) pure virgin olive oil

30 ml (2 tbsp) aceto balsamico (balsamic vinegar)

salt and freshly ground black pepper

2–3 heads radicchio, separated into leaves

10 ml (2 level tsp) dried red basil (optional)

1. Preheat a large 25 cm (10 inch) browning dish for 8 minutes. Remove stem and seed ends of the red peppers and slit the flesh down one side to allow the peppers to be rolled out flat.
2. Quickly place 2 of the flattened peppers, skin side down, in the browning dish, flattening them with a heatproof plate until they have softened and will stay in position. Remove the plate.
3. Microwave on HIGH, uncovered, for 4 minutes, giving the pan a quarter turn halfway through the cooking time.
4. Remove the 2 red peppers, put into a plastic bag and seal. Leave for a few minutes until the skin feels loose. Meanwhile repeat the entire process from (1) to (4) with the second 2 peppers, using a clean dish. Strip the skin from the peppers and discard.
5. Cut the peppers into long fingers and put them in a bowl with the fontina and yogurt. Make a dressing of the yogurt, oil, balsamic vinegar and seasonings. Add this to the bowl and gently toss until coated.
6. Pile the salad on a serving platter encircled with red radicchio leaves. If red basil is available, scatter it over all. Serve with a really good Chianti, Barolo or Amarone.

Curly, & layered Italian bread........ & wine of course.

— SERVING TIP —

If you know a good Italian foodstore which sells the pretty crusty bread called Mantovano, buy some to enjoy with this dish.

MILLIONAIRE'S MUSHROOM TERRINE

This recipe is not for you unless you really appreciate mushrooms. Passionate fungophiles will find the cost of the ingredients acceptable but otherwise find an epicurean millionaire, if you can!

Serves 6

5 ml (1 tsp) fruity olive oil

6–8 fresh bay leaves

4–6 red feuille de chêne lettuce leaves or red batavia

25 g (1 oz) salted butter

3 garlic cloves, skinned and chopped

900 g (2 lb) fresh chanterelles, halved if large

350 g (12 oz) cream cheese

60 ml (4 level tbsp) fresh chives, snipped

3 eggs, separated

5 ml (1 level tsp) sea salt

freshly ground black pepper

5 ml (1 level tsp) coriander seeds, crushed

flat leaf parsley or chervil pluches

Sauce

150 ml (¼ pint) single, or soured, cream

10 ml (2 tsp) balsamic vinegar

herbs of choice

1. Brush or rub a film of oil over the sides and base of a 900 g (2 lb) rectangular microwave loaf dish. Arrange the bay leaves, parallel, along the base and cover with the red lettuce leaves.
2. Put the butter and one of the garlic cloves into a 3.4 litre (3 quart) heatproof casserole and microwave on HIGH for 45 seconds. Add the chanterelles, toss in the butter, and microwave on HIGH, uncovered, for 5 minutes. Pour the dish contents into a sieve and reserve the liquid. Keep both aside.
3. Put the cream cheese, chives and remaining garlic into a food processor with half of the cooked chanterelles. Process in 4–5 short bursts until roughly chopped, or chop the mushrooms by hand and stir into cream cheese with the garlic.
4. Add the reserved mushroom liquor to the contents of the food processor. Add the egg yolks, seasonings and spice and process in short bursts or mix to an even consistency. Do not over process or over mix.
5. Whisk the egg whites until light and fluffy and soft peaks form. Fold the whites into the cheese/mushroom mixture firmly but gently to blend.
6. Spoon half the mixture over the base of the prepared loaf dish. Cover the top with a layer of the flat leaf parsley or chervil. Layer the remaining chanterelles, pushing them down firmly. Spoon over the remaining mixture.
7. Microwave, uncovered, on HIGH for 10 minutes, giving the dish a quarter turn every 2½ minutes. Leave the terrine to stand, uncovered. Once cool, refrigerate for about 1½–2 hours or until the texture is firm to touch.
8. Press down a little to drain off any juices (keep for a sauce) and briskly invert the terrine onto a flat serving plate. Cut carefully, using a sharp knife, into 6, 8, 10, or 12 slices. Stir the juices into the cream and balsamic vinegar with some extra herbs if wished and serve the slices on a pool of sauce. Serve with really first class lacy French baguette and some classic Burgundy.

CHÈVRE PASTRIES ST RÉMY

These filo pastry triangles have a rather Provençal filling of tomato (small cherry tomatoes are perfect because of their shape and fleshiness), tapenade and goat's cheese, which barely has time to melt during cooking. Serve with cherry tomatoes, wine and small Provençal black olives as a snack or as part of a meal.

Serves 4

4 sheets filo pastry (purchased)

50 g (2 oz) salted butter

50 g (2 oz) fromage de chèvre (such as crottin) cut into 16

30 ml (2 level tbsp) tapenade or olive purée, divided into 16

8 leaves fresh basil, halved

16 cherry tomatoes, cut into halves

freshly ground pepper

1. Cut each filo pastry sheet lengthwise into 4, making 16 strips. Pile these on top of each other and cover with damp cloth or plastic to prevent drying out. Microwave the butter on HIGH, uncovered, for 45 seconds or until melted.

2. Brush some butter over a strip of filo. Put a sixteenth portion of cheese and tapenade, half a basil leaf and 2 halves of a cherry tomato, cut sides down, on the right hand side of the pastry. Make 45°-angle continuous rolls and folds from right to left, tucking in any loose pastry to keep the little triangles neat. Place the prepared triangles in one layer on some baking parchment.

3. When the 16 are completed, brush the surface of a 25 cm (10 inch) browning dish with the melted butter (if necessary use a little extra). Arrange 8 triangles like the spokes of a wheel on the dish. Microwave on HIGH, uncovered, for 4½ minutes. Turn the triangles over and microwave for a further 1½ minutes.

4. Remove the triangles from the browning dish. Wash, dry and re-grease the dish and repeat the cooking process with the remaining 8 triangles.

CONCERTINA TOMATOES

Gazing into charcuterie windows in France, I am pleased by the order and symmetry of ranks of tomatoes, slashed almost to their base and filled with slices of hard boiled egg. Why not adapt this 'slash and insert' scheme to cheese, then melt it with fragrant herbs until the tomato flesh is only just hot. If no marmande (beefsteak) tomatoes are available, use smaller tomatoes and reduce the time accordingly (by about ¼ to ⅓). Do use good mozzarella, the oval-shaped type, moist and soft, having been packed in water.

Serves 4

four 250 g (9 oz) marmande (beefsteak) tomatoes
225 g (8 oz) Italian mozzarella cheese (from water buffalo or cow's milk)
12 leaves fresh basil or 4 large sprigs of marjoram or oregano
freshly ground black pepper
freshly ground sea salt (optional)
15 ml (1 tbsp) fruity olive oil (optional)

1. Remove the stalks from the tomatoes and turn them stalk-side downwards. Make 6 parallel slashes in each tomato, cutting about three-quarters of the way to the base. The tomatoes must keep their perfect shape.

2. Carefully cut the cheese into 24 slivers. Cut the leaves of the basil in two, lengthwise, using kitchen scissors, or pull the marjoram leaves or oregano sprigs into 6 for each tomato.

3. Insert a slice of cheese and some herb into each slash in the tomatoes so that they are filled.

4. Arrange the tomatoes around the edge of a large, flat, heatproof serving plate and microwave on HIGH, uncovered, for 4 minutes, giving the plate a half turn halfway through the cooking time.

5. Serve, seasoned well with black pepper, salt and oil, according to preference.

PURSLANE AND PECORINO QUICHES

These little quiches have a delicious filling of lightly-cooked purslane (also known as portulaca kulfa or pourpier). It may be grown by enterprising gardeners, found growing wild, or can be purchased in Greek, Cypriot or Middle Eastern greengroceries or superior grocery stores.

Makes 8

75–100 g (3–4 oz) chopped purslane
2 garlic cloves, skinned and chopped
5 ml (1 tsp) olive oil
8 cooked Liptauer pastry cases (page 77)
8 quail's eggs
50 g (2 oz) pecorino cheese, thinly sliced
45 ml (3 tbsp) natural yogurt
1.25 ml (¼ tsp) cayenne pepper

1. Put the purslane, garlic and olive oil in a heatproof dish and toss thoroughly. Microwave on HIGH, uncovered, for 2 minutes or until the leaves are hot and slightly wilted.

2. Spoon an ⅛th into each quiche case. Break one quail's egg into each (pierce each yolk in one or two places), crumble some cheese around the edge of each egg and spoon some yogurt on top. Add a sprinkle of cayenne.

3. Cover a large heatproof plate with kitchen paper and position the quiches evenly around the edges. Microwave on HIGH, uncovered, for 2½–3 minutes or until the yolks are barely set but hot. Cover and keep warm.

4. Repeat the process with the 4 remaining quiches.

GRANDMOTHER'S AUTUMN MUSHROOMS

A homely dish gains a new lease of life with a cheesy gremolatina and becomes substantial when served as suggested. Select dark, flat, even-sized mushrooms.

Serves 4

50 g (2 oz) butter cut into 1 cm ($\frac{1}{2}$ inch) cubes

450–550 g (1–1$\frac{1}{4}$ lb), or 8, large flat field mushrooms, stalks removed

300 ml ($\frac{1}{2}$ pint) creamy milk

10 ml (2 level tsp) freshly ground pepper

30 ml (2 tbsp) vegetable stock

10 ml (2 level tsp) fécule (potato flour)

salt to taste

Gremolatina Parmigiano

5 ml (1 tsp) fruity olive oil

1 garlic clove, skinned and finely chopped

30 ml (2 level tbsp) chopped parsley

15 ml (1 level tbsp) freshly grated parmesan

finely shredded zest of one lemon

1. Scatter half of the butter over the base of a large casserole dish or 25 cm (10 inch) browning dish. Place 4 mushrooms, gills downwards, on the butter and microwave on HIGH, uncovered, for 3 minutes.
2. Remove the mushrooms from the pan and set aside. Add the remaining butter and mushrooms (plus stalks, finely chopped) to the pan and repeat the process for a further 3 minutes. Return the first 4 mushrooms to the pan and add the milk and pepper.
3. Microwave on HIGH, uncovered, for 3 minutes, basting the mushrooms with the hot sauce from time to time.
4. Blend vegetable stock into the fécule (potato flour) and stir this into the hot sauce, shaking the pan until evenly distributed. Microwave on HIGH, uncovered, for 3 minutes then add salt to taste. Remove the dish from the oven and cover while the gremolatina is made.
5. Put the olive oil, garlic and half the parsley into a measuring jug and microwave on HIGH, uncovered, for 1 minute. Stir in the remaining parsley, parmesan and lemon zest.
6. Serve the mushrooms and their sauce alone or on halved and toasted wholewheat muffins, baps or rolls, or on rice or noodles. Spoon a quarter of the gremolatina on each serving.

CHESTNUT, CELERIAC AND CARROT TIMBALES

Fruitful autumn reminds us of such treats as creamy purées of root vegetables and fresh chestnuts. This recipe comprises a colourful carrot-coated purée, complete with a plump whole chestnut in the centre. Each serving is considerably more substantial than it appears. All the ingredients seem to keep their qualities better when cooked by microwave and the technique for preparing chestnuts is a real labour-saver!

in the prepared bun dish ↑ the strips of carrot Criss-cross

are hidden inside....

Chestnuts, cooked & shelled easily by microwave treatment

Makes 6

225 g (8 oz) long, straight carrots

450 g (1 lb) celeriac, peeled and cut into 6 or 8

2 garlic cloves, crushed

5 ml (1 level tsp) white pepper

150 ml ($\frac{1}{4}$ pint) vegetable stock

225 g (8 oz) fresh chestnuts in the shell

45 ml (3 tbsp) double cream or thick cream

1 egg (size 2 or 3)

Garnish

salad leaves of choice

chervil, chives or dill (optional)

1. Oil and base-line the sides and base of a 6-division bun dish.
2. Scrub the carrots then use a vegetable peeler to make 175 g (6 oz) of long, straight, flexible strips. Line the sides and base of each bun dish with 4 overlapping slices laid criss-cross, leaving 8 tails overhanging the rim.
3. Use a food processor to grate coarsely the remaining carrots and celeriac. Add the garlic, pepper and vegetable stock, cover and microwave on HIGH for 5 minutes. Leave to stand.
4. To shell the chestnuts, cut a lengthwise slash

in each with a sharp knife. Put them on a plate, rinse with water, shake partially dry and microwave 8 nuts at a time on HIGH for 2 minutes, uncovered. Remove and discard the shells. Repeat this process until all are cooked. Reserve the 6 most perfect and chop the remainder, using the food processor. Add the chestnuts to the cooked vegetables with the cream and egg and continue to food process until smooth.

5. Quarter fill each oiled and carrot-lined bun division with some mixture. Push one prepared whole chestnut into each. Spoon the remaining mixture over and around the chestnut. Fold over the carrot tail ends to enclose each timbale neatly. Microwave, uncovered, on HIGH for 3 minutes, giving the dish a half turn during cooking.

6. Cover the timbales and leave to stand for 2–3 minutes. Invert, with one brisk movement, onto a serving plate. Surround with crisp salad leaves and scatter chervil, chives or dill over all. Serve hot, warm or cold, one for each person or three halves to each of four diners.

EDWARD LEAR'S ONION TART

One of Edward Lear's 'Bosh and Nonsense' limericks celebrates an old fellow who, though rather short of a penny 'laid out that money in onions and honey'. This idea rather intrigued me, so I devised a recipe to embody it. Lear would have found the microwave oven a curiosity, I'm sure, and might have greeted it thus (with apologies):

A fellow whose cooking was sloven
Bought himself a new microwave oven
Now he cooks in a trice all the foods that are nice
Time and effort are things he can govern.

In this version of a pissaladière, the onion, garlic, honey and coriander give a special aromatic savour. The tart tastes delicious if some crème fraîche or fromage blanc is served on the same plate. The combination of hot and cold, mild and mellow is fascinating.

Serves 4–6

225 g (8 oz) granary flour
5 ml (1 level tsp) micronized dried yeast (Easy-blend or Easy-bake)
1.25 ml (¼ tsp) salt
150 ml (¼ pint) lukewarm water
700 g (1½ lb) onions, red and white (if wished)
15 ml (1 tbsp) olive oil
45 ml (3 level tbsp) honey
5 ml (1 level tsp) coriander seeds, crushed

1. Mix the flour, yeast and salt together well. Add the lukewarm water and mix to a soft dough. Knead for 5 minutes until satiny and elastic.

2. Leave to stand, covered, in a non-metal bowl over warm water while the filling is prepared.

3. Skin and slice the onions into thick rings. Put most of the oil into a large 25 cm (10 inch) browning dish with the onion rings and trickle the honey all over.

4. Microwave on HIGH for 20 minutes, part covered with some kitchen paper, then remove the paper, stir and microwave on HIGH for a further 5 minutes. The onions should become golden, glazed and the liquid should be a thick syrup.

5. While the onions cook, punch down the dough and leave to rise again. Once the onions have cooked, remove them, clean the pan and brush it with the remaining oil.

6. Roll out the dough to a circle just under 25 cm (10 inch) in diameter. Slide this into the pan, then fold over and punch down an even ridge all round the edge. Microwave on MEDIUM (50%), uncovered, for 2 minutes and then on HIGH for 1 minute. Invert the dough so that the ridge is underneath.

7. Spoon the onions and syrup evenly over the dough. Crush the coriander seeds (using a pestle and mortar or an electric coffee grinder) and sprinkle them over the onions. Microwave on HIGH, uncovered, for 3–4 minutes or until the onions and dough are hot and cooked through.

SERVING TIP

Serve in wedges with fromage blanc battu or crème fraîche, flat leaf parsley or coriander sprigs, and maybe with a red-leafed salad, together with a glass of cool Vouvray or a robust Mercurey.

TUILES OF POTATOES AND ONIONS

Instead of the usual arrangement of horizontal layers of potato and onion, make this variegated gratin-type dish with the vegetables stacked at a 45° angle to the dish, rather like the tiles (tuiles) on a Mediterranean roof. Use good ingredients: Spanish, Italian or French cheese, red potatoes (such as Craig Royal Red, Kerr's Red or Desirée) and beautiful vivid red onions for perfect results. Serve with an accompanying leafy salad.

potato & onion look like tiles on a roof... to continue......

Serves 4–6

550 g (1¼ lb) red onions, skinned
60 ml (4 tbsp) walnut oil
30 ml (2 level tbsp) fresh lemon thyme or thyme, chopped
700 g (1½ lb) red potatoes (even-sized)
2.5 ml (½ level tsp) salt
freshly ground white pepper
25 g (1 oz) salted butter, shaved with potato peeler
25 g (1 oz) cabrales, grana caciocavallo or cantal cheese
25 g (1 oz) walnuts, chopped coarsely
fresh thyme sprigs

1. Slice the onions into .5 cm (¼ inch) slices. Put into a large heatproof 3.4 litre (3 quart) casserole with the walnut oil and thyme. Stir to coat and microwave, covered, on HIGH for 4 minutes or until the onions have softened but still retain their shape.

2. Slice the unpeeled potatoes into .5 cm (¼ inch) thick slices and stack them, at 45° angles, in a medium to large sized oval gratin dish. Layer them alternately with a row of the onions. Continue until all are used. Trickle over the oil and thyme from the pan (using a pastry brush to coat the exposed surface of the potatoes).

3. Cover with cling film and microwave on HIGH for 16 minutes, or until potatoes are tender.

4. Uncover, season well, sprinkle with butter shavings, cheese and walnuts. Microwave, uncovered, for a further minute on HIGH, or until the cheese melts. Garnish with thyme sprigs.

POPPYSEED PASTRY

Here is a tasty pie shell that may be made and cooked in under 15 minutes. Blue (actually black) poppyseeds give a curious but fascinating appearance to all recipes in which they play a part, and impart a desirable nutty flavour. Best results come from prior toasting, easily achieved by microwave, and although this pastry contains a little brown sugar it is largely for colour and texture and does not affect the taste. The pie shell can therefore be used for a huge range of savoury or sweet pie fillings. If possible, reheat the filled pie shells on MEDIUM (60%) power to avoid drying the pastry too much.

Makes a 19 cm (7½ inch) diameter shell

50 g (2 oz) blue poppyseeds
15 ml (1 level tbsp) soft dark brown sugar
30 ml (2 tbsp) cold milk
125 g (4 oz) plain flour
2.5 ml (½ level tsp) salt
65 g (2½ oz) cold butter, cubed

1. Toast the poppyseeds by putting them onto a heatproof plate and microwave, uncovered, on HIGH for 6 minutes, stirring every 2 minutes from edges to centre. Leave to cool.

2. While the poppyseeds toast, dissolve the sugar in the milk. Add the poppyseeds to the flour and salt in a food processor. Add the cold butter and process in 2 short bursts to blend in the butter.

3. With the processor running, quickly pour in the milk mixture and blend for the shortest possible time to achieve a dough. Push the dough together into a ball and roll out on a floured surface to a 25 cm (10 inch) circle. Use to line a 19 cm (7½ inch) inner diameter pie dish, folding under a pastry rim on the lip. Crimp the edges well and prick the pastry all over using a fork.

4. Place a circle of kitchen paper on the base of the pastry and microwave on HIGH, uncovered, for 5 minutes, giving the dish a half turn halfway through cooking time. Remove the kitchen paper. Leave to cool.

─── SERVING TIP ───

This pastry is excellent when filled with leeks in a creamy cheesy sauce (page 57). Similarly, it could easily be filled with hot, freshly cooked vegetables or fruit 'au naturel' sliced into soured cream, fromage blanc or yogurt and egg sauce, perhaps with added cheese for savoury fillings and with spiced, nutty, or sugared nut topping for sweet fillings.

See photograph page 101

LIPTAUER PASTRY CASES

Liptauer is a flavoured cheese which may be found in American-style delicatessens, but is easily homemade. It replaces butter in this pastry (which also contains sesame seeds) to give body, flavour and crispness. The colour of the pastry shells is a curious speckled salmon pink, not at all unpleasing, while the herbs and spices give a surprisingly lively effect, suitable even with a sweet filling. Use this amount of pastry to make eight of the Purslane and Pecorino Quiches (page 73) and sixteen of the small sweet Illusionist's Chocolate Pies (page 117). If not required immediately, roll out the pastry and freeze it, layered with waxed paper or plastic, to use at another time. Alternatively cook, cool, wrap and label the pastries and freeze for future use.

Makes 8 large and 16 small cases

125 g (4 oz) cream cheese
1.25 ml (¼ tsp) salt
2.5 ml (½ level tsp) caraway seeds
5 ml (1 level tsp) tomato purée
1.25 ml (¼ tsp) cayenne pepper or hot paprika
5 ml (1 level tsp) snipped fresh chives
2.5 ml (½ level tsp) mustard seed
225 g (8 oz) plain unbleached flour
50 g (2 oz) sesame seeds
60–70 ml (4–5 tbsp) cold water

1. Mix the first 7 ingredients together to a creamy consistency to make the Liptauer cheese mixture.

2. Add the flour and sesame seeds and cut or rub the 2 together to achieve a crumbly mixture.

3. Add water, gradually mixing with a knife to form a stiff pastry. Wrap and chill for 2 minutes in the freezer. Roll out on a seed-covered or floured surface.

4. To make the larger pastry shells (for the quiches) roll out the pastry until it is 25 cm (10 inches) × 20 cm (8 inches) or large enough to cut out 8 circles × 8 cm (3¼ inch) using a plain cutter.

5. Invert 4 ramekins or small heatproof pots, about 6 cm (2½ inches) in diameter. Brush with oil. Mould the pastry circles over the top so that they form shallow 'cups'. Prick well with a fork. Arrange 4 ramekins around the edges of a heatproof plate and microwave on HIGH, uncovered, for 3–3½ minutes, giving the plate a quarter turn every minute.

6. Remove the cooked pastries and invert them onto a sheet of kitchen paper. Cook the remaining cases in batches of 4 and use them with a filling of your choice.

DRESSED VEGETABLES AU NATUREL

ASPARAGUS PENCILS

These inventions provide a feast for the eye as well as the palate. It occurred to me once that there might be a compromise between whittling away the bases of asparagus (and, alas, wasting them) and cross-cutting the bases (not always effective) to ensure absolute tenderness and efficient cooking. In my technique the bases are sharpened to a point. The 'sharpenings' should be kept, cooked, and added to green mayonnaise, thus securing two pleasures for the price of one! The pencils of asparagus are cooked 'au naturel', using only the water that still clings to them after washing, in one layer on a large flat plate.

Serves 2–4

350 g (12 oz) whole, fresh medium-sized, green asparagus spears

25 g (1 oz) salted butter

freshly ground pepper

1. Holding each asparagus spear as if it were a pencil, sharpen the base with a knife to a 5-cm (2-inch) tapering point. Reserve the sharpenings for another use. Wash the asparagus well and do not dry. Arrange the stalks, parallel and alternating a point with a base, on a heatproof plate.
2. Cover with cling film and microwave on HIGH for 3–4 minutes. Test for tenderness with your fingertips and if very tender asparagus is preferred, microwave for another 1–1½ minutes.
3. Uncover the dish, dot with butter and microwave again on HIGH for 40 seconds. Season and serve each guest a little cluster of pencils in their sauce.

See photograph page 68

GOLDEN COURGETTES WITH POPPYSEED SEASONING

Tender courgettes of the usual (or the rounded patty-pan) shape, cooked 'au naturel', develop a delicate, almost oyster-like, flavour. The topping adds style to a delicious and nutritious dish. Green courgettes can equally well be used, although their texture is a little firmer.

Serves 4

450 g (1 lb) golden courgettes or patty-pan squashes

5 ml (1 level tsp) snipped chives or onion tops

5 ml (1 level tsp) poppyseeds

1.25 ml (¼ tsp) fine sea salt

1.25 ml (¼ tsp) lemon pepper

1. Slice off and discard both ends of each courgette. Pierce each, using a fork, all over in 5 or 6 places.
2. Arrange on kitchen paper on a heatproof plate so that the courgettes are evenly distributed around the edges. Microwave, uncovered, on HIGH for 3 minutes.
3. Turn the courgettes over and microwave on HIGH for a further 3 minutes. Tent the courgettes in foil and leave to stand for 1 to 4 minutes then slice lengthwise, crosswise or halve and slash into fan shape.
4. Make a seasoning of equal quantities of snipped chives (or onion tops) and blue poppyseeds. Add salt and pepper. Sprinkle on the vegetables or pass separately to guests.

See photograph page 45

BABY BEETS WITH ORANGE DRESSING

Some beets are more like fruits than vegetables. It is fresh, evenly-sized baby beets that are required for this recipe and though the stalk ends should be removed (keep them as a salad garnish) the root tails should be left intact. The beets cook 'au naturel' in record time. If larger in size than specified, extend the cooking time by 3–6 minutes, turning the beets over halfway through, as well as rotating the plate. Readiness is indicated by ease of skin removal.

Serves 2 or 4

350 g (12 oz) baby beets (about 8–10), stems only removed

2 oranges, zest finely grated or shredded

30 ml (2 tbsp) hazelnut, walnut or other delicate oil

2–3 shakes tabasco sauce

salt and freshly ground pepper

Garnish

sliced, shredded beet stems and/or leaves (optional) or oak leaf lettuce (feuille de chêne)

1. Wash the beets, remove stem and leaves (keep these aside if in good condition to use as a garnish). Pierce beets in 3 or 4 places with a fork.
2. Place, evenly spaced, around the circumference of a heatproof plate or ring dish, cover with cling film and microwave on HIGH for 5–6 minutes, repositioning the dish once during cooking time and testing for tenderness by feel. Leave the beets to stand while the dressing is prepared.
3. To make the dressing, slice off and discard the orange pith and slice the orange flesh into segments. Halve these crosswise. Squeeze any remaining juice from the membranes over the orange segments, add the oil and tabasco and season to taste.
4. Remove the beets from the dish and, using kitchen paper, quickly enclose each one. Squeeze firmly until the skins have slid off, leaving a clean surface. If this proves difficult, use the blunt side of a knife blade to scrape the skins off. Halve or quarter the beets and toss with the dressing until evenly coloured. Serve while hot or serve warm or cold on a bed of the shredded leaves or some oak leaf lettuce. This serves 2 as a separate course or 4 as an accompanying vegetable.

RED ONION LOTUS FLOWERS WITH PISTACHIO BUTTER

This recipe pleases my artist's eye, for the mild-tasting, ruby-skinned onions with their red striped inner layers are magnificent. Cooked in this way, skin and all, they can be opened out at serving time into the most exquisite lotus flower shapes with rosy 'petals'. Encourage diners to pull off one quarter at a time and, holding the skin in the fingers, eat the butter-dressed onion flesh in one mouthful. Presented this way, onions become an elegant starter or separate vegetable course.

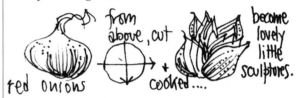

red onions — from above, cut — + cooked.... — become lovely little sculptures.

Serves 4

550 g (1¼ lb), or 4, red onions, evenly-sized

25 g (1 oz) shelled pistachio nuts

15 ml (1 level tbsp) soft butter

2 pinches cayenne pepper

2 pinches sea salt

30 ml (2 level tbsp) chopped fresh parsley or chives

1. Remove the root end from the four onions so that they will stand on their bases easily, but do not remove any skin. Cut through the top of the onions twice at right angles to make a cross cut, but reach no further than halfway down.
2. Position evenly in a ring dish and microwave on HIGH, uncovered, for 6 minutes. Cover and leave to stand while the pistachio butter is prepared.
3. Put the pistachios on a flat heatproof plate with a quarter of the butter, the cayenne and the sea salt. Microwave on HIGH, uncovered, for 2 minutes, stirring the nuts and shaking the dish occasionally.
4. Chop the nuts coarsely or process using a food processor. Stir in the remaining butter and the herbs to make a thick paste.
5. Pull one or two of the outer 'petals' of the onions open to reveal the lotus-like pattern inside and cut down a little deeper to allow inner 'petals' to open out.
6. Divide the pistachio butter between the four onions and serve immediately while they are still steaming.

MANGE-TOUT WITH GARLIC-IN-DISGUISE DRESSING

Mange-tout peas (as opposed to beans of the same description) are one of life's little luxuries as far as I am concerned. Their prettiness, tender-sweet taste and general usefulness in every culinary situation constantly inspire me to find new ways of serving them. This method is child's play and curiously delicious in an unexpected way. The sauce is scented by garlic which, itself cooked 'au naturel', goes almost toffee-like on second cooking and adds interest to the dressing.

Serves 4

---

6 fat garlic cloves, pierced with a fork

---

175 g (6 oz) mange-tout peas, washed

---

60 ml (4 tbsp) natural yogurt, buttermilk or clotted cream

---

5 ml (1 level tsp) tomato concentrate

---

salt and freshly ground pepper

---

1. Put the garlic in a small ramekin or heatproof dish and microwave on HIGH, uncovered, for 3 minutes. 'Pop' the flesh out of the skins and chop coarsely. Keep aside.
2. Arrange the mange-tout peas, water still clinging to them, evenly around a ring dish or large round heatproof dish. Cover with cling film and microwave on HIGH for 2 minutes, shaking the dish to rearrange the peas halfway through. Allow to stand.
3. Cover the dish of chopped garlic with cling film and microwave on HIGH for 1½ minutes, or until hot and sizzling. Stir in the yogurt, buttermilk or clotted cream, the tomato concentrate and the seasonings.
4. Serve each guest with some peas (10–12 each) and a spoonful or tiny pot of the sauce. The peas should be curved into a loop, held at the stem end and dipped into the dressing. They can be eaten in one bite, discarding the stem.

BROCCOLI WITH BLUE CHEESE DRESSING

Broccoli looks ravishing when cooked by this method. There is no water to drain off, the vegetable cooks in the steam generated by the water that clings after washing, and its taste is absolutely perfect, as is the texture: even the stems become delicious! The creamy cheese dressing is a classic accompaniment made while the broccoli is standing.

a choice of particular, or good, known red wine.....

some lovely cheese of classic quality....

and pretty little branches of broccoli, looking like miniature trees, in the countryside & a touch of cream.... what simplicity it has been!

Serves 4

---

450 g (1 lb), or 6 heads, tender, young broccoli spears

Sauce

---

50 g (2 oz) blue cheese (such as Stilton, Blue Vinney, Roquefort or Gorgonzola), crumbled or cubed

---

45 ml (3 level tbsp) red wine

---

60 ml (4 tbsp) cream, soured cream or mayonnaise

---

salt and freshly ground black pepper

---

1. Wash the broccoli well and slice off the long stalks to make the heads approximately the same size. Slice the stem pieces lengthwise into halves, or, if very thick, into quarters.
2. Arrange on a heatproof plate or ring dish with the 'flowering' heads facing towards the centre. Scatter the cut stem sections evenly around the circumference of the dish.

3. Cover with cling film and microwave on HIGH for 2½ minutes. Remove the cling film, turn the heads over, re-cover and microwave on HIGH for a further 2 minutes. Leave to stand for another 2–3 minutes while the dressing is made.
4. To make the dressing, soften the crumbled or cubed cheese with the red wine in a heatproof measuring jug or cup. Microwave on LOW (30%) for 3–4 minutes. Stir with a fork to a smooth consistency and blend in the cream, soured cream or mayonnaise. Taste, adjust the seasonings and pour over the broccoli or serve accompanying it.

See photograph page 46–47

TURNIP NECKLETS WITH BOURSIN

Prepared then cooked by the following technique, perfect little baby turnips remain sweet and decorative. Dill adds a grass-green freshness to this enchanting summer offering.

Serves 4

700–800 g (1½–1¾ lb), or 2 bunches, baby turnips (with green tops)

78 g (2¾ oz) pack Boursin or other full fat soft cheese with garlic and herbs

15 ml (1 level tbsp) fresh dill

1. If the green tops are in good condition, keep the large leaves for a salad. Retain the short stems and little leaves. Wash the turnips well, leaving the water that clings.
2. Using an apple corer, remove a central cylinder (including the stems and roots) from the larger turnips but leave the tiny, marble-sized turnips whole.
3. Put the turnips in a heatproof ring dish and cover with cling film. Microwave for 4–5 minutes, depending on size, or until the turnips are very hot, giving the dish a half turn halfway through cooking time. (The colour should remain unchanged.)
4. Meanwhile put the Boursin, broken up, and the dill, roughly torn, into a food processor or blender with the removed cylinders of turnip. Process briefly until a rough purée has formed.
5. Pile the turnips onto a serving dish and drop a spoonful of the green stuffing into each.

SWEET POTATOES WITH HERBED SUGAR SEASONING

This recipe uses the small, even-sized, red-skinned sweet potato with orange-yellow flesh. If foil-wrapped these could stay hot for 5–6 minutes easily, which is convenient when planning a whole microwave-cooked meal.

Serves 4

700 g (1½ lb), or 5–6, even-sized, red-skinned sweet potatoes

Seasoning

30 ml (2 level tbsp) muscovado sugar

1 pinch mixed spice (optional)

30 ml (2 level tbsp) fresh mint leaves, chopped

whole mint leaves to garnish

1. Scrub, and remove any pointed tails from the sweet potatoes. Pierce all over, using a fork, in 5 or 6 places.
2. Evenly space around the edge of a circular heatproof plate and microwave on HIGH, uncovered, for 3 minutes.
3. Turn the sweet potatoes over and microwave on HIGH for a further 3 minutes, uncovered. Check for tenderness (different varieties can take longer to cook).
4. Remove, cover with foil, and allow to stand for 1 minute. Slice into coin-sized slices, about 1 cm (½ inch) thick. Reassemble on a serving plate and sprinkle with the freshly mixed sugar, spice and mint leaves and serve hot.

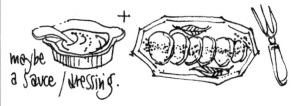

maybe a sauce / dressing.

COOK'S TIP
Some people find that the nutty firm texture goes well with a sauce or dressing such as natural yogurt, mayonnaise, soured cream or a vinaigrette of some kind. Serve this separately for diners to help themselves.
Do not make the seasoning ahead of time: on standing it forms a thick tar-like paste which is difficult to use, although the flavour is not impaired.

BLACK PEPPERS AND PEPPER PURÉE

Black peppers may, during cooking 'au naturel', turn from black to a bright green and/or reddish-orange striped coloration, fascinating to observe. They also remain pleasantly sweet. Dressed with a herbed and fruity vinaigrette they are delicious and simple, but if processed with tahini and vinegar they become a rich sustaining purée, good for use in a multitude of ways.

Makes 2–4

350 g (12 oz) or 2 large black peppers

Dressing

2.5 ml (½ level tsp) coriander seeds, roughly crushed

30–45 ml (2–3 tbsp) vinaigrette of choice

Variation for pepper purée

15 ml (1 level tbsp) tahini paste

30 ml (2 tbsp) white wine vinegar

30 ml (2 level tbsp) chopped fresh herbs

lettuce or chicory leaves

1. Make several large slits around the stem ends of the peppers to allow the steam to escape as they cook.
2. Place the peppers on their sides on kitchen paper and microwave on HIGH, uncovered, for 6 minutes, turning them over halfway through cooking time.
3. Pull out the stem ends and shake out the seeds and central pith, then cut into cubes or strips.
4. Sprinkle with coriander and dress in vinaigrette.
5. For the pepper purée variation, put the cooked peppers, tahini, vinegar and herbs in a food processor. Process roughly then serve in lettuce or chicory leaves with fresh sprinkled herbs. Serve with ficelle, baguette and crusty rolls.

in some pretty, crisp leaves.

PARSNIPS WITH SAUCE ESCOFFIER

Microwave cookery succeeds almost too well sometimes. The humble parsnip cooked by this 'conservative' method is creamy textured and of a sweetness and smoothness almost foreign to the palate. It requires a rough textured, lively sauce or dressing, but then becomes truly unusual whether served as a vegetable accompaniment or as a salad. Make sure that the tail ends are removed and that the parsnips are evenly spaced, then turned, for good results.

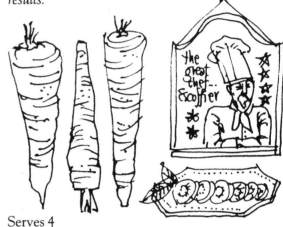

Serves 4

550 g (1¼ lb), or 4, even-sized parsnips, long tails trimmed

Sauce

150 ml (¼ pint) whipping cream

25 g (1 oz) walnuts, coarsely chopped

5–10 ml (1–2 tsp) grated horseradish or horseradish cream

salt and freshly ground black pepper

chopped fresh parsley

1. Clean the parsnips well, leaving the washing water on the skin. Pierce with a fork in 5 or 6 places each side. Arrange around the circumference of a ring or circular dish with the large ends overlapping the slimmer tail ends.
2. Microwave on HIGH, uncovered, for 6 minutes, turning the parsnips over (but leaving them in the same formation) halfway through the cooking time.
3. Remove, leave to stand for 1–2 minutes, then remove and discard stalk ends and very slim tail ends (which may have been overcooked). Slice the parsnips into slim slices and arrange them on a serving dish. Season well.
4. To make the sauce, whip the cream until soft

peaks form, fold in the walnuts, horseradish, seasonings to taste and the parsley. Spoon the sauce over the parsnips and serve hot or warm.

——— **COOK'S TIP** ———

If the parsnips are very big (say 225 g/8 oz) then halve them lengthwise and proceed in the same way. For variation, dress the sliced, cooked parsnip with a generous vinaigrette of balsamic or fruit vinegar, fruity olive oil, chopped nuts and parsley.

BABY PUMPKIN

Many pumpkin and squash varieties are available from late summer well into winter. This recipe uses the still-tender orange-skinned variety which later in the year grow larger and tougher. Pumpkin is fruity and sweet and this recipe makes the best of these features.

Serves 4

---

700 g (1¹/₂ lb) orange-skinned baby pumpkin, green tipped

1 small garlic clove, chopped

2.5 ml (¹/₂ level tsp) salt

2.5 ml (¹/₂ level tsp) freshly ground white pepper

Garnish

coriander or flat leaf parsley

1. Halve the pumpkin crosswise. Remove the stem end and any other pointed section from the opposite end so that each half will stand up easily.
2. Microwave on HIGH, uncovered, for 3 minutes on a heatproof plate. Invert the pumpkin halves so that the cut sides are downwards and microwave on HIGH for a further 3 minutes, then test for readiness. If the flesh resists the pressure of a spoon, microwave for 1 to 2 minutes more, until tender.
3. Leave to stand for 2 minutes.
4. Scoop out the seeds and pith at the centre of the pumpkin (keep aside if wished for other uses). Using a spoon or small ice cream scoop,

remove the flesh in neat scoops and pile on a serving plate.
5. Chop the remaining skin and attached flesh into cubes and put into a food processor with the garlic, salt and pepper and process in short bursts to a rough purée. Spoon the purée into the centre of the scoops and garnish with coriander or flat leaf parsley. Serve warm or hot (reheat briefly for 1¹/₂–2 minutes, cling film covered).
6. Alternatively, cube all the flesh and the skin and reduce to a purée. Serve garnished with flat leaf parsley or coriander sprigs.

THAI WHITE AUBERGINE EGGS

These fascinating small, white, round aubergines make delicious bite-sized hot appetizers, especially with a 'do-it-yourself' accompaniment of seasoned salt and fragrant oil. Show your guests how to help themselves, holding onto the stems. It is well worthwhile looking for an oriental supermarket, particularly a Thai supermarket, where these and other exotica are frequently inexpensive and readily available.

Serves 6

---

350 g (12 oz), or 6, small, fresh Thai aubergines on the stem

To serve

sesame oil

herb and nut seasoning (page 36)

1. Pierce the aubergines in 3–4 places. Position around the edge of a large heatproof plate, about 25 cm (10 inches) in diameter.
2. Microwave, uncovered, on HIGH for 4 minutes.
3. Allow to stand for 2–3 minutes. Cross-cut each aubergine almost through to the stem end so that 4 'petals' are formed.
4. Arrange 4 on each serving plate with a small dish of seasoning and a small dish of sesame oil.
5. Encourage diners to dip the 'petals' of the whole aubergines first into the oil, if used, then into the seasoning, holding the aubergines by the stems. Then bite off each 'petal' one by one.

See photograph page 45

GRAINS, LEGUMES AND HOMEMADE PASTA

CARROTS IN TOFFEE UPON WILD RICE

Here is a recipe which capitalises upon both the tender prettiness of young, new season carrots and the sweet nuttiness of wild rice. Caramel is ideal to unite the two. Spoil yourself one day next spring!

Serves 4

100 g (4 oz) wild rice
2 garlic cloves, skinned and chopped
15 ml (1 tbsp) walnut or hazelnut oil
2.5 ml (½ level tsp) salt
30 ml (2 level tbsp) chopped fresh dill and lovage, mixed
225 g (8 oz) bunch of baby carrots with green tops attached
15 ml (1 level tbsp) butter
50 g (2 oz) caster sugar
30 ml (2 tbsp) mineral water
pinch tartaric acid

1. Pour plenty of boiling water over the rice and leave for about 1 hour. Drain through a sieve, discarding the water.
2. Put the rice, garlic, oil, salt and another 600 ml (1 pint) of boiling water into a medium deep, heatproof bowl or dish. Cover with cling film or a lid and microwave on HIGH for 30 minutes or until the rice is tender. Add the herbs. Allow the rice and herbs to stand for several minutes while the carrots are cooked.
3. Gently scrub the carrots and prick each one several times with a fork. Set out on a heatproof plate, arranged like the spokes of a wheel, thick ends outwards. Cover with cling film and microwave on HIGH for 2–2½ minutes. Set aside and add the butter.
4. Make the toffee by putting the sugar, mineral water and tartaric acid into a browning dish and microwave, uncovered, on HIGH for 2 minutes, stirring at intervals until dissolved.
5. Microwave, uncovered, on HIGH for a further 2½–3 minutes, without stirring, until the caramel colour deepens. Arrange the carrots in a fan design over the wild rice and trickle a lacework of toffee over them.

See photograph page 28

BRIANZA ALCHEMIST'S RISOTTO

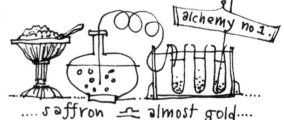

.... saffron ⇌ almost gold ....

Some marriages of ingredients are made on earth but ordained in heaven. Creamy, moist, plump rice grains scented and coloured by saffron is one such example. The fact that an illustrious painter from Brianza first added harmless golden colour to the food at a 14th-century wedding (as a cheaper alternative to gilding it) is a pleasing enough act of fate. But equally so is the delicacy of a dish when all the elements are in harmony, especially when – as here – an effortless and ambrosian dish can be ready in less than 15 minutes. Use only good quality rice from Italy and good quality powdered saffron from a reputable Italian producer (it is the powdered type that particularly enlivens this recipe). Using a ring dish makes the cooking even, the stirring easy and the risk of sticking nil. Serve this lustrous food as a course on its own; it deserves some historical respect.

Serves 4

600 ml (1 pint) hot vegetable stock
50 g (2 oz) salted butter
225 g (8 oz) oval grain, semi-fino Italian risotto rice or arborio
2 small slim leeks, finely shredded
two 1.9 grain (small) sachets good quality powdered saffron
150 ml (¼ pint) frascati, soave or verdicchio wine
50–100 g (2–4 oz) freshly grated parmesan cheese

1. If the stock is cold, put it into a heatproof bowl or jug, cover with cling film and microwave on HIGH until it is boiling, about 4–5 minutes. Keep it covered so it is always warm when being added to the risotto.
2. Put the butter into a large heatproof ring dish and microwave on HIGH for 30 seconds or until melted and hot. Add the dry rice and half of the leek and stir well to coat the rice. Microwave, uncovered, on HIGH for 2 minutes, turning the dish and stirring at least once. Add the saffron and stir again.
3. Pour in 150 ml (¼ pint) of the hot stock and microwave on HIGH, uncovered, for 2 minutes, without stirring, or until the liquid is absorbed.
4. Pour in another 150 ml (¼ pint) of the hot stock and microwave on HIGH, uncovered, for 2 minutes or until the liquid is absorbed. Stir once towards the end of cooking.
5. Repeat step 4 with another 150 ml (¼ pint) of the hot stock. The risotto will have begun to swell and will look moist but will still absorb most of the liquid.
6. Pour in the last measure of the stock to the rice and stir well. Microwave on HIGH, uncovered, for 4 minutes but after 2 minutes put the wine into a heatproof glass jug, cover with cling film and put it into the microwave oven to heat. Give the rice another stir towards the end of cooking time. Add the wine, stir in the remainder of the leeks and microwave on HIGH, uncovered, for a final 2 minutes.
7. Add the freshly grated parmesan, gently stirring it through the moist but creamy golden rice. Cover the dish with a lid or foil and leave to stand for 30 seconds. Accompany the risotto with the same delicious chilled white wine as used in the recipe, and be grateful for small mercies!

See photograph page 66

SEED SPICED BROWN RICE RISOTTO

Toasting spices and seeds to obtain the maximum aroma and colour is always interesting to watch, and in a microwave it is fun and absolutely foolproof. In this recipe, pre-soaking of the rice before cooking means that the microwave oven is free for other uses and only required for a short period at the last minute. Good quality vegetable stock cubes work perfectly well in this recipe.

Serves 4

1.1 litres (2 pints) boiling water
350 g (12 oz) long grain brown rice
20 ml (4 tsp) green cardamom pods
10 ml (2 level tsp) English mustard seeds
10 ml (2 level tsp) alfalfa seeds
10 ml (2 level tsp) coriander seeds
45 ml (3 level tbsp) sunflower seeds
30 ml (2 tbsp) safflower or grapeseed oil
1 dried red chilli, crushed
4–5 fresh bay leaves (or 3 dried), crushed
7.5 cm (3 inch) cinnamon stick, crushed
750 ml (1¼ pints) vegetable stock, boiling

1. Pour the boiling water over the rice, stir several times and leave to stand for 45 minutes. Drain through a sieve until no excess moisture remains, about 15 minutes.
2. Crush the cardamom pods and remove the sticky black seeds. Discard the pods.
3. Preheat a large 25 cm (10 inch) browning dish for 6 minutes. Add the cardamom, mustard, alfalfa, coriander and sunflower seeds. Microwave, uncovered, on HIGH to allow seeds and spice to roast. They tend to pop during this process and darken in colour.
4. Quickly add the oil and the rice, stir well to coat and microwave on HIGH, uncovered, for 1 minute, stirring twice.
5. Pour over the hot stock, add the chilli, bay and cinnamon, cover with a lid and microwave on HIGH for 12 minutes. Leave to stand for 3–4 minutes.
6. Stir well (all the moisture should be absorbed) and serve, perhaps with a handful of fresh herbs of your choice.

CITRUS AND NUT MUESLI WITH SUNFLOWER SEEDS

This versatile concoction can be made once a week for family use. Try it with natural yogurt, fromage blanc, quark, or crème fraîche as a snack, 'energiser' or dessert at any time of the day. Vanilla ice-cream also makes a good companion, but low-fat milk is, of course, what many people will prefer at breakfast time.

Makes about 1.6 kg (3½ lb)

50 g (2 oz) hazelnuts, shelled
75 g (3 oz) sunflower seeds
75 g (3 oz) shelled, roasted and salted almonds
75 g (3 oz) soft dark brown sugar
30 ml (2 level tbsp) malt extract
30 ml (2 tbsp) hazelnut oil
60 ml (4 tbsp) Mexican honey
60 ml (4 tbsp) freshly squeezed orange juice
15 ml (1 level tbsp) shredded orange zest
30 ml (2 tbsp) freshly squeezed lemon juice
5 ml (1 level tsp) shredded lemon zest
500 g (1 lb) 'organic' oats
25 g (1 oz) wheatgerm
75 g (3 oz) oat bran
125 g (4 oz) dried apples
225 g (8 oz) unsulphured dried apricots

1. Put the hazelnuts and sunflower seeds on a large, flat heatproof dish and microwave on HIGH, uncovered, for 5 minutes, stirring from side to centre at regular intervals. Add the almonds.
2. In a large 3.4 litre (3 quart) casserole, put the sugar, malt extract, oil, honey, juices and zests. Stir to mix. Microwave, uncovered, on HIGH for 8 minutes or until thick and bubbling.
3. Add the oats, wheatgerm and bran and stir thoroughly until all the mixture is evenly coated.
4. Spread half the mixture evenly over a sheet of baking parchment 35 cm × 30 cm (14 inches × 12 inches). Slide this onto a non-metal baking tray. Microwave, uncovered, for 4 minutes or until dry and crisp, stirring once. Leave to stand.
5. Repeat the process with the second half of the coated oats, on another piece of similar sized baking parchment. Leave to stand.
6. When both have cooled, crumble them into medium sized pieces. Chop the dried apple into 1 cm (½ inch) strips, using scissors. Mix this and the dried apricots into the muesli with the nuts (broken or chopped). Store in an airtight jar out of direct sunlight.

VOLUPTUARY'S PORRIDGE

My mother believed in decent breakfasts, and still does. We always ate porridge during the winter (followed by a second course) and I feel that it is a sorely neglected treat. This recipe is effortless, lump-free and, with Laphroaig, utterly delicious. It is also very good for the health and morale! The oatmeal I use is not 'rolled oats' type cereal, but the minimally processed kind from wholefood stores.

Serves 4

25 g (1 oz) flaked almonds
50 g (2 oz) medium oatmeal (traditional Scottish type)
15 g (½ oz) wheatgerm
2.5 ml (½ level tsp) salt
600 ml (1 pint) boiling water

To serve

30 ml (2 tbsp) Laphroaig malt whisky
4 fresh figs, quartered (optional garnish)
molasses sugar (to taste)
icy-cold fresh cream (to taste)

1. Mix together flaked almonds, oatmeal, wheatgerm and salt and add in a steady stream to the boiling water in a 3.4 litre (3 quart) casserole. Stir briskly with a fork until smooth, then microwave on HIGH, uncovered, for 7 minutes, stirring only once about a minute before the end of cooking time.
2. Pour the porridge into four serving dishes. Add a teaspoon of whisky to each, stirring gently. Serve with one fresh fig (cross-cut twice, lengthwise, almost to the base and opened out) at the centre, and 'lagoons' of brown sugar and cream.

WILD OATS GOURMET GRANOLA

Muesli and granola-making is a good weekend recreation. This nutritious and delicious food tastes so interesting, however, that it seems a shame to restrict it to the role of breakfast cereal. It may be layered with natural yogurt, cream, or custard as a quick dessert; sprinkled over baked or puréed fruits, and used to coat blue, or cream, cheese balls as an appetizer. Most often, though, it will be appreciated as a first-class homemade breakfast food for the whole family.

Makes about 1.4 kg (3 lb)

60 ml (4 tbsp) soft dark brown sugar
30 ml (2 level tbsp) black treacle
30 ml (2 tbsp) safflower oil
30 ml (2 level tbsp) acacia honey
15 ml (1 tbsp) freshly squeezed lemon juice
30 ml (2 tbsp) unsweetened apple juice
450 g (1 lb) 'Jumbo' (coarse) oats
25 g (1 oz) oat bran
125 g (4 oz) wheatgerm
125 g (4 oz) dried apple ring
125 g (4 oz) sugar-free dried pineapple
275 g (10 oz) dried unsulphured Afghan apricot halves
250 g (9 oz) Afghan raisins
125 g (4 oz) flaked coconut

1. Put the first 6 ingredients into a 3.4 litre (3 quart) casserole, stir well and microwave on HIGH, uncovered, for 8 minutes or until thick and bubbling.
2. Add the oats, bran and wheatgerm and stir thoroughly until the mixture is evenly coated.
3. Spread half the mixture evenly over a sheet of baking parchment, 35 cm × 30 cm (14 inches × 12 inches). Slide this onto a non-metal baking tray. Microwave, uncovered, for 5 minutes or until dry and crisp, stirring once. Leave to stand.
4. Repeat the process with the second half of the coated oats, on another piece of parchment.
5. When both have cooled, break them into medium sized pieces, chop the apple and pineapple into 1 cm (½ inch) strips using scissors. Add the other dried fruits and stir well to mix. Store in an airtight jar out of direct sunlight.

HARLEQUIN BEANS WITH PUMPKIN AND COURGETTES

Black-eyed beans achieve distinction when cooked and served with colourful sweet and sour additions and herbs in this thick 'minestra' type stew. Do not omit the parsley stalks; they help the flavour considerably. The reddish stock makes the pumpkin seem brilliant and the final brief cooking retains the greenness of the courgettes. Serve in generous bowls, with butter or pesto and crusty wholewheat bread.

Serves 4

225 g (8 oz) dried black-eyed beans
2 leeks (white part-only) cut into 2.5 cm (1 inch) slices
2 garlic cloves, skinned and crushed
60 ml (4 tbsp) tomato purée
60 ml (4 tbsp) red wine
30 ml (2 level tbsp) fruit vinegar, such as blackcurrant
1 bunch parsley stems (20–30)
1.1 litres (2 pints) unsalted vegetable stock or water
225 g (8 oz) peeled and cubed pumpkin
225 g (8 oz) courgettes, sliced 1 cm (½ inch) thick) then halved
salt and freshly ground black pepper

1. Pour a generous amount of boiling water over the beans, cover and leave for 2 hours. Drain and discard the liquid.
2. Put the beans, leeks, garlic, tomato purée, wine, vinegar and parsley stems (tied into a bunch for easy removal) into a large 3.4 litre (3 quart) casserole and add stock or water.
3. Microwave, covered, on MEDIUM (50%) for 1½ hours or until beans are tender and leeks have become pulpy.
4. Add the pumpkin and cook on HIGH for a further 10 minutes, uncovered, adding the half moons of courgette after 3 of the 10 minutes.
5. Taste and adjust seasoning. Remove parsley stems. Serve as a thick, sustaining soup-stew, generously scattered with fresh parsley.

TAWNY BROAD BEAN PÂTÉ

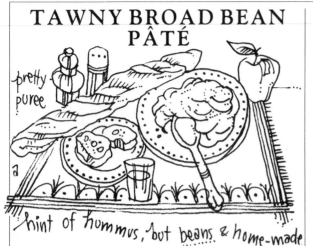

pretty purée

a

hint of hummus, but beans & home-made

Although I may try to deny it, my favourite ways of eating this warm broad bean and tahini purée are upon crusty brown bread spread with salted butter or, alternatively, in a mound drizzled with really good olive oil and accompanied by scoops of crusty garlic bread. Actually most starchy purées do need some oil or fat to make them properly palatable, so I shall stop apologising and simply say – please yourself! The purée has an unusual tawny hue (if a rich brown soy is used) and somewhat resembles a pumpkin purée. When tasted, it is not unlike hummus.

Serves 4

225 g (8 oz) dried Cyprus broad beans (split, skinless)

2 cloves garlic, skinned and chopped

100 g (4 oz) leeks, sliced

5–6 fresh bay leaves

600 ml (1 pint) boiling water

5 ml (1 level tsp) sea salt

freshly ground black pepper to taste

45 ml (3 level tbsp) tahini (toasted sesame seed) paste

15 ml (1 level tbsp) tomato purée

15 ml (1 tbsp) rich soy sauce

45–60 ml (3–4 level tbsp) chopped flat leaf parsley

virgin olive oil

1. Sort through the beans, discarding any foreign matter. Cover with boiling water, cover and leave to stand for 30 minutes. Drain. Put the beans in a large casserole.
2. Add the garlic, leek, bay leaves and the 600 ml (1 pint) of boiling water. Microwave, uncovered, on HIGH for 6 minutes or until tender.
3. Drain the beans (retaining some of the liquid) and put them into a food processor. Remove the bay leaves. Add the salt, pepper, tahini, tomato purée and soy sauce and process to a smooth paste using a little of the cooking water if necessary. Add the parsley and pile up into a creamy mound. Either trickle some oil over all and serve with good bread or serve between mange-tout.

See photograph page 45

CHICKPEA PURÉE WITH LIME AND CHILLI

In recent years hummus has become a favourite snack, enjoyed by babies and octogenarians alike. Often, however, it is so processed that it lacks texture and frequently tastes vinegary. Try making your own; it is both inexpensive and easy. This version contains tahini, no garlic at all (to let the chickpea flavour come through), chilli-flavoured dry sherry and the juice of fresh limes. Some whole peas are scattered around the base of the mound with flat leaf parsley and a trickle of good green olive oil. Crisp salad vegetables should surround the purée and hot, flat breads would always be appreciated. The dish is prepared, cooked and ready within 1½ hours. No overnight soaking is needed.

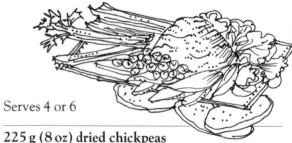

Serves 4 or 6

225 g (8 oz) dried chickpeas

1.1 litres (2 pints) boiling water

5 ml (1 level tsp) salt

30–45 ml (2–3 level tbsp) tahini paste

30 ml (2 tbsp) green olive oil

30–45 ml (2–3 tbsp) chilli-flavoured sherry, or dry sherry with pinch cayenne

freshly squeezed juice of 2 limes

freshly ground black pepper to taste

To serve

a little olive oil

a few reserved cooked chickpeas

flat leaf parsley sprigs

crisp salad vegetables

flat breads to accompany

1. Check over the chickpeas and discard any foreign matter. Pour boiling water over the peas, cover and leave to stand for 30 minutes. Drain well.
2. Put the drained chickpeas into a large casserole, add the 1.1 litres (2 pints) boiling water, cover with a lid and microwave on HIGH for 45 minutes. Drain and reserve about half the liquid.
3. Put most of the cooked chickpeas, all of the salt, tahini, olive oil and chilli-flavoured sherry into a food processor and process, in short bursts, to a thick purée, adding the lime juice and a little of the cooking water to keep the purée from sticking and becoming too solid. Taste and adjust seasonings.
4. Pile the purée upon a serving dish. Trickle some oil over the top, surround with the reserved whole chickpeas, some parsley, salad leaves and bread if wished. Serve with some icy-cold Muscadet, Retsina, Frascati, Vinho Verde or a white Rioja.

MUNG BEAN SPROUT SALAD

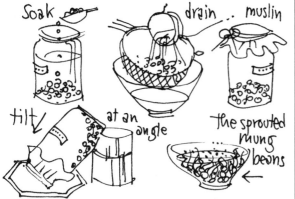

If you wish to use your own freshly sprouted mung beans for this recipe they must be prepared some days ahead. Rinse 30 ml (2 level tbsp) of perfect unsplit beans under running water, put into a large, wide-necked jar, cover with more warm water, close with muslin and a rubber band and leave standing overnight in a warm place. Next day, strain off the water through the muslin. Fill the jar with cold water through the muslin and again strain off the water in the same way. Repeat several times then leave the jar slightly angled with the mouth downwards so that the residual water drains away. Repeat this twice daily. The beans are best left in a warm, dark place for 3 days, at which time they should sprout. Transfer them to a light place (such as a window sill) for one more day, continuing to rinse and drain. Sprouts several inches long should be visible, with developing leaf tips but no musty smell. The yield should be 100–175 g (4–6 oz). Discard husks (which float or sink in a large bowl of water). Drain the sprouts and refrigerate.

Serves 4

100–150 g (4–6 oz) mung bean sprouts

100 g (4 oz) onion, skinned and quartered

2.5 ml (½ level tsp) sea salt, freshly ground

2.5 ml (½ level tsp) garam masala

5 ml (1 level tsp) lime pickle

5 ml (1 tsp) sesame oil

150 ml (¼ pint) homemade tomato sauce

100 g (4 oz) mung beans

To serve

lettuce or batavia leaves

crisp French bread stick

1. Pour 300 ml (½ pint) of boiling water over the 100 g (4 oz) unsprouted mung beans in a deep 3.4 litre (3 quart) casserole. Leave to stand for 30 minutes, covered. Drain the beans.
3. Add a further 450 ml (15 fl oz) of boiling water and the onion. Microwave, covered, on HIGH for 20 minutes. Leave to stand then drain off the water.
4. Separate the onion into 'petals'. Add the salt, garam masala, lime pickle, sesame oil and fresh tomato sauce and toss to mix. Add the sprouted beans and stir gently together. Serve in a circlet of lettuce or other leaves.

— COOK'S TIP —
The salad tastes good spooned into crusty (or between flat) bread, with perhaps a slice of creamy cheese such as farmhouse brie or camembert as an accompaniment. It is delicious at any season of the year.

SAFFRON TAGLIARINI

Pasta-making, once mastered, is one of the most therapeutic pastimes I know. Using a food processor and a hand-operated pasta machine the project becomes child's play. For those without this simple equipment, the rolling out must be done using the heaviest rolling pin available.

Serves 4

125 g (4 oz) unbleached plain flour

two 1.9 grain (small) sachets powdered pure saffron

1.25 ml (¼ tsp) salt

1 egg (size 2)

15 ml (1 tbsp) water, plus 10 ml (2 tsp)

semolina (for dusting)

15 ml (1 level tbsp) coarse salt

15 g (½ oz) unsalted butter

Garnish (optional)

fresh herbs (such as flat leaf parsley, basil or chives)

1. Put the flour, saffron and salt into a food processor and give 1 or 2 short bursts to blend. Add the egg and process again until it has been evenly absorbed (it will resemble crumbs).
2. With the processor motor running, add 15 ml (1 tbsp) water and process until clumps begin to form. Add the next 5 ml (1 tsp) of water tentatively (less may be sufficient) until the pasta forms a cohesive ball. Remove from the food processor, roll generously in flour, divide the dough in half and cover the reserved half in cling film until it is ready for use.

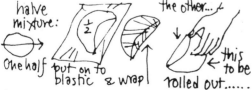

3. Set the rollers of the pasta machine to their widest setting and feed the floured and slightly flattened portion of dough through the rollers. It will emerge a little more flattened.
4. Flour the pasta again on both sides and fold both ends towards the middle so that they overlap. Corrugate it firmly with the fingertips or the side of the hand.
5. Feed the dough, with the folded edges towards the sides of the machine, through the rollers and then repeat the process of flouring, folding and corrugating the dough as before. Repeat this process 5 or 6 times until the dough feels satiny-smooth. You are now ready to thin the dough. From now on do not fold the dough into thirds.
6. Decrease the space between the rollers by one notch and feed the sheet of dough through the rollers again. Continue to decrease the space between the rollers by one notch each time. If the dough feels at all sticky, dust with flour on both sides. Notice that the dough is stretching and thinning. When you get to the last notch but two on the machine the sheet of dough should be the required thickness – about .25 cm (⅛ inch) and will measure about 60 cm (24 inches) in length. Keep the completed sheet aside.
7. Repeat the processes from (3) to (6) with the reserved ball of dough.

8. To make narrow tagliarini, feed each pasta sheet through the narrow cutters, reaching with your other hand to catch the pasta and loop it out of the way as it emerges. Hang up the cut pasta to dry a little or toss gently with some semolina to keep the strands separate. If the pasta is to be used straight away it can be loosely arranged in a sealed plastic bag and laid out flat in a cool place (1–2 days) or a refrigerator (2–3 days) before cooking.
9. To cook the pasta, arrange it evenly in a large, deep, 3.4 litre (3 quart) casserole or dish, sprinkled with 15 ml (1 level tbsp) coarse salt.
10. Pour 1.1 litres (2 pints) of absolutely boiling water over the pasta and microwave immediately, uncovered, on HIGH for 3 minutes, testing for readiness at the end of cooking time. (If preferred, cook for another 30–45 seconds.)
11. Drain the pasta through a colander. Return the casserole, adding the butter, to the oven and microwave, uncovered, on HIGH for 1 minute. Return the drained tagliarini to the casserole,

toss to coat, and serve with herbs of your choice. Have a black pepper grinder at hand.

SERVING TIP

This recipe is so simple and so good that you may wish to make enough to serve 8, for a party. In this case make the recipe twice (do not double the amounts). It takes very little extra time. Most domestic food processors handle smaller volumes of pasta dough better than larger ones. Double the volumes of water and salt and cook the pasta for 5–6 minutes or until the required tenderness is reached. Double the amount of butter.

See photograph page 67

MOREL FUNGHI PASTINATA WITH SALAD GARNISH

le shopping..

morel or morille mushrooms....

FAUCHON Paris

This delicious dish contains morel mushrooms both within the noodles themselves and in the simple sauce which accompanies it, made while the pasta is draining. Dried morels are used because of their outstanding flavour, and the stock is integral to the dish. Because the cooked drained mushrooms make the dough a little moist, do be careful to add the water to the dough very tentatively. Morel mushrooms, even dried, are not exactly inexpensive, but they are a culinary essential for gourmets and a tiny amount goes a long, long way. Ensure top quality from a really good source – smell them, they should be delicious even in their uncooked state. I buy dried mushroom supplies whenever I am abroad in Italy or France, visiting markets and specialist suppliers. Mushrooms do not need to be declared at customs, even though they may seem like riches.

Serves 4

---

7 g (¼ oz) morel mushrooms, dried and crumbled

60 ml (4 tbsp) warm water

125 g (4 oz) unbleached plain flour

1.25 ml (¼ tsp) salt

1 egg (size 2)

15 ml (1 tbsp) water plus 5 ml (1 tsp) added gradually

Sauce

20 ml (4 tsp) reserved morel stock

25 g (1 oz) butter

30 ml (2 tbsp) thick cream

Garnish (optional)

125 g (4 oz) mâche (lamb's lettuce), dandelion, rocket pousses épinards, washed, drained and dried

15 ml (1 tbsp) walnut oil, (optional)

freshly ground black pepper

1. Put the dried morels, crumbled fairly small, into a heatproof jug with the warm water and microwave on HIGH, uncovered, for 1½ minutes or until tender and a dark stock has formed. Strain through a non-metal sieve, press out all the juices and reserve. Discard any grit. Make the pasta dough by putting the drained morels, flour, salt and egg into a food processor and process in several short bursts until it resembles crumbs.
2. For steps 2–7 see instructions under these numbers in Saffron Tagliarini, page 90.
8. To make morel fettuccine, feed each pasta sheet through the wide cutters, reaching with your other hand to catch the pasta and loop it out of the way as it emerges.
9. To cook the pasta, arrange it evenly in a large 3.4 litre (3 quart) casserole or dish sprinkled with coarse salt.
10. Pour 1.1 litres (2 pints) of absolutely boiling water over the pasta and microwave immediately, uncovered, on HIGH for 4 minutes, testing for readiness.
11. Drain the pasta through a colander. Put the reserved stock, butter and cream into the casserole and microwave, uncovered, on HIGH for 50 seconds. Return the drained fettuccine to the casserole, toss to coat and serve with a circlet of oil-dressed salad leaves. Eat immediately, tossing the two together as they are eaten.

See photograph page 66

BUGIALLI'S PARSLEY PASTA SQUARES

Homemade egg pasta, flavoured delicately with parmesan and layered with still-visible green leaves, is typical of the delights that Giuliano Bugialli teaches at his cooking school in Florence. I tasted some of the fruits of this gifted scholar-cook's labours when he demonstrated some of his classic pasta methods in the test kitchen of a specialist cooks' bookshop in London, at the back of the rows of books. My microwave version is less traditional but well worth the effort. Pasta like this reminds me of embroideries in the Uffizi or sketches in a botanist's notebook, so clear is the delineation of each leaf. Serve the cooked pasta in a well-flavoured soup stock or broth (such as Soup Stock Verde, page 20).

Serves 4

125 g (4 oz) unbleached white plain flour
2.5 ml (½ level tsp) salt
30 ml (2 tbsp) freshly grated parmesan (grana)
1 egg, size 2
15 ml (1 tbsp) water
fresh flat leaf parsley leaves, dried

1. Put the flour, salt and cheese into a food processor and give several short bursts to blend. Add the egg and process again until it has been absorbed (it will resemble crumbs).
2. With the processor motor running, add 15 ml (1 level tbsp) of water gradually, and process until it begins to form clumps and then a cohesive ball. Remove from the food processor, roll generously in flour, divide the dough in half and cover the reserved half in cling film until it is ready for use.
3. For steps 3–6 see instructions under these numbers in Saffron Tagliarini, page 90.
7. Lay the completed sheet of dough out flat. Cover one half of it, about 30 cm (12 inches), with separate parsley leaves, not allowing them to touch. (If they all face in one direction your pasta will look particularly beautiful.) Cover the 'leafed' pasta with the other half, folding it carefully on top, and then feed the doubled-over dough once more through the rollers to 'bond' the layers together. If wished repeat. (The pasta should form one well-sealed, decorative strip.) Keep pasta aside.
8. Repeat the processes from (3) to (7) with the reserved ball of dough and the herb.
9. Using kitchen scissors or a cleaver, cut the pasta into 3.5 cm (1½ inch) squares. (Ideally each square will contain one leaf.) Toss the pasta in a little semolina to keep the squares separate. If the pasta is not to be used straight away, it can be loosely arranged in a sealed plastic bag and laid out flat in a cool place (1–2 days) or a refrigerator (2–3 days) before cooking.
10. To cook the pasta, arrange it evenly in a large, deep, 3.4 litre (3 quart) casserole or dish, sprinkled with 15 ml (1 level tbsp) coarse salt.
11. Pour 1.1 litres (2 pints) of absolutely boiling water over the pasta and microwave immediately, uncovered, on HIGH, for 3 minutes, testing for readiness at the end of cooking time. (If preferred, cook for 45 seconds longer).
12. Drain the pasta through a colander. Serve in some hot soup or stock if wished, with pesto (see page 29) and extra cheese, or with a knob of butter, freshly grated cheese and pepper.

See photograph page 66–67

FIVE-SPICED FINE NOODLES

Although this oriental-style pasta can be served very simply, as suggested, with yogurt and herbs, it is also versatile enough to be combined with many other ingredients, for example mange-tout peas (au naturel) and some soft-cooked eggs en cocotte, for a more substantial dish.

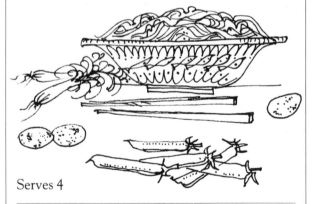

Serves 4

125 g (4 oz) unbleached plain white flour
2.5 ml (½ level tsp) salt
5 ml (1 level tsp) 5-spice powder
1 large egg (size 2)
30 ml (2 level tbsp) snipped chives
20 ml (4 tsp) water

To serve

strained thick natural yogurt

chives

1. Put the flour, salt and 5-spice powder into the food processor and give one or two short bursts to blend. Add the egg and snipped chives and process again until absorbed (the mixture will resemble crumbs).
2. For steps 2–7 see instructions under these numbers in Saffron Tagliarini, page 90.
8. To make narrow tagliolini, feed each pasta sheet through the narrow cutters, reaching with your other hand to catch the pasta and loop it out of the way as it emerges. Hang up the cut pasta to dry a little or toss gently with some semolina to keep the strands separate. If the pasta is not going to be used straight away it can be loosely arranged in a sealed plastic bag and laid out flat in a cool place (1–2 days) or a refrigerator (2–3 days) before cooking.
9. To cook the pasta, arrange it evenly in a large, deep, 3.4 litre (3 quart) casserole or dish, sprinkled with 15 ml (1 level tbsp) coarse salt.
10. Pour 1.1 litres (2 pints) of absolutely boiling water over the pasta and microwave immediately, uncovered, on HIGH for 3 minutes, testing for readiness at the end of cooking time. (If preferred, cook for 30–45 seconds longer.)
11. Drain the pasta through a colander. Return the casserole, adding the butter, to the oven and microwave, uncovered, on HIGH for 1 minute. Return the drained tagliolini to the casserole, toss to coat, and serve with the herbs of your choice. Have a black pepper grinder at hand.
12. Serve noodles tossed in enough natural yogurt to coat the strands, and with a generous addition of freshly chopped chives.

See photograph page 67

PATRICIAN PASTA

My opera singer sister, Patricia, grows huge, succulent, shaggy-leaved basil plants by the score in her greenhouse. It is the best basil I have ever tasted outside Florence, and with a gift of fresh leaves from these superb plants I can make pesto to use and keep. In their honour I have also devised what I consider a classical and properly Patrician pasta dish. Besides basil it uses garlic, parmigiano, and, at serving time, toasted pine nuts (pignolia) with some homemade, stirred in, pesto.

Serves 4

---

125 g (4 oz) unbleached plain white flour

15 ml (1 level tbsp) freshly grated parmigiano cheese

2.5 ml (½ level tsp) salt

15 ml (1 level tbsp) fresh basil leaves, torn small

2 garlic cloves, crushed

1 egg (size 3)

15 ml (1 tbsp) water plus 5 ml (1 tsp) extra if necessary

Garnish

75 g (3 oz) pine nuts

30 ml (2 level tbsp) homemade pesto (page 29)

4 or 8 fresh basil leaves

1. Put the flour, cheese, salt, basil, garlic and egg in a food processor and process in several short bursts until the mixture resembles crumbs.
2. For steps 2–7 see instructions under these numbers in Saffron Tagliarini, page 90.
8. To make fettuccine, feed each pasta sheet through the wide cutters, reaching with your other hand to catch the pasta and loop it out of the way as it emerges.
9. To cook the pasta, arrange it evenly in a large 3.4 litre (3 quart) casserole or dish sprinkled with 15 ml (1 level tbsp) coarse salt.
10. Pour 1.1 litres (2 pints) of absolutely boiling water over the pasta and microwave immediately, uncovered, on HIGH for 3 minutes, testing for readiness.
11. Do not drain the pasta, but leave to stand, covered. Meanwhile put the pine nuts on a heatproof plate and microwave on HIGH, uncovered, for 7 minutes or until lightly browned. Drain the pasta. Add the pesto and nuts to the pasta in its pan. Microwave on HIGH, uncovered, for 1½ minutes or until very hot. Stir the fettuccine, pesto and nuts gently and serve with a garnish of whole basil leaves.

—————— **SERVING TIP** ——————
A good Barolo or Florentine wine would not go amiss with such a dish.

See photograph page 67

JELLIES, CREAMS, MOUSSES AND FRUITS

PASSION FRUIT SOUFFLÉS WITH SAUTERNES

Fruit and the eloquence of good golden sauternes (make sure it has that perfect 'honeyed' taste) combine easily and well in this simple dessert. Do not be tempted to use bottled or preserved passion fruit pulp: it loses the sharpness necessary here. Have the biscuits gently warmed for these icy cold dishes.

Serves 4–6

15 g (½ oz) powdered gelatine, or 10 ml (2 level tsp) agar agar
30 ml (2 tbsp) sauternes
15 ml (1 tbsp) freshly squeezed lemon juice
150 ml (¼ pint) freshly extracted passion fruit pulp (from 7–8 fruits)
2 eggs (size 2)
pinch salt
30 g (2 oz) icing sugar

To serve

crêpes dentelles, tuiles or langue de chat biscuits
4–6 (60–90 ml) sauternes

1. Stir the gelatine (or agar agar) into the sauternes and lemon juice in a heatproof measuring jug or cup and leave to soak until firm. Microwave, uncovered, on HIGH for 45 seconds, then stir in the passion fruit pulp and stand over ice to cool, stirring from time to time, until the mixture begins to set (take care not to allow sides and base to become firm). This should take about 10–15 minutes.
2. Using an electric beater, or rotary beater, whisk the eggs, salt and icing sugar over hand-hot water until light and very pale.
3. Whisk the almost-setting gelatine or agar agar mixture into the eggs and pour quickly into dishes, stemmed glasses or custard cups, making sure that the surface is smooth. Chill for 1½ hours.
4. Pour 15 ml (1 level tbsp) of sauternes over each soufflé. Serve with crisp biscuits, warmed for a few seconds in the microwave oven.

DAY LILIES DE BELDER

leafing through the pages... a surprise...

Leafing through the garden and food pages of Harpers and Queen magazine recently I came upon some ideas (using fresh flowers, herbs, green leaves and aromatics) which I found very sympathetic to the way I feel about such things – not 'cute and chic' but grounded (pardon the pun) in good sense, taste, colour and texture. Jelena and Robert de Belder nurture an arboretum in Belgium where visiting students can learn about the exotic herbs, vegetables and flowers which thrive there. My adaptation of their excellent idea also employs microwave praline, and is served with a pool of golden liqueur. Day lilies (not the ordinary varieties) are very perishable, delicate edible lilies which are rarely on sale in florists, but scented roses may be substituted.

Serves 4

8–12 yellow and/or orange day lily blooms

2 egg whites (size 2)

25 g (1 oz) caster sugar

150 ml (¼ inch) whipping cream

2.5 cm (1 inch) cube fresh root ginger, skinned and finely grated

30 ml (2 level tbsp) pistachio praline (page 120)

Aurum liqueur or yellow Chartreuse (optional)

1. Check the blooms for cleanliness (discarding any caterpillars or foreign matter).
2. Using an electric whisk, whisk the egg whites until soft peaks form then add the sugar gradually until a stiff meringue results. Whip the cream until soft and frothy then fold one into the other, with the ginger and praline, which has been reduced to powder manually or in a grinder.
3. Fill each bloom with some mixture and stand upright, packing them into a basket or dish inside a folded napkin.
4. Serve with the liqueur and pour a little pool onto the plate for dipping. Eat the lilies with your fingers. Serve with some very cold champagne or more of the same Aurum and Chartreuse used in the recipe.

SUMMER FRUITS JELLIED WITH CASSIS

oh for summertime.......

Individual jellies filled with the real reds of summer – fresh raspberries, strawberries and redcurrants – also contain wine and cassis to create a glow of exceptional rosiness. Use 90 ml (6 tbsp) timbale moulds if you have them, or small, straight-sided bun dishes, or ramekins, so that they present pretty shapes when turned out. Each jelly sits on a pool of cassis, with calligraphies of cream, to delight the eye and the tongue, traced at intervals around the edge. This will make a lovely party dessert, yet is simple enough for everyday use with a wine of less superior quality.

Makes 4–6

10 ml (2 level tsp) sachet powdered gelatine or 10 ml (2 level tsp) agar agar

45 ml (3 tbsp) cold water

60 ml (4 tbsp) crème de cassis de Dijon

300 ml (½ pint) Aligoté or other crisp white burgundy

50 g (2 oz) fresh redcurrants, separated from their stems

50 g (2 oz) fresh raspberries

50 g (2 oz) fresh strawberries, hulled and halved

To serve

crème de cassis and thick cream

1. Stir the gelatine (or agar agar) into the water in a heatproof bowl or jug and leave to soak until firm. Microwave, uncovered, on HIGH for 45 seconds or until melted. Mix in the crème de cassis and the wine. Stand the bowl over ice to cool, stirring at intervals to make sure it does not begin to set at the sides and base.
2. Prepare and check over the fruit, drying any moist berries upon kitchen paper (the fruit is best left unwashed, as long as it comes from a reliable supplier).
3. Stand the bun dishes, moulds, glasses or ramekins together on a tray or shallow dish. When the jelly is on the point of setting (after 30–35 minutes), stir the fruit very gently through it, to mix evenly, and turn into the containers. Refrigerate until fully set (about 2 hours or more).
4. To unmould, wrap the containers in a hot damp cloth, or hold briefly in warm or hot water. Cover with a large flat plate and invert in one brisk movement, to free the jellies. Repeat this process, if necessary, until all jellies are unmoulded.
5. Spoon a little cassis carefully around each jelly to form a pool. Drop 4 or 5 'dots' of thick cream around each. Swirl each (clockwise or anti-clockwise) into a pretty spiral, using the tip of a skewer or satay stick. Serve quickly, before the effect is dimmed.

See photograph page 104

GELÉE AGIA SOFIA

Soon I intend to make a trip to Turkey to visit some of its many architectural and archaeological treasures – and to sample its splendid cuisine. Until then I amuse myself devising dishes such as this: a rather grand Byzantine dome, filled with decorative fruits. A garland of foliage is pretty and most appropriate. Star fruit (carambola) are available from specialist greengrocers, oriental foodmarkets and certain supermarket chains. They are used whole, skin and all. Although one might wish agar agar to be used instead of gelatine, the amount needed gives a rather unpleasing texture and so is, to my mind, unacceptable here.

Serves 4

---

two 15 g (1/2 oz) sachets of powdered gelatine

300 ml (1/2 pint) Nierstein or similar wine

300 ml (1/2 pint) white grape juice, unsweetened

150 ml (1/4 pint) clear apple juice, unsweetened

5 fresh dessert pears (with stems), peeled

2 ripe yellow star fruit, thinly sliced

2 cinnamon sticks

---

1. Stir the gelatine into 60 ml (4 level tbsp) of the Nierstein in a large heatproof bowl or jug. Leave to soak until firm. Microwave, uncovered, on HIGH for 1 minute, or until melted. Stir into the wine, with the grape juice and half of the apple juice. Leave to cool over ice.
2. Meanwhile, put the pears, on their sides, and star fruit slices into a ring dish with 1 cm (1/2 inch) boiling water, cover with cling film and microwave on HIGH for 3–4 minutes, or until hot but still firm. Turn the pears over and leave to cool. Dry the pears on kitchen paper.
3. Using an apple corer, remove the base core sections of the pears (not as far up as the stem), twist and remove this central portion, so that the pears still look intact.
4. Break the cinnamon sticks cross-wise, into 4 equal pieces. Part-insert two cinnamon pieces into the lower sides of two pears and push the remaining two pears on to the free ends. Use the remaining two cinnamon sticks to form the two pairs into a 'construction' of four.
5. Tie the four stems together using chive stems or else some narrow silk ribbon.
6. Invert the four-pear 'construction', positioned carefully with the stems downwards, into a 1.1 litre (2 pint) bombe mould or similar domed container. Put the fifth pear in the centre.

7. Drain the star fruit (discard liquid) and dry the fruit on kitchen paper. Position the star fruit round the pears and pour the jelly gently over. Refrigerate until really firm (5–6 hours) or overnight.
8. To unmould, rinse the jelly briefly under warm to hot water, until you can feel it loosen slightly. Holding the serving dish over the top, quickly invert it, in one brisk movement, and remove mould. Refrigerate for a few minutes.
9. Decorate with a garland of flowers and foliage. This cool dessert makes a stimulating conversation piece.

See photograph page 104

HERB-SCENTED CELTIC CREAM

One languid summer day at a friend's house we were offered a deliciously simple meal of stuffed baked aubergines and leafy salad followed by fresh berries piled into a bowl and accompanied by an Irish pottery jug of what appeared to be thin cream. Great was our surprise and delight to discover that it was a fragrant sauce, composed of scented leaves, cheese and cream. My version employs both geranium leaves and very well chopped fresh (and I must stress fresh) bay leaves to impart a haunting, delicate fragrance. There is currently much misunderstanding about the true bay (Lauris nobilis): unlike its cousins (Mountain laurel, Cherry laurel) it is perfectly harmless in reasonable quantities (the others are considered bad for the health) and cooked and used fresh it has long been a standfast of European cookery. Really fresh leaves have an enchanting taste. Try them: the dried variety do not compare.

Serves 6–8

---

12 fresh bay leaves cut into shreds with scissors

6–8 rose, lemon or ginger-scented geranium leaves, crushed

300 ml (1/2 pint) single cream

50 g (2 oz) caster sugar

2 egg yolks (size 2 or 3)

225–350 g (8–12 oz) natural cottage cheese (puréed in a food processor or blender)

---

1. Chop up or bruise the leaves thoroughly. Put

them into a 900 ml (1½ pint) heatproof jug or
bowl and add the cream. Microwave,
uncovered, on HIGH for 2 minutes to allow the
flavours to infuse. Leave to stand, covered, for
10 minutes. Strain off the liquid and discard the
leaves, squeezing them dry.
2. Return the cream to the heatproof jug and
add the sugar and egg yolks. Whisk briefly then
microwave, uncovered, on LOW (30%) for 5
minutes or until thickened, stirring from time to
time.
3. Stir the custard into the puréed cheese to
obtain a smooth sauce.

FRESH FRUIT CHOCOLATE CREAMS

*This is a version of chocolate fondue: chocolate
melted perfectly with cream and other additions to a
dipping consistency. At each diner's setting there
should be a small silver fork or satay stick, an
(optional) dish of icy water, and a selection of fresh
seasonal small fruits, all with their stems, hulls,
leaves and greenery intact. Guests prepare their own
fruits to dip into the communal fondue, and then eat.
Participant sport!*

Serves 4–6

700 g (1½ lb) fruit: select from lychees, fresh dates, cherries on the stem, wild strawberries, physalis (Cape gooseberries), grapes, red or white currants on the stem
350 g (12 oz) good quality dark chocolate
90 ml (6 tbsp) double cream
5 ml (1 level tsp) ground cinnamon
30 ml (2 tbsp) dark rum, brandy or whisky

1. Select suitable fruits and arrange attractively
on serving plates. Put a small glass ramekin of
ice-cubes and iced water by each plate, if
wished, and a utensil for dipping.
2. Break the chocolate into 1 cm (½ inch)
pieces in a heatproof serving bowl. Add the
cream and cinnamon. Microwave, uncovered, on
HIGH (60%) for 3 minutes, or until chocolate is
softened and creamy. Stir well and add the rum.
3. Place on the table, keeping the bowl warm
over a candle flame or other apparatus.
4. Encourage diners to dip a piece of fruit into
the fondue, harden the chocolate (if wished) in
the iced water then eat.

KUMQUAT CUSTARD CREAMS

*Little pots of creamy custard, delicately flavoured
with discs of kumquat and an orange sauce, prove an
effective variation on a classic theme. A spoonful of
thick strained yogurt adds contrast of texture.*

Serves 4

4 fresh kumquats, sliced crosswise into 8 or 10
45 ml (3 level tbsp) caster sugar
60 ml (4 tbsp) water
250 ml (8 fl oz) creamy milk
15 ml (1 level tbsp) vanilla sugar
1 cinnamon stick, crushed into pieces
2 eggs and 1 egg yolk (size 3), lightly whisked

1. Layer the kumquat slices, overlapping,
around the base of 4 microwave-proof ramekins
or china pots, 7.5 cm (3 inch) diameter and
75 ml (3 fl oz) capacity.
2. Put the sugar and 15 ml (1 tbsp) of the water
into a straight sided porcelain or pyrex dish.
Microwave, uncovered, on HIGH for 3 minutes.
3. Add the remaining water and microwave,
uncovered, for 3 minutes until caramelized,
turning the dish twice during cooking.
4. Quickly trickle the caramel over the
kumquats in the ramekins or pots. Cool.
5. Put the milk, vanilla sugar and crumbled
cinnamon stick into a large heatproof measuring
jug. Microwave, uncovered, on HIGH for 2
minutes then leave to stand for 2 minutes. Pour
the milk onto the whisked eggs then strain the
custard mixture back into the prepared ramekin
dishes. Position them, evenly spaced, around
the edge of a heatproof plate.
6. Microwave, covered loosely with cling film,
on LOW (30%) for 5½ minutes, giving the
plate a quarter turn every 1½ minutes. Carefully
remove the hot ramekins. At this stage the
centres should appear definitely undercooked
but the residual heat will complete the cooking
process while they stand.
7. Cover the ramekins with a double thickness
of kitchen paper. If they are to be eaten warm,
leave them to stand for 5–8 minutes.
8. If the custards are to be turned out, leave
them to stand as above then refrigerate for at
least 1½ hours. Invert each custard in one rapid
movement onto its serving dish. Once cooked,
the fruit will have floated through the custard
and the caramel dissolved to a pale syrup.

SWEET RENAISSANCE CURDY

In these days of culinary sophistication we sometimes forget how good many old English 'receipts' actually were. One such sauce (warmed softened butter whipped light with sugar then combined with egg yolks, butter, brandy and nutmeg, all achieved in front of a blazing fire and/or over bowls of hot water) can be wonderfully 'reborn' using the microwave oven. This is not a dish for dieters, those with liver problems or dyspeptics! It is rich fare and a little tends to go a long way. However, if the sauce is folded through some low-fat, natural yogurt and topped with fresh fruit, it will adequately serve 6. I present this dish icy-cold in stemmed liqueur glasses with lacy gaufres, tuiles or amaretti biscuits.

Serves 6

50 g (2 oz) soft dark brown sugar

45 ml (3 tbsp) freshly squeezed lemon juice

75 g (3 oz) salted butter

2 egg yolks (size 3)

60 ml (4 tbsp) low fat natural yogurt

15 ml (1 tbsp) brandy or whisky

pinch freshly grated nutmeg

To serve

200 g (7 oz) low fat natural yogurt

6 fresh cherries on their stem (or 6 gooseberries)

crisp biscuits

1. Put the sugar and lemon juice into a large, shallow measuring jug set within a bowl containing 150 ml (¼ pint) boiling water. Microwave, uncovered, on HIGH for 30 seconds or until hot and sugar dissolves when stirred. Add the butter, egg yolks and yogurt all at once and whisk vigorously using an electric whisk.
2. Microwave, uncovered, on LOW (30%) for 6 minutes, stirring from sides to centre every few minutes or until smooth and thickened.
3. Allow to cool a little, then stir in the liquor and nutmeg. Leave to cool completely, for at least 2 hours. It will become mayonnaise-like in consistency.
4. Serve marbled with yogurt in decorative glasses topped with the fresh fruit and accompanied by crisp biscuits.

FRUITED BRIE MOUSSE WITH CARAMEL LACE

Imagine breaking through a burned caramel and grape topping to find an icy-cold brie mousse beneath! The most important stage in this recipe is to cook the caramel to the correct dark golden colour so that it sets almost immediately when it touches the near-frozen desserts. For those who need to prepare ahead or are merely forgetful, these delicacies may be made and frozen in advance. Allow the desserts to ripen in the refrigerator for approximately 1 hour for perfect results. Encourage your guests to give a sharp tap with their spoon to uncover the delicious rich mixture beneath.

Serves 4–6

275 g (10 oz) muscatel or other white grapes, halved and seeded

15 ml (1 level tbsp) caster sugar

125 g (4 oz) ripe brie, cubed

15 ml (1 level tbsp) Cointreau

15 g (½ oz) sachet of gelatine (or 1 level tbsp) or 10 ml (2 tsp) agar agar

45 ml (3 level tbsp) cold water

225 ml (8 fl oz) double cream, chilled

Caramel

50 g (2 oz) caster sugar

30 ml (2 tbsp) water

pinch tartaric acid (or cream of tartar)

Decoration

6–8 grapes, halved and seeded

1. Put the grapes and sugar in a heatproof dish, cover with cling film and microwave on HIGH for 2 minutes.
2. Add the cubed brie and stir into the grapes. Cover again with cling film and microwave on HIGH for 15–20 seconds. Add the Cointreau and reduce the mixture to a coarse purée using a food processor in short bursts.
3. Pour the mixture into a shallow, freeze-proof plastic container, cover and fast freeze for 20 minutes or until the mixture is cooled and firm.
4. Stir the gelatine or agar agar into the water in a large heatproof measuring jug and leave to 'sponge' until firm. Microwave, covered, on HIGH for 1 minute or until melted and allow to cool a little. Stir in the purée and return to the

freezer for a further 5–8 minutes or until almost freezing.

5. Whip the cream until soft peaks form. Fold the almost-setting cheese mixture into the cream and divide the mixture between 4 or 6 heatproof pots. Return to the freezer.

6. To make the caramel, put the 50 g (2 oz) sugar with the 30 ml (2 tbsp) water and tartaric acid into a 25 cm (10 inch) diameter browning dish or rectangular glass dish, about 1.1 litres (2 pints) volume. Microwave, uncovered, on HIGH for 2 minutes. Stir until dissolved.

7. Microwave, uncovered, for a further 2½–3 minutes, without stirring, but tilting the pan (wearing oven gloves) to avoid hot spots. It should become a uniform dark golden brown.

8. Remove the pots from the freezer and decorate with grapes (cut surfaces down). Wearing gloves, spoon trickles of the molten caramel in a criss-cross pattern over the surface of the desserts to achieve a lacy effect. Allow the caramel to cool and serve within one hour for best results (although caramel stays fairly crisp if kept cool for up to 5 hours).

SANTA ROSA MOUSSE

This dessert could also be called a fool, but its mousse-like quality derives from the egg white which has been added to the crème fraîche, marbled throughout the mixture. Use the dark, flavourful plums specified if at all possible.

Serves 4

---

450 g (1 lb) Santa Rosa plums, halved, stones removed

---

30 ml (2 level tbsp) flower-scented honey

---

15 ml (1 tbsp) slivovitz, quetsch, mirabelle or other plum spirit

---

1 egg white (size 2 or 3)

---

pinch salt

---

30 ml (2 level tbsp) caster sugar

---

60 ml (4 tbsp) crème fraîche or lightly whipped cream

---

1. Put the halved plums, with the washing water still clinging to the skins, into a microwave ring dish. Microwave, uncovered, for 4 minutes or until tender. Mash, food process or blend to a rough pulp. Allow to cool somewhat. Stir in the honey and slivovitz.

2. Whisk the egg white and salt in a small, high-sided bowl using an electric beater, rotary beater or whisk, until foamy. Add sugar and continue to whisk until soft peaks form. Fold the cream into the egg white, then fold this mixture through the plums, using large, easy movements of the spatula so as not to lose the lightness, or over mix.

3. Spoon into individual goblets, bowls or custard cups and serve cool.

a cool & classy dessert...

COOK'S TIP

If no plum spirit is available, white rum, tequila or vodka could be substituted, but with different results.

RAMBUTANS IN SCENTED SYRUP

Rambutans are tropical fruits (rather like lychees) with thick, dark red-brown and hirsute skins that tend to discourage or horrify potential diners. The skin peels off easily, however, to reveal a delicate, pale succulent flesh beneath.

Makes 450 g (1 lb)

---

350 g (12 oz) fresh rambutans

---

150 ml (¼ pint) Moscatel or Moscat wine

---

10 ml (2 tsp) champagne or white wine vinegar

---

10 cm (4 inch) cinnamon stick, crushed

---

1 whole vanilla pod, slightly bruised

---

75 g (3 oz) caster sugar

2.5 ml (½ tsp) orange flower water

---

1. Peel the rambutans and discard the rough dark skin. Keep the peeled fruit aside.

2. Put the wine, vinegar, cinnamon and vanilla pod into a heatproof glass jar or china pot. Cover with cling film and microwave on HIGH for 2 minutes. Remove cling film and check flavour for scentedness.

3. Add the caster sugar and stir until dissolved. Add the fruit and microwave on HIGH, uncovered, for a further 3 minutes or until the syrup is boiling. Allow to cool and stir in the orange flower water. Cover with a non-metal top and store in the refrigerator as a short to medium term preserve. Serve with cheese or with creams, yogurts, mousses and ices.

MACEDONIA AL MARSALA

A gently scented and spiced syrup permeates receptive fruits in this delicate party dessert. I prefer to leave in the stones and seeds of the fruits (including watermelon) and thus the flavours stay fresh, the goodness intact. If preferred, an orange-fleshed canteloupe or charentais could take the place of watermelon (though the vividness would be lost).

Serves 6–8

...scented fruits in the softness of a marsala syrup....

75 g (3 oz) vanilla sugar
¼ nutmeg, freshly grated
15 ml (1 level tbsp) preserved ginger, sliced into shreds
100 ml (4 fl oz) freshly squeezed orange juice
15 ml (1 level tbsp) shredded orange zest
30 ml (2 tbsp) freshly squeezed lime juice
150 ml (¼ pint) Marsala
225 g (8 oz) fresh cherries, stems removed
225 g (8 oz) nectarines, sliced into eighths
225 g (8 oz) muscat grapes, stems removed
125 g (4 oz) wild strawberries
125 g (4 oz) fresh blueberries
225 g (8 oz) watermelon, cubed or in balls

1. Put the vanilla sugar, nutmeg, ginger and orange juice into a large, heatproof (preferably glass) serving dish and microwave on MEDIUM (60%), uncovered, for 2 minutes, stirring, until dissolved and very hot.
2. Add the zest, the lime juice and Marşala, then all the prepared fruit and stir to make sure the fruit is covered.
3. Refrigerate, covered with cling film, just long enough for the syrup to cool (but not chill) and its perfume to pervade the fruit.
4. Uncover just before serving and present with lacy biscuits if wished, but no cream.

HIGHLAND BROSE

The Scots have long been connoisseurs of good food and drink. In this recipe, four of their nation's famous products triumph all at once. The dessert looks superbly appropriate served in old Georgian goblets on a silver tray, with a spray of seasonal heather. It is simplicity itself to prepare: the microwave oven dispenses with the need for overnight standing.

Serves 4

50 g (2 oz) 'organic' oats (not rolled oats)
60 ml (4 tbsp) dry white wine
75 ml (5 level tbsp) Scottish heather honey
75 ml (5 tbsp) Glenfiddich or Macallan malt whisky
200–225 g (7–8 oz) Cream Crowdie cheese (or quark)
50 g (2 oz) Scottish raspberries

To decorate

20 ml (4 tsp) Scottish heather honey

1. First toast the oats. Put on a heatproof plate and microwave, uncovered, on HIGH for 4 minutes, stirring 3 to 4 times during cooking. Keep aside.
2. Put the white wine and 75 ml (5 level tbsp) of honey into a measuring jug, cover with cling film and microwave on HIGH for 7 minutes. Stir and add most of the oats and all of the whisky. Leave to stand for 5–8 minutes, covered, then fold in the cheese to make a smooth mixture.
3. Spoon into four medium-sized, 125 ml (4 fl oz) wine glasses, goblets or glass dishes. Sprinkle the reserved oats on top, divide the raspberries between the four servings, and spoon a little honey over each. Serve while the honey still gleams, and the desserts are faintly warm (accompanied, perhaps, by a wee dram of the inimitable whisky).

Mango fan salad with tandoori dressing (and poppadums) (page 52) and Dill, yogurt and leek tart (page 57) in Poppyseed pastry (page 76).

OVERLEAF
Geranium flower ice cream (page 114), Saffron and poppyseed babka (page 106) with Lemon and limonnaya cordial (page 123). Beside the cordial one Orange flower fougassetta (page 109).

CAKES AND LOAVES

CROESUS CAKE

Depending on the greed and avidity of your guests, this cake will feed from between 6 to 12 people. It is uncompromisingly rich, like its namesake, and takes a surprisingly short time to make (and an even shorter time to devour, especially when freshly made). Coffee and chocolate are the predominant tastes but the cake is drenched with a syrup of crème de cassis, vodka and coffee while it cools, giving a wondrously sumptuous effect. It is then coated in melted chocolate (easy in a microwave cooker) and whipped cream and should be served, to my mind, to sustained applause.

Serves 6–12

75 g (3 oz) plain unbleached flour
1.25 ml (¼ level tsp) salt
5 ml (1 level tsp) baking powder
60 ml (4 tbsp) cocoa
100 g (4 oz) dark soft brown sugar
75 g (3 oz) brazil nuts, chopped or food processed
100 g (4 oz) butter
15 ml (1 level tbsp) coffee granules
15 ml (1 tbsp) hot water
2 eggs (size 3)

Syrup

30 ml (2 tbsp) crème de cassis
15 ml (1 level tbsp) coffee granules
15 ml (1 tbsp) hot water
30 ml (2 tbsp) vodka, white rum or gin

Coating

100 g (4 oz) chocolat pâtissier (or good dark chocolate)
225 ml (8 fl oz) whipping cream

1. Sieve the flour, salt and baking powder with the cocoa, then add the sugar and nuts.
2. Put the butter into a heatproof measuring jug and microwave on HIGH, uncovered, for 30–45 seconds or until melted. Dissolve the coffee in the water. Add the butter, coffee and eggs, all at once, to the dry ingredients. Beat well to give a smooth mixture then pour into a 1 litre (1¾ pint) heatproof glass pudding bowl which has been previously lined with cling film. Stand the bowl on a trivet or roasting rack.
3. Microwave on HIGH, uncovered, for 5 minutes, giving the bowl a half turn halfway through the cooking time. (During cooking the cake may rise a little above the lip of the bowl but this is not important.)
4. Allow the cake to stand for 4–5 minutes. Meanwhile make the syrup. Combine the ingredients in order, stirring well. Pierce the cake all over with a skewer and drizzle the syrup all over it. Cling film the surface and cool the cake, rapidly if wished by fast-freezing it for 20 minutes. Remove from the bowl.
5. To make the chocolate coating, break the chocolate into small pieces and put it into a small heatproof jug or bowl, adding 15 ml (1 tbsp) of the whipping cream. Microwave on HIGH, uncovered, for 2 minutes, stirring twice to obtain a creamy smooth consistency.
6. Spoon or, using a wide, soft pastry brush, paint the chocolate coating over the inverted 'bombe' of the cake. Fast-freeze again, if wished, for 5–8 minutes or until the coating is set.
7. Whip the remaining cream until stiff and spread it over the chocolate-covered cake using a spatula or palette knife. Keep the cake in a cool place but do not refrigerate.
8. Serve the cake in slices, with perhaps a glass of vodka (especially the superb buffalo grass scented variety). Alternatively, iced rum or gin could be served in tiny glasses as 'digestifs'.

Summer fruits jellied with cassis (page 95) and Gelée agia sofia (page 96) complete with ribbon.

SAFFRON AND POPPYSEED BABKA

While undertaking research recently, my peregrinations took me to the Polish cultural centre, where I tasted some superlative almondy poppyseed cake. It was baked in a fluted ring mould then dusted all over with icing sugar. I resolved to invent a microwave version, and decided that adding semolina for texture and saffron for scent and colour would be worth a try. Do not substitute almond flavouring for almond essence; there is a considerable difference. If the latter is unavailable, use an almond liqueur instead.

Serves 4–8

25 g (1 oz) blue poppyseeds

125 g (4 oz) ground almonds

50 g (2 oz) semolina

1.9 grain (small) sachet pure powdered saffron

5 ml (1 level tsp) baking powder

3 eggs (size 3), separated

75 g (3 oz) caster sugar

75 g (3 oz) butter, melted

45 ml (3 tbsp) milk

5 ml (1 level tsp) almond essence

icing sugar for dusting (optional)

1. Oil a 1.4 litre (2½ pint) fluted, deep, heatproof china, pottery or glass ring dish. Measure the dry ingredients into a mixing bowl and blend well.
2. Whisk the egg whites until soft peaks form, then, in a separate bowl standing over hot water, whisk the egg yolks until light and frothy. Add the sugar and continue until very light and pale.
3. Place the butter in a heatproof jug and microwave on HIGH for 35–45 seconds, then add the milk and almond essence.
4. Pour these into the dry ingredients, fold in the egg yolks and mix gently but thoroughly, then fold in the egg whites, keeping the mixture as light as possible. Pour or spoon evenly into the prepared ring dish. Microwave, uncovered, on HIGH for 4 minutes, giving it three quarter turns during the cooking time. Allow the cake to stand for 3–4 minutes then turn out and dust generously with the icing sugar if wished. This cake is delicious, warm or cold, served plain or with yogurt, cream or crème fraîche.

See photograph page 102–103

COURGETTE AND GREEN GINGER CAKE

Do you dare to serve your friends and family a green cake? This fascinating confection utilizes tender courgette flesh and two types of ginger, and makes no attempt to conceal its components, all of which are delicious but unusual to say the least. The frosting is of the American type: it uses cream cheese instead of butter and limes give unmistakable style.

Serves 6

2 eggs (size 2)

225 g (8 oz) caster sugar

150 ml (¼ pint) safflower or grapeseed oil

10 ml (2 tsp) green ginger wine

225 g (8 oz) unskinned courgettes, finely grated

50 g (2 oz) crystallized ginger, chopped

150 g (5 oz) plain flour

10 ml (2 level tsp) ground ginger

2.5 ml (½ level tsp) ground nutmeg

5 ml (1 level tsp) baking powder

2.5 ml (½ level tsp) salt

Decoration

175 g (6 oz) cream cheese

60 ml (4 tbsp) icing sugar

shredded zest and segmented flesh from 1 lime

chopped crystallized ginger (optional)

1. Base line a 23 cm (9 inch) microwave ring mould with baking parchment.
2. Beat the eggs, sugar, oil and green ginger wine in a large mixing bowl. Add the courgettes and crystallized ginger and sieve the remaining dry ingredients into the mixture before stirring. Do not over mix.
3. Spoon the mixture into the prepared ring mould and cover lightly with baking parchment. Microwave on HIGH for 9 minutes, giving the dish a half turn halfway through cooking time.
4. Leave the cake to stand for 5 minutes then turn out and allow to cool.
5. Make the frosting by beating the cheese and icing sugar together. Stir in the finely shredded zest and lime flesh. When the cake is cool, apply frosting with a palette knife. Decorate with thinly chopped crystallized ginger if wished.

FRESH RASPBERRY RING CAKE

This delicious fresh fruit cake, layered and with perfect undamaged fruits still visible inside, is best eaten while still warm and fresh. To keep the lightness, work quickly and fold together gently but firmly before the mixture settles. It looks and tastes pleasing if the centre is filled with extra berries (a considerable volume is needed) in which case it will serve 8 or so as a dessert with whipped cream.

Serves 4–6

---

125 g (4 oz) fresh raspberries (reserve 6)

---

175 g (6 oz) plain unbleached flour

---

5 ml (1 level tsp) baking powder

---

grated zest of ½ lemon

---

3 eggs (size 3), separated

---

pinch salt

---

75 g (3 oz) caster sugar

---

50 g (2 oz) butter

---

45 ml (3 tbsp) milk

---

15 ml (1 tbsp) lemon juice

---

1. Oil a fluted mould; a glazed ceramic deep Kugelhopf dish, capacity 1.1 litres (2 pints) and 20 cm (8 inch) diameter is fine. Arrange 6 raspberries evenly round the base.
2. Sieve the flour and baking powder and add the lemon zest.
3. Separate the eggs and whisk the egg whites with a pinch of salt until soft peaks form. Whisk the yolks with sugar until thick and mousse-like.
4. Melt the butter in a small heatproof dish, uncovered, on HIGH for 1 minute, then add the milk and lemon juice. Pour the liquid, all at once, into the dry ingredients. Add the egg yolk mixture, blend well and gently fold in the egg whites. Pour half the mixture into the prepared mould. Scatter over half of the berries, pushing them well down into the mixture.
5. Mash the remaining berries with a fork and fold them into the remaining cake mixture. Pour into the mould.
6. Cover with a sheet of baking parchment and microwave on HIGH for 4 minutes, giving the mould a quarter turn every minute. Leave to stand for 3–4 minutes. Pull the cake inwards gently from the sides and from the centre. Invert in one brisk movement onto a serving dish. Allow to cool and dust with icing sugar. Eat within one day, or the fruit discolours.

WANDA'S APPLE AND HONEY CAKE

Each Christmas I receive the gift of native honey from an old and treasured friend in New Zealand. Used sparingly it lasts a whole year, reminding me of the giver, as does this cake. Eat it warm with fresh coffee and/or with a little 'trou' of Calvados.

Serves 4–8

---

75 g (3 oz) butter

---

125 g (4 oz) plain unbleached flour

---

5 ml (1 level tsp) baking powder

---

10 ml (2 level tsp) ground mixed spice

---

100 g (4 oz) soft dark brown sugar

---

250 g (9 oz) apples, Cox's Orange Pippins

---

50 g (2 oz) roasted, salted cashew nuts, chopped

---

30 ml (2 tbsp) milk

Syrup

---

60 ml (4 tbsp) New Zealand white clover honey

---

30 ml (2 tbsp) dry cider or Muscadet

---

30 ml (2 tbsp) Calvados or applejack brandy

Decoration (optional)

---

142 ml (5 fl oz) soured cream or crème fraîche

---

1. Oil a 900 ml (1½ pint) heatproof fluted ring dish. Keep aside.
2. Put the butter into a cup and microwave on HIGH, uncovered, for 45 seconds or until melted. Keep aside.
3. Sift the flour, baking powder and spices into a mixing bowl and add the sugar. Cube the apples, skin and all, and add, with the chopped nuts, to the dry ingredients.
4. Add the melted butter and milk and stir briefly but firmly to blend the ingredients. Spoon or pour the mixture into the oiled dish and microwave on HIGH, uncovered, for 5 minutes, giving the dish 4 quarter turns during the cooking time. Leave the cake to stand for 2 minutes then invert onto a serving plate.
5. Meanwhile put the honey and cider or wine into a cup and microwave on HIGH, uncovered, for 45 seconds. Stir well to dissolve and add the Calvados. Drizzle this syrup all over the cake. Spoon a 'frosting' of soured cream around the top of the cake and serve while still warm. As an alternative, leave the cake to cool, then chill and serve sliced with a separate serving of cream.

HEALTHY LOAF

This loaf contains three types of flour as well as wheatgerm, bran, raisins and malt – a lively selection of ingredients. It is dense and spongy in texture, rather dry but excellent toasted. If sliced thin, the bread makes an excellent accompaniment to all sorts of vegetable dishes or with spreads, cheese or egg dishes. It is not crusty, but a microwave with a browning facility can briefly brown it at the end of the cooking time. Otherwise it can be browned under a conventional grill.

Makes 1 large loaf

225 g (8 oz) granary flour	
125 g (4 oz) white flour	
50 g (2 oz) soya flour	
2.5 ml ($\frac{1}{2}$ level tsp) salt	
25 g (1 oz) wheatgerm	
25 g (1 oz) unprocessed oat, or other, bran	
75 g (3 oz) seedless raisins	
7.5 ml ($1\frac{1}{2}$ level tsp) or $\frac{1}{2}$ sachet micronized dried yeast (Easy-blend or Easy-bake)	
300 ml ($\frac{1}{2}$ pint) warm water	
45 ml (3 level tbsp) pure malt extract	

1. Put the flours, salt, wheatgerm, oat bran, raisins and dried yeast in a large non-metal mixing bowl and stir to mix. Stir the warm water with the malt until dissolved, then pour all at once into the dry ingredients and mix to form a soft dough. Knead briefly in the bowl three or four times. Leave to rise, loosely covered with cling film, on a rack above hot water, until doubled in bulk. Punch down. Divide the dough into 4 even-sized balls.
2. Oil a 450 g (1 lb) heatproof glass or plastic rectangular loaf dish. Pack the 4 balls, one at a time, into the dish so that they give a corrugated curved dome effect. Leave to rise, loosely covered, above hot water for a little while.
3. Microwave on HIGH, uncovered, for 6 minutes, giving the dish a quarter turn every 2 minutes. Remove the loaf from the dish and allow to cool on a wire rack.
4. If you have a browning facility, brown the loaf briefly, if wished, or remove and place for a short time under a preheated conventional grill to brown, but do not allow it to dry out.

COUNTRY-STYLE HERB AND PUMPKIN BREAD

The surface of this unusual bread is covered with a bright green layer of flat leaf parsley – an unusual concept and one which will only work in a microwave oven. The salt content counteracts the sweet mildness of pumpkin and the bread tastes even better with a generous sprinkling of black pepper.

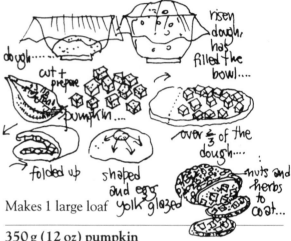

Makes 1 large loaf

350 g (12 oz) pumpkin	
175 g (6 oz) wholemeal flour	
100 g (4 oz) strong plain white flour	
15 g ($\frac{1}{2}$ oz) or 1 sachet micronized dried yeast (Easy-blend or Easy-bake)	
10 ml (2 level tsp) salt	
60 ml (4 tbsp) olive oil	
450 ml (15 fl oz) lukewarm water	

Topping

1 egg yolk	
25 g (1 oz) flat leaf parsley, finely chopped	
25–50 g (1–2 oz) pine nuts	

1. Remove the seeds and pith from the pumpkin. Pierce the skin and flesh several times and microwave, uncovered, on HIGH for 6 minutes, turning it over halfway through cooking time. Allow to cool.
2. Put the 3 flours, the yeast and salt into a non-metal mixing bowl and mix to distribute the ingredients evenly. Pour in the olive oil and warm water, mix to a soft dough and knead for 5 minutes until the dough is smooth, satiny and elastic.
3. Put the dough into a lightly oiled mixing bowl and cover with cling film. Stand on a rack

over warm water and allow to rise until the dough has doubled in size, about 20–25 minutes.

4. Punch down the dough, knead again briefly and leave to rise for a further 20 minutes.

5. Pat or roll out the dough to a 25 cm (10 inch) circle. Remove and discard the pumpkin skin and cut the flesh into 1 cm (½ inch) cubes. Cover two-thirds of the rolled dough surface with the pumpkin, then fold the dough twice to enclose and layer the pumpkin.

6. Give the dough a quarter turn and roll and fold again, working gently so that the pumpkin does not break the surface of the dough.

7. Pat out to an even 15–20 cm (6–8 inch) circle. Drop the egg yolk on top and, using your fingers or a pastry brush, rub it all over to coat.

8. Scatter the parsley and pine nuts all over the surface of the dough and press firmly into place. Slide the dough onto a piece of baking parchment and place on a pizza tray, a grooved roasting tray or a browning dish.

9. Microwave, uncovered, on MEDIUM (50%) for 5 minutes, giving it 2 quarter turns during cooking. Then microwave, uncovered, on HIGH for a further 6 minutes, giving it 2 more quarter turns during cooking.

10. Remove and allow to stand for 3–4 minutes. Slice and serve warm with soups, cheese, egg dishes or salads.

See photograph page 45

ORANGE FLOWER FOUGASSETTAS

Fougasse is a flat bread from the South of France region. Slashed, spread open and shaped, it is cut and opened out into a lacy, fabric-like texture. These miniature versions are crisp and aromatic enough to be eaten like biscuits. They are also good with creamy mousse-type desserts and ice creams.

Makes 8

700 g (1½ lb) strong plain white flour

5 ml (1 level tsp) salt

15 g (½ oz) sachet micronized dried yeast (Easy-blend or Easy-bake)

45 ml (3 level tbsp) light soft brown sugar

150 ml (¼ pint) boiling water

300 ml (½ pint) cool to lukewarm water

45 ml (3 tbsp) grapeseed or safflower oil

Flavouring

4 oranges, freshly shredded zest and juice of

10–15 ml (2–3 tsp) orange flower water

20–30 ml (4–6 level tsp) light soft brown sugar

Glaze

2 egg yolks

15 ml (1 tbsp) orange flower water

45 ml (3 tbsp) orange juice and a little reserved orange zest

1. Put the flour, salt and dried yeast into a large non-metal mixing bowl and stir ingredients well to mix.

2. Dissolve the sugar in the boiling water then add the 300 ml (½ pint) of warmish water, judging measures carefully to end up with a lukewarm liquid. Stir this and the oil briskly into the dry ingredients, mixing to form a soft dough.

3. Knead for 5 minutes on a lightly floured surface until the dough is smooth, satiny and elastic.

4. Put the dough into the (lightly oiled) mixing bowl and cover with cling film. Stand on a rack over warm water until the dough has doubled in bulk, about 20–30 minutes.

5. Punch down the dough, knead again briefly and leave to rise for a further 20 minutes. Divide the dough into 8 parts.

6. Shape into balls and then roll the balls flat. Sprinkle on some of the orange zest, the orange flower water and brown sugar.

7. Fold the 4 corners of each fougassetta into the middle and fold completely over to enclose the filling. Roll out to a roughly 20 cm (8 inch) oval and slash or slit with a knife or scissors 12–15 times. Pull out into a lacy pattern. Slide onto some baking parchment.

8. Microwave one at a time on MEDIUM (50%) for 3 minutes, or until puffed, giving a half turn halfway through cooking time.

9. Brush with a glaze made of the egg yolk, orange flower water, some of the orange juice and the reserved orange zest. Microwave on HIGH for 1–1½ or 2 minutes, or until firm but not hard. Repeat the process with the remaining seven. Eat while still fresh.

See photograph page 103

BANANA AND COCONUT TEA BREAD

Bananas baked 'au naturel' in their skins, before being skinned and sliced into a spicy, nutty loaf, give a specially interesting flavour and colour contrast to this straightforward but delicious tea bread. The coconut used is the wide, curly variety, not the old-fashioned desiccated coconut.

Makes a 700 g (1½ lb) loaf

350 g (12 oz) or 2 ripe bananas
90 g (3½ oz) wholewheat flour
5 ml (1 level tsp) baking powder
50 g (2 oz) plain unbleached flour
175 g (6 oz) light golden soft sugar
150 ml (¼ pint) safflower oil
2 eggs (size 1), lightly beaten
50 g (2 oz) flaked coconut shreds

1. Pierce both bananas 3 times on each side and then microwave on HIGH for 2 minutes. (The colour of the skins may darken.)
2. Leave to stand for 5 minutes, then peel and chop the banana flesh into slices. Set aside.
3. Put the remaining ingredients, in order, into a large mixing bowl and mix gently and minimally until all the dry ingredients are incorporated.
4. Stir in the banana, then spoon or pour into a 1·1 litre (2 pint) rectangular, heatproof, glass baking dish which has the sides and base lined with baking parchment and the opposite ends lightly oiled.
5. Put a strip of foil over the mixture to overlap the shorter ends of the dish. This will ensure even cooking. Place the dish on a trivet or roasting rack. Microwave, uncovered, on MEDIUM (50%) for 9 minutes, giving a quarter turn every 2 minutes.
6. Increase power to HIGH and microwave for

another 2 minutes. Remove the foil from the edges and microwave on HIGH for a further 2 minutes. Leave to stand for 2–3 minutes, then turn out and serve sliced as tea bread.

GRANARY SODA BREAD

This daisy-shaped loaf is rough, moist and textural. It is also delicious, looks homely and, if made and eaten within a quarter hour (spread with butter and a trickle of honey) it is irresistible.

Makes 1 large loaf

100 g (4 oz) unprocessed oat or wheat bran
350 g (12 oz) granary flour
10 ml (2 level tsp) bicarbonate of soda
10 ml (2 level tsp) cream of tartar
7.5 ml (1½ level tsp) salt
15 ml (1 level tbsp) brown sugar
60 ml (4 tbsp) safflower or rapeseed oil
300 ml (½ pint) milk
45 ml (3 tbsp) freshly squeezed orange juice

Decoration

honey and alfalfa seeds

1. Mix the first 6 ingredients in a large bowl. Add the oil, milk and orange juice all at once and stir well to form a soft dough. Knead lightly.
2. Shape into a 17.5 cm (7 inch) round and slide on to some baking parchment. Mark into 8 or 12 sections using a knife. Push fingers into each mark to make indents, thus forming 'petals'.
3. Microwave on MEDIUM (50%) for 5 minutes, giving a quarter turn twice. Microwave on HIGH for a further 3 minutes, giving a quarter turn twice.
4. Brush or trickle circlets of honey over the top and sprinkle with alfalfa seeds if wished.
5. Microwave on HIGH for 1 more minute. Take the bread out of the oven and slide on to a cooling rack. Leave for 1 minute then turn it over and peel away the parchment. Leave for 2 minutes and then invert. Eat while warm.

See photograph page 47

BOSTON BROWN BREAD JUG LOAVES

Recently I read in Evan Jones' American Food about a New England housewife called Anna whose bread was so like her own lazy character that her husband devised his own recipe called 'Anadama bread'. Whether from Rockport or Boston, there is no doubt that easy breads of this type, raised with yeast (Anadama) or baking powder and bicarbonate of soda (Boston) are worthwhile and delicious. Cornmeal can be found in health food stores and specialist delicatessens.

Makes 2 loaves

125 g (4 oz) plain unbleached flour
10 ml (2 level tsp) baking powder
50 g (2 oz) wholewheat flour
75 g (3 oz) cornmeal
75 g (3 oz) black treacle or molasses
300 ml (½ pint) milk
50 g (2 oz) butter
5 ml (1 level tsp) bicarbonate of soda

1. Line with cling film 2 containers, such as heatproof measuring jugs, of 8.5 cm (3½ inch) diameter bases and 1.1 litre (2 pint) capacity to allow for rising.
2. Sift the first 4 ingredients into a bowl. Put a large heatproof bowl on the scales, reset the scales to zero, and weigh 75 g (3 oz) of treacle.
3. Pour a quarter of the milk, all the butter and bicarbonate of soda into the black treacle. Microwave on HIGH, uncovered, for 1 minute, then stir to mix.
4. Add the remaining milk, pour the liquid into the dry ingredients and stir to form a moist, batter-like mixture.
5. Pour half the mixture into one prepared jug and microwave on 50% (MEDIUM) for 5 minutes or until the mixture feels firm at the centre. Then microwave the second loaf.
6. Cool the bread for 2–3 minutes before turning out. Serve with soups, salads or for tea.

MALTED YOGURT SCONES

Scones cooked in a microwave oven have light, spongy texture but no crispness (unless there is a browning facility). These scones are quick, delicious and have a malted top surface to provide a colourful and nutritious extra. Eat them while still warm, or rewarmed, opened for fruit preserves or, if you feel profligate, sandwiched with added clotted cream, crème fraîche or thick cream.

Makes 12

50 g (2 oz) unsalted butter, cubed
50 ml (2 fl oz) natural yogurt
50 ml (2 fl oz) water
125 g (4 oz) seedless raisins
125 g (4 oz) plain flour
125 g (4 oz) wholewheat flour
15 ml (1 level tbsp) baking powder
1.25 ml (¼ tsp) salt
30 ml (2 level tbsp) pure malt extract
15 ml (1 tbsp) hot water
30 ml (2 level tbsp) toasted sesame seeds (see page 36)

1. Put the butter into a large heatproof mixing bowl and microwave on HIGH, uncovered, for 45–60 seconds or until melted. Stir in the yogurt and the first measure of water. Add the raisins.
2. Add the flours, baking powder and salt all at once, mix to form a soft dough but do not over mix.
3. Pat out gently to form a 15 cm (6 inch) square. Using a 5 cm (2 inch) cutter, cut out 12 scones, reshaping the dough as necessary toward the end. Arrange the scones evenly, in rows of 3, on baking parchment. Microwave on HIGH, uncovered, for 4–4½ minutes or until well risen.
4. Put the malt and hot water in a heatproof mug or jug and microwave, uncovered, on HIGH for 30 seconds. Brush this all over the top of the scones and sprinkle with the sesame seeds. Eat while the scones are still warm and sticky.

—— **SERVING TIP** ——
These scones are also tasty served with a slice of creamy brie or camembert inside.

ICED AND HOT DESSERTS

FROZEN MOUSSE LA COUPOLE

I enjoy drinking, dining and people-watching in cheerful café-restaurants such as La Coupole in Paris, while guessing what intrigues are taking place at the tables of the gregarious arm-waving habitués. (I also long for a letter to be waiting for me on the elegant letter board, but have yet to be pleasantly surprised.) Under La Coupole's dome I sip Pastis, Ricard or Pernod while surveying the menu. This mousse, dome-shaped and anise-scented, is a suitable reminder. It is delicious.

Serves 6–12

300 ml (½ pint) freshly-made smoky China tea (such as Lapsang Souchong)

100 g (4 oz) caster sugar

15 ml (1 level tbsp) freshly squeezed lemon juice

60 ml (4 tbsp) Pastis, Ricard or Pernod

2 eggs (size 2)

15 g (½ oz) powdered gelatine, or 10 ml (2 tsp) agar-agar

45 ml (3 tbsp) cold water

300 ml (½ pint) double cream

20–30 star anise seeds (extracted from seedheads), crushed

To serve

6–12 whole star anise seedheads (for decoration)

45–90 ml (3–6 tbsp) Pastis, Ricard or Pernod

1. Put half the tea and half the sugar into a heatproof measuring jug and microwave, covered, for 2 minutes on HIGH, stirring until a syrup forms. Add the lemon juice and remaining tea. Cool over ice and add the liquor.

2. Break the eggs into a medium bowl, add the remaining sugar and whisk, using an electric beater, until the mixture becomes thick and mousse-like.

3. Stir the gelatine into the cold water in a heatproof jug or bowl. Leave to soak until firm. Microwave, covered, on HIGH for 1 minute or until melted, then stir into the cooling syrup. Leave over ice, stirring from time to time, for 15–20 minutes or until nearly setting.

4. Whip the cream until it forms soft peaks.

5. Fold the almost-setting aniseed-gelatine mixture into the egg mixture with the cream and fold in the crushed star anise seeds.

6. Turn into a lightly oiled 1.1 litre (2 pint) freeze-proof bombe mould or dome-shaped freeze-proof bowl. Cover, seal and leave to set. Freeze for 2½–3 hours, or until firm at the edges and just set in the centre. Stand the bombe mould or bowl briefly in cool or warm water, then invert onto a serving dish.

—— **SERVING TIP** ——

Serve slices on a pool of the liqueur, 7.5 ml (½ tbsp) per serving, with one whole anise seedhead as an edible decoration. Many orientals believe star anise seeds help digestion: so encourage diners to nibble the seeds.

POMEGRANATE GRANITA

In this recipe, hollowed pomegranate shells are filled with a highly-flavoured granita made from their own juices. They rest amid a crown of grapes, reminiscent of a Chardin, Goya, Dufy or de Stael painting come to life. Pomegranate seeds (some of which are reserved in the shell lids) always seem fitting symbols of fecundity and Persephone's sojourn

in the underworld. In hot countries the sweet astringency of these fruits is a protection against thirst. Try to select fresh, juicy specimens. It is worth paying for one fruit to break open and squeeze-test for juiciness, before you pay for more. (Use the juice from this extra fruit in the base of a tall glass, topped up with champagne, for a cocktail accompaniment to this luscious dessert.)

Serves 4

4 juicy pomegranates, about 900 g (2 lb)

100 g (4 oz) caster sugar

shredded juice and zest from 2 lemons

shredded juice and zest from 2 tangerines or clementines

2.5 ml (½ tsp) orange or geranium flower water

450 g (1 lb) small, seedless dessert grapes on the stem (such as Italian King's Ruby or muscat)

1. With the pointed crowns facing upwards, cut through each fruit (using a sharp, serrated, stainless steel knife) about a third of the way from the top. Remove the lids.
2. Extract the juice from the larger portions by squeezing them over a lemon squeezer (crush any runaway seeds in a non-metal sieve or strainer, if necessary). Measure the liquid; there should be about 300 ml (½ pint).
3. Put the sugar, pomegranate juice and 2 kinds of zest into a medium heatproof bowl and microwave on HIGH, uncovered, for 2 minutes. Stir, then microwave on HIGH for a further 2 minutes or until syrup forms.
4. Cool the syrup over ice, stir in the juices and orange flower water. Pour into a shallow freezeproof, heatproof plastic container and fast freeze for 2 hours or until frozen to a slush, stirring from sides to centre after 1 hour and 1½ hours.
5. Arrange the grapes on one large or four individual chilled serving dishes, so that they form a support for the large pomegranate shells.
6. Stir well and put scoops of the frozen granita into each of the chilled, prepared shells. Rest the upturned lids close by.

COOK'S TIP
If the granita is made in advance and has hardened, soften or 'ripen' it in the microwave oven for 15–20 seconds on HIGH, covered. Stir gently for a minute or so, until crumbly smooth.

See photograph page 48

MANGO AND KUMQUAT GRANITA

Fresh kumquats, those fascinating little fruit (of which green pips, flesh, orange skin and all are eaten), taste refreshingly sharp as well as aromatic. Combined with the mango (scented and mellow) and fresh grapefruit juice, then polished to a resolute finish with Cointreau, they become sublime. Serve on icy dishes with a decorative garnish of sliced kumquats and orange blossom.

Serves 4–6

225 g (8 oz) kumquats, sliced thinly, crosswise

75 g (3 oz) caster sugar

450 g (1 lb) ripe mango, 225 g (8 oz) after preparation

300 ml (½ pint) grapefruit juice, freshly squeezed

30 ml (2 tbsp) Cointreau (1 miniature bottle)

1. Put the sliced kumquats into a food processor with the sugar and chop finely. Remove the chopping blade and put the bowl (it must not contain metal parts) into the oven. Microwave on HIGH, uncovered, for 3 minutes. Stir well.
2. Put the blade back on the food processor and into the bowl put the mango, skinned and stoned, with the grapefruit juice and Cointreau. Process to a smooth purée and cool over ice. Fast freeze in a shallow container for 3 hours, stirring after each hour from edges to centre, until frozen to a slush.
3. Remove from the freezer and stir with a gentle, rhythmic motion for 1–1½ minutes or until very smooth-textured (but not crumbly) ice results. This will give a perfect creamy scoop when removed with a spoon. Serve on cold dishes or in stemmed glasses, decorated with kumquats if wished.

GERANIUM FLOWER ICE CREAM

This barely-cooked custard cream is flavoured with orange and (available from oriental food stores) geranium flower water, frozen until firm, stirred once, and then re-frozen. It is 'faintly and quaintly' scented, as a friend remarked. If you have lemon-scented geranium growing in the garden, place a small leaf – washed, dried and chilled – in each goblet, glass or dish. Add scoops of ice cream and balance a wafer biscuit to one side, if wished.

Serves 4–6

3 fresh eggs (size 3)

100 g (4 oz) icing sugar

300 ml (½ pint) whipping cream

60 ml (4 tbsp) geranium flower water or 4 lemon-scented geranium leaves, crushed

5 ml (1 tsp) triple-strength orange flower water

1. Using an electric beater, whisk the eggs in a medium, high-sided bowl until frothy. Add the sugar all at once, continuously beating until the mixture becomes pale and light.
2. Meanwhile, pour the cream (containing crushed leaves if they are used in place of the geranium flower water) into a large heatproof measuring jug. Microwave on HIGH, uncovered, for 3 minutes or until scalding hot.
3. Remove the geranium leaves (if used) with tongs, squeezing off any cream. Pour the scalding cream onto the eggs in a steady stream with one hand, while whisking continuously with the other hand. Cool over ice then add the other flavourings.
4. Pour into a shallow, freezeproof, heatproof container, cover and fast-freeze for 2 hours. Stir thoroughly from sides to centre and top to bottom (or it will form layers). Freeze for a further hour. Serve in scoops, garnished as suggested or alternatively, present it in crisp, tulip-shaped, 'coupelles' biscuits.

See photograph page 102

CAPTAIN MORGAN'S COFFEE GRANITA

Some people say that Her Majesty's Navy will never be the same – now that the daily tot of rum is, alas, no longer supplied. But whether you have access to Navy rum, Pusser's rum or simply good quality dark rum, it certainly makes all the difference to this sorbet. It must be stressed that to be successful the coffee must be top quality and a hundred per cent fresh. If the ice has been frozen for much longer than the suggested time it will have hardened. Soften or 'ripen' it in the microwave for 40 seconds on HIGH, uncovered, then proceed as in step 3.

Serves 4–6

50 g (2 oz) medium roast, freshly ground coffee, filter fine

125 g (4 oz) caster sugar

15 ml (1 tbsp) dark rum (or more)

To serve

tiny edible flowers (optional)

chocolate sticks or wafers (optional)

1. Pour 600 ml (1 pint) boiling water over the freshly ground coffee, stir well, cover and leave to infuse. Strain twice through a non-metal sieve. Stir the sugar into a quarter of the coffee and microwave on HIGH, uncovered, for 2 minutes. Stir and microwave on HIGH, uncovered, for a further 2 minutes. Add the rum and stir into the remaining coffee and cool over ice.
2. Pour into a shallow, freezeproof plastic container and fast freeze for 2½ hours or until frozen to a slush, stirring from side to centre after 1 hour, 1½ hours and 2 hours.
3. Beat well then spoon or scoop the frozen grainy-textured granita into serving glasses or dishes, accompanied by edible flowers and/or chocolate sticks or wafers.

JADIS ET GOURMANDE CHOCOLATE POTS

The best chocolates I have ever eaten were bought, many times, as a gift from specialists in Paris called Jadis et Gourmande. My friend Maurice would expertly choose a different selection from their air-conditioned shelves just before each visit to London. Some had gold leaf embedded in them and others a calligraphy in white chocolate. There were veritable sculptures of nuts, while others would be filled with pralines, liqueurs and creams. They would be packed tumbled, yet with great élan, in an immaculate white glazed cardboard box tied with the unmistakable ribbon, and sealed. This recipe should use similar superb dark chocolate to give it the proper style. Serve cool or chilled in pretty pots or custard cups.

Serves 4–6

40 g (1½ oz) unsalted butter
45 ml (3 level tbsp) cornflour
2 eggs (size 3)
350 ml (12 fl oz) creamy milk
45 ml (3 level tbsp) vanilla sugar
50–75 g (2–3 oz) good quality dark chocolate or chocolates, chopped finely
15 ml (1 tbsp) cognac

1. Put the butter in a heatproof 900 ml (1½ pint) bowl or jug and microwave on HIGH, uncovered, for 1 minute.
2. Add the cornflour and microwave, uncovered, on HIGH for a further 45 seconds.
3. Whisk the eggs with a quarter of the milk and stir in the sugar. Add the remaining milk to the butter and flour mixture, mix well and microwave on HIGH for 3 minutes, stirring frequently.
4. Whisk the hot sauce into the egg and milk mixture, cover loosely with cling film and return to the microwave oven. Microwave on HIGH for a further 1½ minutes. Whisk thoroughly. Add the chocolate and whisk until dissolved (if necessary, microwave on HIGH for a few seconds). Allow to cool slightly.
5. Stir in the cognac, then pour or spoon into 4 or 6 individual pots, cups or glasses.

POMMES CARAMELISÉES NORMANDE

New season's apple chunks taste beyond compare when cooked and served in this simple manner. But do not attempt the recipe using faded apples of indeterminate age. The fruit must be small, crisp and sharp flavoured for perfect results. The Normandy fromage blanc makes a far better accompaniment than cream or yogurt, having a lightness and freshness which blends superbly with the rich caramelized apple. Purchased galettes or buckwheat pancakes can be halved, folded into cones and then filled with the fromage blanc as a pretty garnish, or the two can simply be passed separately to guests.

Serves 4

775–900 g (1¾–2 lb) small crisp new season's apples (such as Cox's Orange Pippins)
50 g (2 oz) unsalted Normandy butter
50 g (2 oz) soft dark brown sugar
15 ml (1 tbsp) dry cider or Muscadet
2 buckwheat galettes (crêpes Bretonnes) or more if wished
125 g (4 oz) fromage blanc battu or fromage frais

1. Preheat a 25 cm (10 inch) browning dish for 8 minutes on HIGH. Meanwhile peel, quarter and core the apples.
2. When the pan is hot, add the butter and sugar and stir quickly to distribute the mixture evenly. Add the apples (evenly distributed) and microwave on HIGH, uncovered, for 8 minutes, shaking the pan once or twice. Do not stir the apples.
3. Remove the apples to a warm serving dish, caramel sides upwards. Cook the butter-sugar caramel for a further 2 minutes then add the cider or wine and stir quickly. Pour the sauce over the apples. Briefly microwave the galettes (evenly distributed in the oven and overlapped if necessary) then halve and twist into cones. Spoon some fromage blanc into each. Serve with the apples and eat while warm and fragrant.

TARTE ZAGARA WITH PÂTÉ SUCRÉE

This delicious citrus-flavoured tart takes its name from the Sicilian (but originally Arabic) word for citrus flower, the perfume of which impregnates that countryside so memorably. The softish biscuit pastry contains just enough cinnamon to provide a contrast to the fruitiness of the filling, which should be very gently set. Serve this tart in tiny, elegant slivers (perhaps 3 per person) with a flourish of yogurt if wished, and a twist of lemon.

Serves 8

75 g (3 oz) salted butter, cubed
150 g (5 oz) plain flour
40 g (1½ oz) soft dark brown sugar
5 ml (1 level tsp) ground cinnamon
1 egg yolk (size 3)
5 ml (1 tsp) iced water

Filling

3 eggs (size 3)
3 egg yolks (size 2)
1 lemon, shredded zest and juice
1 orange, shredded zest and juice
5 ml (1 level tsp) citrus flower water
90 ml (6 tbsp) thick strained natural yogurt
50 g (2 oz) caster sugar

To serve

thick strained natural yogurt (optional)
lemon twists (optional)

1. Put the butter, flour, sugar and cinnamon into a food processor. Process in short bursts until the mixture resembles fine crumbs.
2. Add the egg yolk and water and process in one or two bursts (as little as possible) to achieve a cohesive dough (it may not appear to go into a ball but will do so with hand pressure). Wrap in cling film and chill for 20 minutes before use.
3. Have ready a 20 cm (8 inch) flan or tart dish (preferably with a removable base, or else lined with baking parchment or cling film). Flatten the pastry ball then, using finger pressure, shape the pastry to cover the base and sides. Prick pastry all over using a fork. Place a circle of kitchen paper over the pastry base. Microwave

on HIGH for 4–5 minutes or until firm. Leave to cool. Remove the paper.
4. Lightly whisk the filling ingredients until smooth, and pour into the pastry. (It should very nearly fill it.) Microwave on MEDIUM (50%) for 10 minutes then reduce the power to LOW (30%) and microwave for a further 17 minutes. Eat whilst still warm.

SESAME SHORTCRUST PASTRY SHELL

Here is a delicious way of adding taste and goodness to shortcrust pastry. Because sesame seeds toast so perfectly in the microwave oven, it is effortless to make and gives style to whatever filling it accompanies, including bananas and rum (page 117). The pastry is also good used warm or cold with a raw fruit and natural yogurt filling, as long as it is filled and eaten within a relatively short time. Brandied berries in vanilla sugar may also be spooned into this pie shell.

Makes a 19 cm (7½ inch) diameter shell

50 g (2 oz) sesame seeds, toasted (see seasoning page 36, step 3)
15 ml (1 level tbsp) dark soft brown sugar
30 ml (2 tbsp) cold milk
125 g (4 oz) plain unbleached flour
2.5 ml (½ level tsp) salt
65 g (2½ oz) cold butter, cubed

1. Dissolve the sugar in the milk, stirring well. Add the cooled sesame seeds to the flour and salt in a food processor. Add the cold butter and process in 2 short bursts to blend in the butter.
2. With the processor running, quickly pour in the milk mixture and blend for the shortest time possible to achieve a dough. Push the dough together into a ball, wrap and chill in the freezer for 2 minutes. Roll out, on a floured surface, to a 25 cm (10 inch) circle. Use to line a 19 cm (7½ inch) inner diameter pie dish, folding under a pastry rim (on to the lip) and crimping the edges firmly. Prick the pastry all over using a fork.
3. Place a circle of kitchen paper on the base of the pastry and microwave on HIGH, uncovered, for 5 minutes, giving the dish a half turn halfway through cooking time. Remove the kitchen paper and leave the pastry to cool.

BRIGITTE'S BANANA TART

This idea I learned from a friend in Paris. She made a pâte brisée version in her attic kitchen near the Bastille while I watched. The speed and simplicity, and the final delicious taste as it was brought to the table (where once glue-makers practised their art in what was then a 'quartier artisanal') really impressed me. In my version a sesame pastry is used (page 116) which works well in the microwave. The effect of using a food processor for slicing the bananas is curious – they emerge wafer thin but still cohering and can then easily be piled into the pastry shells for a very special smooth effect. Don't omit the kiwi fruit; it is an integral part.

Serves 4–6

1 kg (2 lb) very firm bananas, unpeeled
30 ml (2 tbsp) dark rum
30 ml (2 level tbsp) dark soft brown sugar
19 cm (7½ inch) diameter pre-cooked sesame shortcrust pastry shell (page 116)
5 ml (1 level tsp) finely shredded lime or lemon zest
1 large kiwi fruit, skinned

1. Peel and thinly slice the bananas using a food processor. Gently mix in the dark rum and half of the sugar. Spoon this filling into the pastry shell.
2. Sprinkle the zest over the surface. Slice the kiwi fruit crosswise into 16 thin slices. Overlap these to make a circle on top of the bananas. Sprinkle the remaining sugar into the central portion of the bananas.
3. Microwave on MEDIUM (50%), uncovered, for 10–12 minutes or until very hot. Serve absolutely plain (without cream or yogurt) accompanied perhaps by a glass of chilled dark rum containing a twist of lime or lemon.

——— COOK'S TIP ———
To slice bananas by hand to the required thinness takes a long time. Thick chunks may taste similar but will not achieve the peculiar creaminess which makes the texture of this dish so interesting.

ILLUSIONIST'S CHOCOLATE PIES

To combine a savoury cheese pastry case with a raisin, chocolate and liquor filling may seem a little ambitious. It works miraculously well, however. The sight of the squares of chocolate, each melted but perfect (the name MENIER can still be read accurately on each) is singularly surreal and the sizzle of the liquor 'cooking' as it trickles over each little hot tart is truly fascinating. Some people find these not unlike Christmas mince pies, and for this reason the optional creamy topping is included: it completes the illusion. Use a good fruit brandy such as poire, framboise, quetsch, fraise or something exotic like boukha (Tunisian fig eau de vie) if you can find it. Eat these while still warm.

Makes 16

175 g (6 oz) uncooked Liptauer pastry (page 77)
175 g (6 oz) seedless raisins
75 g (3 oz), or 16 squares, chocolat Menier, or similarly slim, good dark chocolate
60 ml (4 tbsp) eau de vie de fruit

Topping

50 g (2 oz) cream cheese
30 ml (2 tbsp) eau de vie de fruit

1. Roll out the pastry thinly to about 27.5 cm (11 inches) square, and cut 16 circles of pastry.
2. Invert 4 heatproof glasses, plastic cylinders or ramekins and brush them with oil. Mould the pastry circles over the top so that they form shallow 'cups'. Prick well using a fork. Arrange the 4 glasses or ramekins with their pastry 'cups' around the edge of a large heatproof plate. Microwave on HIGH, uncovered, for 2 minutes.
3. Remove the pastry cases, invert and place on a heatproof plate lined with a sheet of kitchen paper. Add ¹/₁₆th part of the raisins to each cup and put a square of chocolate in the centre of each. Microwave on HIGH, uncovered, for 1½ minutes.
4. Remove the plate from the oven and pour some liquor over each tart (it will sizzle!). Allow to stand while the remaining 3 batches are cooked. If necessary, reheat the 16 briefly before eating.
5. To make the topping, work the cheese and the liquor together until smooth. Spoon a small portion on top of each tart.

SATURNALIA PUDDING

A simply-made and lighter-than-usual version of Christmas Pudding, cooked in a ring dish and, believe it or not, ready to be used on the same day. Make it to serve within 30 minutes (the time it needs to stand). If it must be made ahead then reheat, cling-film covered, on HIGH for 4 minutes. Serve with Jamaican Rum Sauce.

Serves 8

125 g (4 oz) dark soft brown sugar
250 g (9 oz) brown wheatmeal flour
2.5 ml (½ level tsp) salt
15 ml (1 level tbsp) baking powder
10 ml (2 level tsp) ground cinnamon
5 ml (1 level tsp) ground nutmeg
5 ml (1 level tsp) mixed spice
10 ml (2 level tsp) coriander seeds (crushed)
125 g (4 oz) shelled pecan nuts, chopped
125 g (4 oz) shelled macadamia nuts, chopped
125 g (4 oz) shelled brazil nuts, chopped
125 g (4 oz) seedless raisins, chopped
125 g (4 oz) dried figs, quartered
250 g (9 oz) carrots, coarsely shredded
4 eggs (size 3) beaten
125 ml (4 fl oz) safflower oil
150 ml (¼ pint) stout
30 ml (2 level tbsp) molasses

1. Lightly oil and base line a 2 litre (4 pint) 9 inch diameter ring dish.
2. Put the first 8 dry ingredients into a large mixing bowl and stir until well blended. Add the nuts, raisins and figs, chopped using kitchen scissors. Make a well in this mixture and add the shredded carrot.
3. Whisk the eggs and safflower oil together. Put the stout and molasses into a heatproof jug and microwave on HIGH, uncovered, for 30 seconds, then stir. Blend all the ingredients, stirring to give a moist mixture, with no pockets of flour showing. Do not overmix.
4. Carefully turn the mixture into the prepared dish. Cover with a circle of baking parchment and microwave on LOW (30%) for 38 minutes, or until an inserted skewer comes out clean. Stand, covered, for 25–30 minutes and then turn out.

Jamaican Rum Sauce

25 g (1 oz) butter
30 ml (2 level tbsp) plain flour
1.25 ml (¼ tsp) ground allspice
1.25 ml (¼ tsp) ground cloves
300 ml (½ pint) single cream
60 ml (4 tbsp) dark rum
45 ml (3 level tbsp) muscovado sugar

1. Put the butter into a 900 ml (1½ pint) heatproof measuring jug. Microwave, loosely covered, on HIGH for 30–45 seconds. Stir in the flour and spice and microwave on HIGH for 15–20 seconds.
2. Slowly stir the cream into the roux, whisking constantly. Microwave, uncovered, on HIGH for 3 minutes, stirring every minute.
3. Cool a little. Stir in the dark rum and muscovado sugar until well blended.

APPLE AND ORANGE BLISS

This recipe (arrived at quite by chance) epitomises simplicity and goodness. I first made it while illustrating to a child how differently microwave ovens cooked food. 'Look,' I said 'chopped apples can cook uncovered, with no water, no sugar and without visible change, yet taste excellent.' Puréed with fresh orange juice it became jelly-like and tasted superb!

Serves 1

225 g (8 oz) or 3 small apples (preferably Cox's Orange Pippins)
150 ml (¼ pint) freshly squeezed orange juice

1. Cut the apples (cores and stems removed if wished) into 8 or 12 segments each. Put on a heatproof plate and microwave on HIGH for 3 minutes, giving the plate a half turn halfway through cooking time.
2. Put into a blender with the orange juice. Blend until smooth. Rub through a non-metal sieve, or serve as it is, warm or chilled.

SWEETMEATS, TISANES AND COCKTAILS

ALMOND SWEETMEATS CLAUDIA

These small, sweet almond paste confections are less sweet and more delicate than much commercially made marzipan, and can be flavoured at will. (This mixture also makes an excellent covering for cakes, or a basis for petits-fours.) The flavour of the apricots matters hugely: old-style dry, slightly freckled, dappled apricots with sharp taste give the best results by far. I once collaborated with the cookery writer Claudia Roden, who was passionately concerned that I obtain the correct apricots (of this very same quality) for a photograph of one of her dishes. This preoccupation with excellence greatly impressed me, and I have named these sweetmeats in her honour.

Makes 56 (minimum)

225 g (8 oz) ground almonds

225 g (8 oz) granulated sugar

125 ml (4 fl oz) hot water

few drops rose or citrus-flower water (triple distilled)

15 ml (1 level tbsp) shredded orange zest

125 g (4 oz) ground almonds or ground pistachio nuts

28 shelled pistachio nuts

28 small sharp-flavoured dried apricots

To serve

ground almonds and petits-fours cases

1. Put the 225 g (8 oz) of ground almonds into a food processor (with grinder-mixer blade in position).
2. Put the sugar and hot water into a large heatproof measuring jug or bowl. Microwave, uncovered, on HIGH for 2 minutes. Stir well to dissolve all the sugar.
3. Microwave, uncovered, for a further 5 minutes (without stirring) until the syrup reaches the soft ball stage (a candy thermometer will register 115°C/240°F).
4. Pour the hot syrup into the feed tube of the running food processor. Process continuously until the mixture clumps into a sticky paste, adding the rose or citrus-flower water and zest.
5. Remove the still-warm and sticky almond paste from the food processor and knead it with the extra ground nuts (use an electric grinder for pistachios) into a pliable mixture, on a clean dry surface. (Marble is ideal for this.)
6. Form the paste into one long cylinder, 25 cm (10 inch). Halve and then quarter crosswise. Wrap all but one of the pieces in cling film to keep the mixture easily workable. Divide the quarter portion into eight. Enclose one pistachio nut in one apricot, folding it over (or insert pistachio if apricot opens easily) then enclose this stuffed apricot in a portion of almond paste. Use clean hands (otherwise it marks) to shape. Squeeze and knead each into a compact ball. Continue this process until all 28 are complete, unwrapping each cylinder of paste as needed. Store in an airtight container.
7. To serve, cut each sweetmeat into halves or quarters and set each in one of the petits-fours cases, with a dusting of ground almonds.

— SERVING TIP —
These old-fashioned sweets are excellent served with espresso coffee and liqueurs after dinner, or in place of dessert.

TOFFEE AND NUT CLUSTERS

These fresh nuts, encased in a thin layer of gleaming toffee, are not exactly inexpensive but do constitute a real treat on occasions. Moreover, there are no suspicious additives and the high protein content of the nuts makes them, to me, an acceptable sweetmeat. They look beautiful wrapped carefully as gifts, or on a tall glass bonbonnerie stand, in place of dessert, with cheese and vintage character port.

Makes 450 g (1 lb)

50 g (2 oz) glucose syrup

250 g (9 oz) granulated sugar

50 ml (2 fl oz) water

5 ml (1 level tsp) raspberry vinegar

75 g (3 oz) shelled macadamia nuts

75 g (3 oz) shelled hazelnuts

75 g (3 oz) shelled brazil nuts

1. As long as it is not metal, put the container of glucose syrup into the oven and microwave on HIGH, uncovered, for 1½–2 minutes, or until the contents are soft enough to measure. Place on the scales and remove 50 g (2 oz) to a deep 2.3 litre (4 pint) casserole.
2. Add sugar, water and vinegar and microwave, uncovered, on HIGH for 5 minutes, stirring occasionally until the sugar has completely dissolved. (Tilt the dish from time to time as well.)
3. Microwave on HIGH, without stirring, for a further 6 minutes, tilting the dish as the toffee browns (use gloves for this).
4. Have the nuts arranged in small clusters on lightly oiled baking parchment. Quickly pour the toffee over each cluster to make separate 'pools'.
5. Once the toffee and nut clusters are quite cool, wrap in cellophane or waxed paper and store in an airtight jar.

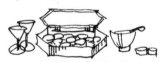

VARIATIONS

If crushed to a powder the clusters will make a sort of praline, but the nut content is too high for a traditional praline, delicious though it is. If preferred, make and pour the toffee over 125–175 g (4–6 oz) shelled pistachio nuts. Once powdered, this makes a delicious pistachio praline.

CHOCOLATE, CREAM CHEESE AND ORANGE 'FUDGE'

Actually not a fudge at all, this confection is so delicious and creamy in texture that it defies any other description. The orange flavour comes from adding crumbled dried rind (page 38) to the cooked fudge. If none is available, use fresh orange zest, stirred well in.

Makes 64 pieces

225 g (8 oz) good quality dark chocolate (such as Menier) broken into squares

450 g (1 lb) icing sugar, sifted

pinch of salt

15 ml (1 tbsp) creamy milk

25 g (1 oz) butter, cubed

75 g (3 oz) good quality cream cheese, cubed

5 ml (1 tsp) vanilla essence

175 g (6 oz) hazelnuts

30 ml (2 level tbsp) crumbled dried citrus peel (page 38)

1. Base line and lightly oil a 20 cm (8 inch) dish or cake tin. Put the chocolate in a small heatproof bowl or jug and microwave on HIGH for 2 minutes. Beat vigorously.
2. Sift the icing sugar and salt into a large bowl. Stir in the milk, butter pieces, crumbled cream cheese, melted chocolate and vanilla essence. Microwave, uncovered, on HIGH for 2 minutes then beat vigorously until smooth.
3. Sprinkle half of the roughly chopped nuts and half of the citrus peel into the base of the prepared dish or tin. Quickly pour over the fudge then sprinkle the top with the remaining nuts and peel, pushing them well down into the fudge. Mark and cut into 2.5 cm (1 inch) squares. Store in an airtight jar.

PEACH AND PISTACHIO CARAMELS

When my sisters and I were small, Sunday afternoon was the one time we were allowed into the kitchen to make toffee, fudge, coconut ice and hokey pokey (also called honeycomb). Much mischief was indulged in, but the sharing, laughing and quarrelling, and finally the proud achievement of producing and offering the sweets to our bemused parents, are joys never forgotten. The following recipe is an updated version of a sweetmeat we used to call Russian toffee.

Makes 64 pieces

100 g (4 oz) sweetened condensed milk

250 g (9 oz) granulated sugar

300 ml (½ pint) double cream

50 g (2 oz) butter, cubed

15 ml (1 tbsp) vanilla essence

pinch salt

15 ml (1 tbsp) freshly squeezed orange juice

100 g (4 oz) dried peaches, cut into .5 cm (¼ inch) shreds

50 g (2 oz) shelled pistachio nuts

1. Put the can of condensed milk on the scales and weigh before removing the required amount, spooning it into a deep 3.4 litre (3 quart) heatproof china or glass casserole. Have ready an oiled, 20 × 20 cm (8 × 8 inch) square dish or tin.
2. Add the sugar, cream, butter, vanilla essence and salt to the casserole. Microwave on HIGH, uncovered, for 5 minutes, stirring occasionally to dissolve the sugar. (No grittiness whatsoever should remain.) Add the orange juice. Microwave on HIGH, uncovered, for a further 10 minutes without stirring. The caramel appears light golden brown on the surface but below it has caramelized to a darker brown. The temperature should register just below 116°C (240°F) on a candy thermometer.
3. Remove the hot casserole carefully and beat, using a wooden spoon, to mix the darker areas with the lighter. The colour will become uniform and the texture velvety smooth.
4. Working quickly, scatter over the peach pieces and nuts and smooth the mixture into the prepared dish. Mark the caramel into 2.5 cm (1 inch) squares with an oiled knife. When cold, wrap the pieces in waxed paper or cellophane and store in an airtight jar.

ROSE TRUFFLE PETITS-FOURS

These chocolate truffles are made in the usual way, but flavoured with rose petals and rose flower water. Then, instead of using paper petits-fours cases, I use fresh rose petals in which to serve them. Inset crystallized rose petals on top if wished. These sweet delights are very perishable, so must be kept chilled and eaten within a few days.

175 g (6 oz) couverture-grade white chocolate

50 g (2 oz) cream cheese

15 ml (1 tbsp) fresh thick cream

5 ml (1 tsp) triple-strength rose flower water

75 g (3 oz) ground almonds

25 g (1 oz) fresh rose petals

1 egg yolk (size 2)

To coat

15 ml (1 tbsp) fraise, framboise or poire eau de vie

25 g (1 oz) cocoa powder or chocolate vermicelli

100 g (4 oz) fresh perfect scented rose petals

Decoration

30–36 crystallized rose petals (optional)

1. Break up the chocolate finely and put in a medium heatproof bowl. Microwave, uncovered, on HIGH for 2½ minutes or until melted.
2. Stir in the cream cheese (in pieces), cream, rose water, almonds and finally 25 g (1 oz) rose petals. Beat until smooth. Beat in the egg yolk and fraise and roll into marble-sized balls (about 30–36).
3. Roll in cocoa or chocolate vermicelli. Keep chilled.
4. Serve each of the petits-fours in a double 'cup' of two overlapped rose petals and decorate with crystallized rose petals if wished. Accompany, perhaps, with some of the same fruit brandy used in the recipe.

— COOK'S TIP —
These should be eaten while still chilled, and not left for long at room temperature.

MOTHER'S APRICOT SWEETMEATS

When visitors came to the house on festive or celebratory occasions, or whenever my mother felt especially indulgent, she would make (or allow us to make) this delicious recipe. I quote it almost from memory: my mouth has never forgotten the tastes nor the fun of participating. These confections will keep, ideally, in an airtight jar or tin (my mother had shelves of such things) for some weeks. They are rarely given the chance in most households, I have discovered.

Makes about 48

50 g (2 oz) sesame seeds
100 g (4 oz) desiccated coconut
275 g (10 oz) dried apricots
300 g (11 oz) medium juicy oranges, cubed
60 ml (4 tbsp) sweetened condensed milk
125 g (4 oz) ground almonds

1. To toast the sesame seeds, spread evenly on a flat heatproof plate. Microwave, uncovered, on HIGH for 8 minutes, stirring every 2 minutes. Spread the 100 g (4 oz) of desiccated coconut to be toasted on a flat heatproof plate. Microwave, uncovered, on HIGH for 5 minutes, stirring every minute. Leave to cool.
2. Put the apricots (chopped), orange and condensed milk into a food processor and process until a sticky mass results.
3. Add half the toasted coconut, the sesame seeds, almonds and process again, in short bursts, until the mixture is well blended. Divide into 48 portions. Squeeze each ball into a compact shape the size of a walnut.
4. Roll in the remaining toasted coconut (there should be approximately 48 balls).
5. If they are to be eaten fresh, no drying is necessary. But if they are to be kept for a long period, space them, 8 at a time, in a circle on some kitchen paper and microwave on LOW (30%) power for 4 minutes, then repeat process with remaining balls.
6. Allow to cool completely, label and store. (If wished, each may be wrapped in cellophane or waxed paper.)

VARIATIONS

Roll the balls with toasted sesame seeds instead of desiccated coconut.
Use a mixture of half dried figs and half dried apricots.
Use the equivalent weight of kumquats instead of the orange.
Add a spoonful of whisky, brandy or rum to the mixture and increase the dry ingredients somewhat.
Substitute honey, molasses or treacle for parts of the sweetened condensed milk.

GREEK ISLAND 'TEA'

Greece has a powerful effect upon many visitors who then become passionate about its charms. One of the phenomena which causes the holidaymaker delight is the ease with which aromatic herbs may be gathered on hillsides, near the sea, beside the dusty winding roads. These herb bunches may travel back home, to grace the kitchen wall. Greek tsai (tea) can be made with a number of herbs, but one of the most common is wild faskomilo (sage). Pungent English sage does not taste the same, but could also be substituted, with different effects. This drink is peace-inducing and makes one ruminative. Should you find yourself there, tsai may be purchased in the market of Anthinas Street, Athens.

6 stems (with leaves) of faskomilo or dried sage, halved
600 ml (1 pint) boiling water
juice of ½ a lemon
30 ml (2 level tbsp) Greek hymettus honey

To serve

lemon slices (optional)
Greek Metaxa brandy (optional)

1. Put the sage and boiling water into a tall heatproof jug (leave room for expansion), cover with cling film and microwave on HIGH for 2 minutes. Leave to stand, covered, for 2 minutes.
2. Add the lemon juice, freshly squeezed, and the honey, using the sage twigs as 'stirrers' to dissolve the honey. Embellish with lemon slices, if wished, and sip while the beverage is hot.
3. Alternatively, add a little Metaxa (Greek brandy) if wished, for a hot healthful 'cocktail'.

GARNET RASPBERRY LEAF TEA

This old-fashioned infusion has the colour of smoky garnets, and a sharp, sorrel-like astringency to spark an initial shock to the taste buds. If wished, spoon 15 ml (1 tbsp) of Chamberyzette Vermout (strawberry-flavoured vermouth) onto each glass or cupful for added pleasure. For fainthearts double the honey measure.

Makes 8 glasses

600 ml (1 pint) boiling water
15 g (½ oz) fresh raspberry or loganberry leaves (20–30), torn
6 fresh raspberries
45 ml (3 level tbsp) raspberry vinegar
30 ml (2 level tbsp) heather honey
120 ml (8 tbsp) Chamberyzette Vermout (optional)

1. Pour the boiling water over the torn leaves in a 1.2 litre (2 pint) heatproof measuring jug. Microwave on HIGH for 3 minutes, stirring vigorously once.
2. Cover with cling film and leave to stand for 2 minutes. Strain through a non-metal sieve and add the fresh raspberries, crushed thoroughly with a fork. Add the vinegar and the honey. Leave to stand for 2 more minutes. Strain again. Garnish with fresh raspberries and their leaves.

MINTED TEA SYRUP (FOR COCKTAILS)

Close to the Jardin des Plantes in Paris is a discreet little mosque with a courtyard garden and tiled Salon de thé. Here one can sip hot minted tea and enjoy the quiet murmur of North African, French, tourist and student voices. The hot scented tea refreshes the senses and the spirits. Although one can buy mint impregnated tea, I prefer to buy dried mint 'tisane' and gunpowder (green) tea from specialist suppliers (the Drury Lane Tea and Coffee Co., London) and make my own syrup. Combine with Bourbon in mint julep or with sliced fruits.

Makes 450 ml (15 fl oz)

90 ml (6 tbsp) green tea and dried mint, mixed (preferably Algerian, Tunisian or Moroccan)
300 ml (½ pint) boiling water
handfuls of fresh spearmint or peppermint leaves and stems, well crushed
45 ml (3 level tbsp) unsweetened lemon juice
90 ml (6 tbsp) scented liquid honey

1. Pour the boiling water over the tea in a large heatproof jug or pot and add the fresh leaves, stirring vigorously, crushing the stems as much as possible. Cover with cling film or a lid and microwave on MEDIUM (60%) for 4–5 minutes, or until very hot. Leave to stand for 5 minutes.
2. Strain through a non-metal sieve, adding the lemon juice and honey and stirring well to dissolve. (If necessary cover and microwave on HIGH for a further 1 minute.)
3. Allow to cool. Bottle, label and store in a cool dark place (preferably the refrigerator.)

LEMON AND LIMONNAYA CORDIAL

Limonnaya, the subtle lemon-scented vodka, is used in the making of this 'fresh lemon cordial' base. If unavailable, use a clean clear-tasting alternative, such as Absolut.

225 g (8 oz) caster sugar
450 ml (15 fl oz) boiling water
3–4 lime leaves, crushed (optional)
shredded zest and squeezed juice of 6 lemons
10 ml (2 level tsp) tartaric acid
10 ml (2 level tsp) Epsom salts
300 ml (½ pint) Limonnaya vodka

1. Pour the sugar, water, lime leaves (if used), lemon juice and zest into a large heatproof jug. Stir, then cover with cling film and microwave on HIGH for 5 minutes or until very hot.
2. Stir in the tartaric acid and the Epsom salts (magnesium sulphate) and again cover. Leave to grow completely cold. Add the vodka and stir thoroughly. Pour into a sterilized glass bottle (see page 41). Cork firmly, label and refrigerate.

See photograph page 103

CHERRY RATAFIA

This pretty fruit liqueur will grace your store cupboard and delight your guests. But if you can resist the temptation to eat the fruits, you can make this an everlasting ratafia by topping up the syrup as it is used with more sugar and liquor (gin is specified but kümmel or aquavit are acceptable substitutes). I have one such (now three summers old) containing tiny damsons picked during one autumn holiday in Eure et Loir, near Chartres. Use this ruby-red liquor sparingly; it is strong and should be savoured.

Makes 450 g (1 lb) jar

225 g (8 oz) fresh black or morello cherries
50 ml (2 fl oz) hot water
50 g (2 oz) caster sugar
8–10 juniper berries, crushed
150 ml (¼ pint) dry gin (or other white spirit)

1. Remove stalks (discard these) from cherries and prick each fruit to the stone several times with a cocktail stick.
2. Place cherries in a sterilized 450 g (1 lb) jar (see page 41). Mix the water and sugar and pour over the cherries.
3. Microwave, uncovered, on HIGH for 1½ minutes. Cover and invert (or give a very gentle shake or stir) to dissolve the sugar. Uncover and microwave on HIGH for a further 30 seconds.
4. Add the juniper berries and leave to cool slightly.
5. Pour in the gin and seal immediately, using a non-metal screw-top lid. Shake very gently to blend the flavours. Leave in a warm place for 4 days, inverting the jar once a day. Label, store and use within 3 months if not kept topped up.

CREOLE BUTTERED BRANDY SUSTAINER

Hot buttered rum drinks and their ilk seem to have had a place in culinary folklore, frequently being described more as medicines than frivolities. (I have a theory that described thus, they would remain the preserve of the privileged 'sufferer' who could then indulge his or her appetite with no fear of criticism, or cries of profligacy!) Preferably use low-price,

fruity brandy bought on holidays abroad rather than age-old cognac. It does seem to banish the blues, this sustaining beverage! Add some jazz, a bowl of spicy gumbo, beans and rice and you'll give an authentic creole touch to the darkest evening!

Serves 1

15 ml (1 level tbsp) unsalted butter
30 ml (2 level tbsp) molasses sugar
2.5 ml (½ level tsp) ground cloves
2.5 ml (½ level tsp) ground nutmeg
2.5 ml (½ level tsp) ground cinnamon
1.25 ml (¼ tsp) ground allspice
125 ml (4 fl oz) cognac or brandy (or bourbon or dark rum)
1 twist lemon zest

1. Put the butter, sugar and spices into a large heatproof mug, goblet or tumbler. Microwave, covered, with cling film on HIGH for 1½ minutes, or until there is a distinct aroma. Stir well.
2. Stir in half of the cognac, cover in cling film then microwave for a further 1 minute, or until hot and bubbling.
3. Uncover and stir in the remaining cognac, add the lemon and enjoy the fumes as you savour the mellow tastes.

SOUTHERN BELLE COCKTAIL

a Southern belle of a peachy drink.....

A soothing hot drink suitable for many occasions should be made in the same vessel from which it will be drunk, so as not to miss the delectable fumes!

Serves 1

150 ml (¼ pint) peach nectar (fresh peach juice)

| 15 ml (1 tbsp) freshly squeezed lemon juice |

| 2.5 ml (½ tsp) freshly shredded lemon zest |

| 1 slice fresh peach (or other seasonal fruit) |

| 3 cloves |

| 45 ml (3 tbsp) Southern Comfort |

1. Put the first three ingredients into a large heatproof mug or heatproof glass (with holder). Add the fruit studded with cloves.
2. Cover with cling film and microwave on HIGH for 1½ minutes or until hot, but not too hot to drink.
3. Uncover, stir in the Southern Comfort and enjoy both the scented steam and the beverage at once.

COOK'S TIP
The drink may be cooled over ice then served as a long drink, with dry champagne as a mixer.

TEQUILA SUNSHINE

This 'hair of the dog' cocktail packs a punch: its first innocent fruity taste is of carrots and orange – a clever façade behind which the tequila hides. But in fact, if preferred, the liquor may be omitted for a pleasant brunch or lunch non-alcoholic cocktail.

Makes 700 ml (1¼ pints)

250 g (9 oz) young carrots, scrubbed and thinly sliced

| 50 ml (2 fl oz) vegetable stock |

| 300 ml (½ pint) freshly squeezed orange juice |

| 1.25 ml (¼ tsp) angostura bitters |

| 3 shakes tabasco sauce |

| 2 egg whites (size 3) |

| 90 ml (6 tbsp) golden tequila (optional) |

| cayenne pepper |

1. Put the carrots and vegetable stock in a heatproof ring dish, cover with cling film and

microwave on HIGH for 4–5 minutes, or until the carrots are very tender indeed. Leave to stand for 2 minutes.
2. Put the carrots and their stock, half the orange juice, the bitters and tabasco into a blender and blend to a smooth purée. Add the remaining juice, the egg whites and the tequila. Blend again, until frothy and white.
3. Pour into 4 or 6 glasses, each containing 2 ice cubes. Serve sprinkled with a little cayenne, and short straws for drinking, if wished. An edible decoration could also be added.

CAROB COCKTAIL CREAM

Many people prefer carob to chocolate, so here is a recipe for a homemade cocktail syrup, to which may be added alcohol of choice, to decorate and serve at will.

Makes 600 ml (1 pint)

2 cinnamon sticks, crushed

| 45 ml (3 level tbsp) molasses sugar |

| 30 ml (2 level tbsp) carob powder |

| pinch allspice |

| 1.25 ml (¼ tsp) freshly grated nutmeg |

| 300 ml (½ pint) hot, freshly-brewed coffee |

| 90 ml (6 tbsp) dark rum, rye whisky or armagnac |

| 150 ml (¼ pint) single cream |

1. Stir the cinnamon, sugar, carob powder and spices together in a heatproof measuring jug. Stir in the hot coffee. Cover with cling film and microwave on HIGH for 2 minutes. Sir well.
2. Strain over 6 ice cubes and once it has cooled, stir in the rum, whisky or armagnac along with the cream.

SERVING TIP
Serve chilled, in long elegant glasses for sipping, as an after-dinner digestif, particularly at festive occasions.

STRAWBERRY SCELTO COCKTAIL

This exquisite fruit cocktail gives new insights into strawberries as a cocktail ingredient, supplying stunning scentedness and brilliant colour. It is strong in flavour, so some may wish to serve it as a spritzer – with a dash of sparkling water or, more wickedly, with dry champagne. If a non-alcoholic version is preferred, omit liquors and substitute one tablespoon of grenadine or crème de cassis (though I feel the effect is not at all the same). The result is a delicious summertime tipple, good for parties. Store in the refrigerator for several days and use as required.

...the scent of berries & the colours too... last on for days....

freshness...

Makes 600 ml (1 pint)

225 g (8 oz) fresh strawberries, hulled
75 g (3 oz) caster sugar
150 ml (¼ pint) boiling water
2.5 ml (½ level tsp) tartaric acid
150 ml (¼ pint) iced water
6 cubes of ice, crushed
60 ml (4 tbsp) fraise (eau de vie)
60 ml (4 tbsp) dry gin

1. Quarter the strawberries, but do not wash them.
2. Put the sugar and half of the water (boiling) into a large heatproof jug with the tartaric acid. Microwave, uncovered, on HIGH for 1½ minutes, stirring once.
3. Put the strawberries into a blender or food processor with the hot syrup and blend or process until foamy and smooth. Add the iced water, the ice cubes and the two liqueurs. Blend or process again.
4. Serve in a chilled jug, perhaps with some extra ice (no more than 6 cubes), the mixer of your choice and some crushed fresh strawberry leaves and blossoms.

See photograph page 48

HOLLIER COCKTAIL

My father was a geologist, a geographer and a passionate, orderly gardener. He loved his rows of leeks and potatoes, the gooseberries and currants, which he nurtured. The fruit trees and their progress – Peasgood Nonsuch and Orleans Reinette, for example – were watched with a protective eye. One year we made 'rum' from marrows, and another year, parsnip wine. The preserves were legion; flowers always graced our table. Although my father rarely drank cocktails, I'm sure he would have approved of the garden-fresh tastes of this offering.

Makes 450–600 ml (¾–1 pint)

300 ml (½ pint) unsweetened clear apple juice
zest from 1 lemon, in one continuous curl
juice of 1 lemon, freshly squeezed
60 ml (4 tbsp) clover honey
2 cinnamon sticks, halved lengthwise
1 head of rowan berries, or loganberries, crushed
2 sprigs of lemon-scented verbena, crushed
1 eating apple, old-fashioned variety
8 ice cubes

To serve

150 ml (¼ pint) whisky
fresh mint sprigs
up to 150 ml (¼ pint) sparkling mineral water or soda (optional)

1. Put half the apple juice, all the lemon zest, juice, honey, cinnamon, crushed berries (still on their stem) and the scented leaves in a large heatproof glass jug. Cover with cling film and microwave on HIGH for 4 minutes. Leave to stand.
2. Strain off the liquid and cool over ice. Return it to the jug with the remaining juice, the apple (freshly segmented), ice cubes, whisky and mint. Stir.
3. Serve in long glasses, topped up with sparkling water if wished.

....garden goodnesses.....

—— COOK'S TIP ——
Add a fresh head of berries, if wished, for their beauty.

INDEX